BIG LIFE

JAZZ SUMMERS

QUARTET

First published in 2013 by Quartet Books Limited
A member of the Namara Group
27 Goodge Street, London W1T 2LD
Copyright © Jazz Summers 2013

A catalogue record for this book
is available from the British Library
ISBN 978 0 7043 7330 3
Typeset by Josh Bryson
Printed and bound in Great Britain by
T J International Ltd, Padstow, Cornwall

I dedicate this book to my brother Don Ottignon, and to my three beautiful daughters, Katie, Rio and Georgia.

And to everyone who is in it.

[The following tapes were recorded in the south of France during the winter and early summer of 2012. The speaker's name is Jazz Summers. The recordings were made by Joe Stretch.]

PART ONE

PART ONE

TAPE #1
(5TH JANUARY 2012)

Jazz

I don't wanna write a book. There's some great books about the music industry. Some classics. Full of people getting pissed and on coke in the morning. Walter Yetnikoff's book, for example. He was crazy. He hardly remembers the eighties. You run the biggest record label on earth, you run a circus. They marched him out the door in the end.

[Pause]

I wanna write a book that changes people's lives.

[Long pause]

There're two kinds of musical star: Artists and Designers. Although having said that, in the fifties and the sixties, a lot of acts were neither. People would find a good-looking guy with a nice voice, hand him a pair of tight trousers, give him a quiff and find him a song down Tin Pan Alley. And then suddenly you'd have Billy Fury or John Leyton or whoever.

But then you get the Beatles, a rock band, who started off playing covers, of course, but then, as they started to write their own songs, they became Artists. And others followed. Jimmy Hendrix was an Artist.

In the seventies, the Art became a little indulgent, with Prog Rock and all. So Punk came along and cleared all that stuff out. From then on, the basic parameters of pop music had been roughly laid out, and so by the eighties, a new kind of musician appears: The Designer. George Michael, for example. His dad was an

1

immigrant who came to England from Cyprus to build a better life. He wanted George to be an accountant. George was brought up middle class. He's the ultimate Designer. He probably won't like me saying this. But he really studied what Elton John and Queen did. He studied it and he made sublime music on the back of those studies. Although George was capable of Artistic moments, too. Listen to 'Careless Whisper', and that song, what's it called, 'A Different Corner'. Listen to them. They aren't works of Design.

In the eighties, there were a lot of middle-class people who viewed being in a rock band or a pop band as a good career move. There was money to be made. I wonder if a middle-class kid really thinks like that these days. Maybe they want to design Apps for iPods. Ray Charles: he's an Artist. I'll give you another Artist: Prince. I don't know what his background is, but he oozes Artistry. He was only ever going to dance and play music. I'm not sure about Bob Dylan. I think he's got a bit of the Designer about him and that's no bad thing. At least not in theory. Richard Ashcroft from the Verve. He's an Artist.

Paul McCartney's interesting. He's an Artist, for sure; anyone who writes 'Maybe I'm Amazed' or 'Blackbird' is a genius Artist, but everyone treats him like a God, so he starts making music like a Designer and his records these days sound like it. David Bowie's an Artist and a Designer simultaneously and that makes him special.

The truth is this: if people haven't got much, they create a lot. Take this week: I'm managing three acts who are all in the same position, OK. La Roux, Scissor Sisters and Klaxons are all trying to return after huge Artistic and commercial success. It's not easy. Maybe fame and money disorientate the Artistic temperament. Maybe that's just a fact. What do we want to be, creators of great beauty, or rich? I know what I think.

TAPE #1

Success leads to very serious partying – I've seen it many times. I've seen great artists burn their fucking brains out. I've seen it recently. I've never taken acid. I once saw a bloke jump out a window into a fishpond. But I do like 'Lucy In The Sky With Diamonds' – the song. I think the drugs of the sixties were purer. I think acid can open up other dimensions. It helps you to see beyond the basic three. But drugs these days are commercialised. They're fucked up – dipped in all sorts of stuff. I think drugs these days *shut* your mind. Dope's no good. My French girlfriend used to paint rows of beautiful trees, OK – plane trees, mulberries and poplars. But that was before she started smoking too much. These days she paints black squares.

Really, the creative process ain't that different from the process of becoming a human – becoming a good person. Integrity, authenticity, honesty; they're not easy things to be. If they were, the world would be full of authentic, honest people, and it's not, is it?

I think a person who's creative has the ability to tap into the Universe, OK. Out there in the Universe is everything that's ever been and everything that ever will be. A true Artist can channel that through them. A lot of great songs were written in a minute, did you know? It just comes, *bam*, from the Universe. When you get famous and the pressure comes on, your mind closes down and fear comes in, and stress, and your channel to the Universe is somehow lost. I'm certain of that.

Michelangelo said he didn't do the sculpture, God did, and he just peeled the marble away. And it's the same with songs really. The Universe writes the song. An Artist's capacity to channel the Universe is what makes them special people. But, sadly, selling ten million records can sometimes convince Artists that *they* wrote the songs. They believe themselves to be geniuses and that corrupts them. I'm a manager. I have to set Artists free, as free as they were when they didn't realise they were free. It's my job to remind them that their relationship with the Universe is more important than their relationship with their record company.

Right at this moment, my act Scissor Sisters are really stuck. Truthfully, I should tell them to climb the Himalayas and live in a hut for a year. It's the same with Klaxons and La Roux. They're so talented, but they're a bit fearful. I tried to persuade George Michael to go to India once. The real India, not the new one. The Himalayas. He needed to go somewhere where people wouldn't recognise him, to alter his perception of himself and the Universe. The energy would have flowed from the summit of Everest, through George Michael and down through the Gangees. But he didn't fancy it. I think he went to LA.

[Long pause]

I'd like some mint tea. Could you drink some?

I wanna write a book about people becoming free.

My French Girlfriend's Eyebrow in 1990

I was having lunch with my girlfriend Marine in a restaurant on Spring Street, New York. It was a sunny day and she was severely chic, Marine. On the table next to ours were three young men.

'This band I've found,' one of them was saying. 'Jazz Summers wants to sign them to Big Life. He's *obsessed* with them. He keeps trying to call up the singer. He's already talking to *radio* about them.'

One of Marine's plucked eyebrows elegantly rose. And the more the guy talked, the higher and more inquisitive her eyebrow became.

'Jazz Summers?' said another guy. 'You wanna be careful. I met a man once who'd been dangled out a window by Jazz Summers. I heard he burned a venue to the ground in Houston.'

I put my napkin on the table. Marine was looking a little alarmed. I went across to their table and coughed lightly.

'You guys work in the music industry, I couldn't help overhearing.'

'That's right. We're at Epic. Him and me. This guy's a manager.'

'Epic,' I said. 'A few years ago I managed a big band on Epic Records in the UK. They were on Columbia over here.'

'Oh, yeh? Who was that?'

'Wham!'

'Wham?'

'This Jazz Summers,' I said. 'He wants to sign your band?'

'Well …'

'Tell me something. What does he look like?'

The guy leapt from his seat and sprinted out of the restaurant so fast. Bullshitters, I thought. Slick, cock-sure cowards. You meet them in the music industry from time to time. Bravado for breakfast. Cocktails for lunch.

I never burned a venue to the ground. I've never even hit an A&R man. I locked one in a cupboard once, as punishment for some racism and sexism.

King's Cross

A lot of people talk nonsense about success. They'll tell you success is going triple platinum then having lunch with Liza Minnelli. It's not. I've had dinner with Liza. For me, success is simple: if I really love a piece of music, get it recorded, get it released and it sells *one* copy – that's a success. Because it means you've created something.

BIG LIFE

You've added something to the world. You've contributed a piece of music to life.

Dad was in the army when he was thirteen. He didn't have a home. In those days, the army could raise you, give you an education, some qualifications. They'd train you. They trained Dad to be a musician. He left the army in the thirties and joined the dole queues of the Great Depression.

It wasn't illegal downloads that had musicians lined up in those queues in the thirties, it was the decline of silent cinema. Dad used to soundtrack Charlie Chaplin films, or Buster Keaton, and he played at Sadler's Wells for a bit, too. He drummed in some good bands – he was mega-talented, but he ended up working as a labourer.

I was in love with Dad a bit. He had my life planned out for me. He didn't want me to end up like him. When I was four, I remember telling my cousin Pat that when I was nine I'd go to military school, and when I was fifteen I'd join the army and learn a trade. Dad really drummed that future into me.

And it happened like that, more or less. I went to Gordon Boy's Military School in Woking aged twelve. That place was tough. You were fighting for your virginity. We all got bullied beyond belief. I signed into the army in Brighton in 1959. Me and Dad listened as the bloke told me there was no way out once I signed on. You couldn't even buy yourself out in those days. I'd be in the army for eleven years and six months. The bloke handed me the form and I felt dizzy. I remember holding the pen, thinking, what am I doing here? The bloke asked me if I understood the consequences. I nodded and wrote my name.

England was all fucking foggy. I went up to military school in Yorkshire. Sitting alone on the train, watching the fields and the dark towns, I did the sums. I'd be twenty-seven by the time I got out. It would be 1971. As it was, it was '59, and it was night by the time I stepped onto the platform at Harrogate. Cliff Richard was number one with 'Travelin' Light'.

Hamburg Here I Come

The army apprentice school was on Penny Pot Lane in Harrogate. I used to go to Newcastle quite a bit to see my cousin Jackie. I went there for Christmas 1959, aged fifteen and a half. We used to go to a youth club on a Sunday night to dance and meet girls. It was run by St John's church and they'd get a band in.

I was waiting for the band to begin one evening when my cousin Jackie came over and said, 'Jazz, you've gotta play drums.' The band's drummer hadn't shown up and Jackie had told the guitarist, who I think she fancied, that I could play a bit.

'Without the band we can't dance,' she said. 'You're great.'

So I did. I played. I busked it. The singer wanted to be Buddy Holly. That was fine by me. I'd only ever played in a trad jazz band before. We played Peggy Sue, some songs by the Shadows and an instrumental tune called 'Rocking Goose'. Afterwards, the band asked me where I'd come from. They said they were off on tour to Germany on fifteen quid a week. They had an agent and were travelling via the Hook of Holland.

'You gotta go with them, Jazz,' Jackie said. 'Will you?'

'Yes,' I said. 'I will.' I didn't say I was in the army. It wasn't a cool thing. 'Just give me a few days to sort something out.' Going off to Hamburg was a cool thing - to go on a road with a band, to earn fifteen quid a week. That was twelve times more than I was earning in the army. I *had* to get out. I sat on the train home thinking, fuck it, what a dream.

BIG LIFE

I returned to Penny Pot Lane and got hold of a copy of the *Manual of Military Law*. I looked up the section on apprenticeships. You could leave anytime in the first four weeks, it said, but I'd already gone past that. Then it said if the army couldn't offer you an apprenticeship in your chosen field, you could ask to be discharged.

They were training me to be a radio technician, which is all about colours, in a way, different coloured wires. The next day, during the practical bit where it's all 'Connect green wire to blue terminal', I deliberately fucked it up. When the sergeant told us to turn on our circuits, everyone's worked but mine. Mine smoked and made a sharp, electrical cracking sound. The room filled with the smell of burning plastic.

'What the *fuck* are you doing, Summers?' The sergeant was standing over me. He looked like he'd been wired up wrong, too. 'That's blue, not black, that's brown, not green!'

'I'm a bit colour-blind,' I said.

'A bit?'

'Slightly.'

I went for a test. I messed it all up on purpose and got called before the Company Commander. He had this miserable moustache and looked so old I thought he could easily have fought in the Boer War.

'What other trade do you want to do?' he said. 'You could be a draughtsman, a motor mechanic, an armourer. What about a chef, Summers? You could be a chef. We could send you to the catering corps.'

'I really want to be a radio technician.'

'You *can't*, Summers. You're colour-blind. *Think*, Summers. We'll have to discharge you. I'm giving you couple of days to make a choice.'

Fantastic, I thought. That's it. I'm out. Hamburg here I come.

8

TAPE #1

Working Your Ticket

Two days later, I got called back to the same office by a stern sergeant major – his eyes and nose were as sharp as knives and his mouth was lipless and mean.

'Go into that cubicle, Summers. There's a phone. Your father's on the line.'

I went into the cubicle and picked up the phone. I'd not been on the phone many times.

'Right you,' Dad said. 'You're working your ticket.'

'Dad, I'm colour-blind.'

'Don't you give me that colour-blind bullshit.'

'You know I'm colour-blind. Slightly.'

'I know what you're doing, son. You're working your ticket. I won't have it. You're staying in the army. And if you try to come out, you've got no home to go to.'

I said, 'Fuck off' and put the phone down. That's the first time I ever told Dad to fuck off.

A bunch of bands went out to Hamburg that year. The Beatles, of course. But I didn't go. The army paid for me to go and talk to Dad. He had a friend who ran the Medical Corps band. 'If you wanna do music,' Dad said, 'at least do music in the army.' I auditioned, and I got in, but it wasn't quite the same as playing with the band in Newcastle. I didn't feel as free, marching around a parade square, playing third percussion. I transferred out of the band to train to be a radiographer.

Dexys

When I was eighteen, Dad had a heart attack. I remember his funeral. I was really distressed, but I sat there thinking, it's all right for you, you're off and gone. I've got nine years to do in this fucking army. I was living in the military hospital in Woolwich by then, working as a radiographer. I played in a jazz band at weekends and a rock band during the week.

I was introduced to Dexedrine by an army nurse…I think his name was Chris. Everyone warned me off Chris, calling him a 'nancy boy'. But he loved music and he'd come to my gigs and supply me with Dexys. When I wasn't taking Dexys, I was pissed on pints of bitter and Scrumpy. I took a lot of drugs in the army. And I was missing so many opportunities. One band I drummed for opened for Freddy and the Dreamers in Bristol. I couldn't get out of my army duties, so I never got the gig. Whenever I gigged I'd have people coming over saying, 'Fucking hell, you're good. What are you doing?'

Once you told them, they lost interest. There was prejudice against soldiers. It was OK in the early sixties cos everyone had short hair. You could just about get away with it. But then long hair came in. When the sixties started swinging, I was fucked.

The Cuckoo's Nest

In the weeks running up to my radiography finals I lived on Dexys. I used to steal them from the hospital if Chris wasn't around. I'd made money gigging and I rented a flat in London. I got in shit for it, but I was always in shit in the army. I hated it. One of the guys who shared this flat was gay. He got out of the army simply because he was gay – it was seen as a mental illness. I was inspired by this. I read up the symptoms of being manic-depressive and went off to Tidworth in Wiltshire for the summer.

When I got back, I didn't talk much. That was the start. I fell silent. Having been the life and soul of the party, you know, the rock 'n' roll soldier, I came back from Tidworth and I was suddenly very introverted. I didn't clean or clip my nails, left cigarette ash on my hands, wore the same collar everyday. I sighed all the time and I moved extremely slowly. I used to hear people taking the piss out of me. But after six weeks of sighing my plan wasn't quite working. I needed to do more.

In those days, X-ray departments had darkrooms with huge wash tanks to wash the fixer from the X-rays. Water flowed continuously in and out of those tanks, so I decided to block the outflow with a clump of X-ray film. The room beneath the darkroom was the sergeants' mess. I turned their ceiling into this big bubble and then, when they all went in for breakfast, it was like it was raining indoors.

Within two hours, I was being interviewed by the hospital psychiatrist, a strange Colonel who regularly groomed his eyebrows with licked fingertips. In my research, I'd learned that most manic-depressives were treated as out-patients and then were quickly let go after a few months. That was my dream. But this Colonel had other ideas.

'OK,' he said, smoothing those eyebrows. 'I think we need to send you to Nettley. And I think we should send you today.'

Nettley was a huge fucking Victorian hospital on the south coast that was built to treat casualties of the First World War. They'd send them back from the Somme, up Southampton Water to Nettley.

Most of Nettley was derelict by the sixties. The only thing left was the mental health wards. I was put in the modern bit, the South Ward, the worst in the hospital, for the most insane. It was a gloomy, dirty place, full of long deserted corridors. This was the age of Electro-Convulsive Therapy. This was *One Flew Over The Cuckoo's Nest* before it fucking came out. All the other patients were

BIG LIFE

either silent or violent. I lay there in a bed with no one to talk to. I just had to get through it; no one who got sent to Nettley went back into the army. I used to see these frazzled-looking guys getting guided back to their beds from the ECT room. I was twenty.

Jigsaw Puzzle

I was made to do an inkblot test. I figured I'd either say, 'It looks like a pelvis,' or, 'It looks like someone looking at me.' If you say 'pelvis', well, you might be a bit sexually orientated, but you're basically sane. I was supposed to be a manic-depressive, so I tried to get the middle line. I said 'pelvis' and was prescribed pills.

I was sleeping in wards of twenty beds full of schizos and paranoid schizos. My shoelaces, belt and razor blade were confiscated and I had to take tablets. I'd see people going down for ECT all day.

Because I was a medical trainee, I occasionally saw people I knew. This guy called Nick, for example, came to see me. We'd played a bit of hockey together in the past.

'Jazz, Jesus, how are you?'

'Nick, I'm not nuts.' I grabbed his collar. 'You've got to help me.'

'Don't worry. We'll look after you.'

'I'm not nuts, Nick. I'm not mad. I've gotta get out the fucking army.'

'OK, Jazz. It's good to see you.'

'No, you don't understand. I've gotta play drums.'

'Jazz, you don't have to worry. I'm serious. You won't suffer.'

I was on white tablets and blue tablets. They made me take them. The white tablets would be a bit of a downer. The blue made me feel strange. They weren't psychedelic, sadly, so I'd sit around,

12

thinking about what I should say the next inkblot reminded me of. Maybe it didn't remind me of a pelvis.

The next time I saw Nick, I was prepared. I talked to him like you would anyone. I talked about hockey and going out drinking. I reminded him of when I'd tripped over him and his girlfriend shagging by a canal. I reminded him of when he'd been so pissed I'd had to carry him home.

'You *are* OK,' he said, 'aren't you? You're working your ticket.'

'*Yes!* You've gotta help me. What's in my notes?'

'Lardactum,' he said. 'The white tablets are Lardactum. The blue ones are Stellazine. You've overdone it, sunshine. They think you're a simple schiz.'

My heart was beating like mad.

'Nick, what do I do?'

'Stabilise yourself. Keep taking the tablets, but stop acting mad. Talk more. They'll move you to West Ward, then East Ward, then finally North Ward. Do the occupational therapy – jigsaws and whatnot. It'll take about six weeks, then there'll be a few tests and a meeting, then you'll be discharged. Nobody returns to the army from here. They're observing you, Jazz. You're scheduled for the ECT room.'

I started doing the jigsaws. I made a rug. It was a nice rug and I found I enjoyed jigsaws. West Ward. More jigsaws. East Ward. A slightly inferior rug – a D-shaped one for my mum's hearth. North ward. I was close, after five years in the army, to being free. I could feel it. They let me out into Southampton for a day. I was with this guy who had amnesia. I had to look after him a bit. We talked, but he kept forgetting. It was a nice day, really. He liked to gamble so we went down the bookies. We tried the horses, but won nothing, and he really wasn't sure who he was. We went down the cinema and saw *The Longest Day* – that was a mistake. It was all army glory crap. I bought *Melody Maker*. I wanted to get on the phone and talk to people I knew in bands. But I phoned my mum instead. I told her I'd be out in a week and, though she was worried, we were looking forward to seeing each other.

The following Monday, I shared a waiting room with a bunch of other patients who were being considered for discharge. One by one, they went into the meeting room and, after not much time, they came out free. I went in last. I was asked to take a seat in the middle of a long table. There was a load of people there: nurses, warrant officers, doctors. Sunlight streamed through a huge window that looked down Southampton Water. My inquisitor, a naval captain, was gaunt with a salt and pepper beard. He sat at the end of the table, silhouetted by sunlight. In five minutes' time, I thought, I'll be out.

'What do you understand, Summers, by the proverb, *people in glass houses shouldn't throw stones*?'

'I'm not sure, sir.'

'How do you feel now, compared to when you arrived? Do you feel different?'

'I feel much better, sir.'

'I'll ask you again. Do you feel any different from the day you came in?'

'Yes, sir.'

'How, Summers?'

'I used to feel scared, sir. I feel OK today. I'm better.'

'Well, Summers, we don't agree.' I looked around the room. Everyone was staring at me; all these fucking stern men who'd all been born to stern Victorian parents, covered in stripes and gold medals. 'In fact, we *know* you're no different now than the day

14

you came in. We know, Summers, that you've been malingering, working your ticket. This is a sham, boy!'

I told myself that the doctor was testing me, that he was bluffing, trying to force a confession from me.

'I'm sorry, sir,' I said. 'But, that's not true. When I arrived here I was ill. You've given me tablets and rest. I'm different now.'

'We're going to court martial you for malingering, Summers. With a bit of luck, you'll be sent to military prison for six months.'

The sun went behind a cloud and his face focused and I saw a simple hatred in his eyes. I looked over his shoulder, right down Southampton Water, to the sea. It was clear no rubber stamp would be thumping my discharge papers any time soon.

'If you wish to court martial me, sir, then court martial me. When I arrived here I was ill. I'm sorry sir, I really do feel different.'

I was asked to leave. For a while, I sat alone in the empty waiting room. I got to thinking about Nick and about whether he was the type that betrays. When I was summoned back, the atmosphere in the room was different. You could tell there'd been an argument. The room stank of sweat and cigar breath. As I sat, the doctor stood.

'You know it and we know it, Summers,' he said. 'You were pre*tend*ing. Nevertheless, we're sending you back to Woolwich. You're going to be Nettley's one success. If we see you again, we will throw the *book* at you.'

I didn't have to ask which book. A big heavy depressing book full of painful rules. The *Manual of Military Law*.

It was 1965. The Beatles were at number one with 'Help!' and I returned to London with six army years ahead of me. I can still *buy* music, I thought. I can still *make* music, maybe. But, oh, fucking hell, I was devastated. I felt so close. I'd sighed for three months. I'd made rugs. I'd said so many ink smudges reminded me of pelvises. I'd been to Nettley and nearly had my mind fried. All for nothing.

[Long pause]

I was in a lounge bar once with George Michael, not far from the Great Wall of China. We were listening to this Filipino guy sing 'Careless Whisper'. It was as though George himself was up there singing it. I told George a bit about my time in the army, about how I was stationed in Hong Kong, where all the gigs were owned by the Filipinos. They're unbelievable mimics of Western pop. Even in the 1960s they were. Every club had a band, every bar – all of them Filipino. Hong Kong was the first time in my life when I couldn't get a gig. I don't think George knew what the fuck I was talking about.

TAPE #2
(6TH JANUARY 2012)

Conversation #1

People used to sit down at the Marquee and listen to music. Except that guy called Jesus who danced to everything. Remember him? Then Punk happened and people stood up and the labels didn't have a fucking clue. What?

Don't they teach you English at Legal School? Deal breaker means deal breaker, not fucking 'send me another email'. No, I'm not going anywhere near those dysfunctional fuckers. I'm not interested in players. They'll all be fucked in a few years anyway. I'm interested in getting my artists away. All those executives earning fifteen million dollars a year. They're just milking it. And in reality they're not making money. I wouldn't get close enough to fucking smell them. I might go and see Mike…Alison? Have you ever worked with her?

[Pause]

I've got a friend called Kevin who's a stubborn old git. He says to me, Jazz, we're old men. I said, remove the fucking 'we'. I'm not an old man. I'm here. I work. I love music…we'll start in five minutes. I've gotta speak to Tim and Tony Beard first. I should tell you about Malacca. I went with a Malaysian bargirl in Malacca. She gave me a dose. I had to go on antibiotics. I couldn't drink for six weeks and I had snakies – those horrible dreams you get when you stop drinking. Other than that I played a lot of hockey and gigs… Hiya Tim, how's it going?

17

BIG LIFE

The Shades of Blue

I had six years to do in the army – couldn't have felt more depressed, but then a great thing happened: I fell in love. Head over heels. She was called Di Chapman and we had a fucking full-on relationship. It was passionate. She was beautiful. I'd sneak into her room in the nurses' home and we'd make love rampantly. Me and a friend used to sneak in together. Sometimes frigid nurses sounded the alarm if they woke to the sound of shagging. One night I had to climb out of Di's third storey window to evade capture. I dangled there for half an hour in the middle of the night, clinging to the face of the Royal Herbert Hospital, standing on a tiny little ledge on my tip-toes. My mate got caught and did a month in Colchester military prison. He was never the same after that.

[Pause]

I'd have died if I'd fallen from that window, you know. I risked everything for Di. She pulled me up into her room with her bed sheet. She dumped me for a Para after six months. That broke my heart. Couldn't sleep or eat or anything. I begged Jim Swain, the army's Chief Radiographer, to post me. 'Post me,' I told him. 'Post me as far away from England as you can.'

I flew to Bahrain in a small, angry-sounding Britannia Airline propeller plane. From Bahrain to Columbo, Sri Lanka, from there to Bangkok, from Bangkok to Hong Kong, where the port was crawling with American soldiers, sailors, screaming seabirds and hundreds of different accents and languages. The war was on in Vietnam and the USS *Enterprise* was docked in the harbour, flying the stars and stripes. The Red Guard were marching up and down the Chinese border. I was sat on a bench. A bunch of seagulls perched on some nautical rope and watched me smoke.

TAPE #2

I got a cozy little job in charge of a small X-ray department. My Chinese clerk, a good guy called Harry Kwan, taught me some Cantonese and I got a Chinese girlfriend. I moved in with her in fact. Musical instruments were cheap so I saved for a drum kit quickly. The problem was there was no gigs. The Filipinos had it sewn up.

There was a guy in the X-ray department who could play trumpet and piano at the same time. It was pretty cool. I found a double bass player who I'd played hockey with back in England. We got a band together and went to the sergeants' mess and did a gig there for beer money and a good supper. We got a bit of repertoire together.

I met an Australian guy who booked the Ocean Terminal, a proper venue, a really big place with a couple of lounges, but no music playing. I went drinking with him. We drank San Miguel, I remember. San Lig, the Chinese called it. 'Eee San Lig, ng goy,' I remember saying – two San Miguel. We drank twenty bottles each and then shared a bottle of Scotch in the Professional Club, a recently plush but now dingy dive, home to everyone in Hong Kong who wanted to get completely out of it – police, gangsters, prostitutes, soldiers, judges. At our most pissed, I convinced the guy that he should have music in the lounges at the Ocean Terminal. And I told him to fuck the Filipinos and hire us. He was pissed as punch, I suppose, and he gave us three nights a week.

That was pretty cool for a while. Everything was bubbling. I was playing music and partying and I was pretty happy. But then one day, out of nowhere really, I got posted to Malaysia. I got three days notice. They were short of radiographers. I had to say goodbye to my Chinese girlfriend, who was actually a pretty good singer.

[Pause]

19

BIG LIFE

Actually, I never said goodbye to her. She was away in Japan with her dad. Her parents owned ballrooms in Hong Kong. We used to laugh a lot, me and her. Her voice wasn't nasal at all. She sang 'Yellow Bird'. Do you know that song? [Sings] Yellow bird, up high in banana tree…We'd make fun of each other, our differences. I was enchanted and falling in love with her. I wrote her a letter, saying goodbye, and left it with her grandmother.

Having been the life and soul of the Professional Club, Hong Kong, I suddenly found myself sitting alone on a hard bed in Terandak Camp, Malaysia. I was in the middle of the jungle, in the middle of monsoon season. I sat there, looking out my small window, watching a monkey on a tree branch trying to shelter from the rain. A moment later, rain fell so heavily that the monkey and its tree were obscured completely. It was like a sheet of steel, the rain. Right when I was thinking that this was one of the most miserable moments of my life, this guy came in and says, 'Jazz, it's great you're here! I heard you were coming. I need a great drummer.'

'Who are you?'

'My name's Bernie. Have you got a drum kit?'

'Oh, yeh, sure, it's over there in my rucksack.'

Everyone knew I played drums. Everyone knew I loved music. This guy Bernie had a gig in an army families club. I played, of course – blagged a kit from somewhere, and we sounded pretty good. The nice thing about Malaysia was it was fucking beautiful and suddenly I had a gig. The problem was we were playing to army people and Bernie wasn't too hot on keyboards. We did miserable covers and boring standards, bloody 'Fly Me To The Moon' and awful Cliff Richard songs. It wasn't going well, really, until we re-jigged the line-up, switched Bernie to sax and found Pete McLane, who could sing 'I Feel Good' like James Brown.

TAPE #2

We started doing Stax material – the Four Tops, the Bee Gees. Pete knew an Australian who was killer on keyboards. We put a Caucasian band together. Our plan was to pretend to be a real pop band from England. We called ourselves the Shades of Blue.

We grew our hair as long as we could and we went round doing gigs. A record company called Life Records was running a competition to win a record deal. We went along and, after playing one song, the boss of Life Records, this Chinese guy, sat there gobsmacked. We sounded like whoever we wanted to sound like.

'Don't enter the competition,' he said. 'You're too good.'

He signed us up and took us to Kuala Lumpur to record an EP. It was four tracks, two of our own and two covers. We covered 'Reach Out (I'll Be There)' by the Four Tops. We did our own arrangement.

We had this manager we called…I can't remember. We called him 'The Commy Manager'. He used to turn up with a copy of Mao's *Little Red Book*. His problem was he was an idiot so we got rid of him. Although I was the youngest member of the Shades of Blue, I started looking after the band. I did a deal with Tiger Beer so we always had plenty to drink. In fact, Pete and I used to drink a crate of Tiger Beer each a day. I'd put my last can in the fridge for the morning. I remember once I woke and found someone had nicked it. I was over at the hospital eating eggs and bacon and, as I picked up my knife and fork, I noticed my hands were shaking. I was twenty-two and I had the DTs. Delirium Tremors. I put the cutlery down and tried to steady myself. I held my hand out in front of me and watched it shake. In those days, you could get beer from the hospital. We gave it to the soldiers who donated blood. I went and drank one of those beers at eight thirty in the morning.

I did us a deal with Rothmans cigarettes, too, so we could smoke. I actually ended up doing some hand modelling for Rothmans. My

21

hands were on billboards all over Singapore. We had beer, cigarettes and we played in Kuala Lumpur clubs. Our plan worked; everyone thought the Shades of Blue were a proper band from England. People would recognise us. I'd go into bars and see our records on the jukebox. Nobody knew I was a radiographer or that we were all soldiers.

They used to have a chart countdown on Saturday night radio. And it was all stuff like the Bee Gees and the Beatles. And then once they'd done the chart, they played our record, and I remember them saying, 'This is a song that *should* be in the Malaysian chart. It's from the Shades of Blue and it's out on Life Records.' He was gay, the DJ, and he fancied our bassist big time, I think, which was handy for us, but tough for our bassist, who we called Spock for some reason; I think we liked *Star Trek*.

After that one radio play, our gigs went crazy. We got played more and more. We did television. We toured. We did swanky private shows. We had so many gigs that I was struggling to do my shifts in the X-ray department. I was having to bribe people with crates of Tiger and packets of Rothmans to cover for me at the hospital. We'd leave the army base and get driven to gigs in limousines and sports cars.

I bribed the guy who ran the Naffi, the army shop, with crates of Tiger. He agreed to buy loads of copies of the Shades of Blue single and, in those days, the Malaysian chart was made up of wholesale and not over-the-counter sales. I got the Naffi to buy twelve hundred copies on the understanding we'd buy them back and sell them at our gigs. I also got the bloke who stocked Malaysian jukeboxes to buy a load. That week, we entered the charts at number six, then the boss of EMI Malaysia complained and we got disqualified. Major record labels have always been killjoys, you see!

22

TAPE #2

One Saturday night in July 1967, we'd played in Singapore. American soldiers were there on R&R – they'd come for five days with wads of cash to spend on girls and drugs, before going back to the jungle. They were so young and I'd feel sorry for them, sitting at the bar, talking about life, not knowing whether they'd be dead or alive by next week. This American comes up to me that night and says, 'You guys. You guys are great.' He was one of those suave, husky-voiced Americans, but nice, you know, polite and super-confident. 'I'm Major Cord. The entertainment officer for the Third Airborne. Can I speak to your manager?'

'I'm afraid not. We don't have one.'

'OK, son. Well, how would you feel about playing Nam?

'Nam?'

'Vietnam.'

'That might be tough.'

'If you come to Nam for eight days, you could play seven or eight gigs.'

'Where?'

'A couple of clubs in Saigon. The rest in bases.'

'What about the Vietcong?'

'We'll take care of those guys. You see, son, if we move you by helicopter, we never stop firing. If we move you by truck, we never stop firing. They stay away. And my guys are gonna love you. We could fly you into Saigon from Bangkok. Can you get there?'

I did a deal. The Yanks could get hold of anything. I agreed to play a week of gigs in Vietnam in exchange for a Farfisa organ, three Fender guitars and amps, a Ludwig drum kit and a whole bash of Zildjian cymbals; all to be picked up in Saigon and for us to take back to Bangkok once we'd done the gigs. Plus $500 each, which was a fucking fortune in 1967, all supplied and paid for by the US government. I was pretty sure we could all wangle ten days' holiday. You couldn't get that quality of musical instruments anywhere, no matter how much money you had, but the Americans could get anything. Major Cord and I shook on it.

'So where do you guys live?'

'We move around a lot. You can contact me here...'

I gave him the number of the X-ray department back in Terendak Camp. It was to a phone in the back office that didn't go through the main switchboard. I told him it was the number of a friend's place in Malacca.

'Call between two and four on Monday,' I said.

Vietnam would be the first serious tour for the Shades of Blue. It wasn't quite what I'd dreamt of, years earlier, when I'd dreamed of touring Germany, following in the footsteps of the Beatles, but a Vietnam tour was better than nothing. All I really wanted was to play, to sit on that stool and bang those drums. I'd have toured hell's inner circle if the Devil was keen on our music. Especially if he'd offered us a Farfisa organ and a Ludwig drum kit.

Major Cord called on Monday at one. A sergeant took the call and, quite honestly, he's this real wet fuckwit, this sergeant, who couldn't take an X-ray to save his fucking life. He had an army brain, too; washed completely clean by endless rules. I guess the phonecall went like this:

'Hello, this is Major Cord from the Third Airborne. Is Jazz Summers there?'

'No,' says Sergeant Fuckwit. 'He's in the darkroom.'

'The darkroom? Right, OK, well, I'm calling to discuss the Shades of Blue gigs in Vietnam. Could you take a message?'

'I'd be happy to.'

TAPE #2

'Tell Jazz the flight leaves a week on Friday at 5pm. Tell him we'll pay $1500 before then $1500 after. Tell him not to go to the main terminal in Bangkok. The US Air Force have got our own terminal, half a mile south on the right. Tell him I'll see him in Saigon.'

The sergeant never said anything to me when I came out of the darkroom at two. Within an hour, I was arrested. Two military policemen marched into the X-ray department and grabbed me. So I'm sat in the back of this van, thinking, What the fuck is this about? I was driven to the Brigade Headquarters and there, outside the brigadier's office, standing in a row looking pretty fucking nervous, were the Shades of Blue. All except the keyboard player; he was Australian.

'Left, right, left, right, mark time, atten*tion*. Left turn.'

We were marched into the office of the head of the Commonwealth Brigade, Brigadier Niven, who everyone said was the actor David Niven's brother, but he wasn't. Behind the brigadier was a row of colonels and majors in charge of our respective units. He did look a little like David Niven. He was the type of person who says 'orf' instead of 'off'. A pure, upper crust, condescending, Sandhurst man.

'So,' he said. 'You are all members of a pop band called the Shades of Blue. Is that correct?'

'Yes, sir,' we replied in unison.

'Which one of you is Summers?'

'Me, sir.'

'And are you the manager, Summers?'

'Kind of, sir. And the drummer.'

'Have you got any idea, Summers, why you're all in front of me? Have you ever been in front of a brigadier before?'

BIG LIFE

'No, sir.'

'So, we can assume there's something serious going on, can we?'

'I suppose so, sir.'

'So *why* do you think you're all here.'

'I honestly don't know, sir.'

Niven's desk was mahogany and huge. Behind him, framed in elaborate gold, was a portrait of the young Queen. She was surrounded by photographs of army cricket teams, posing in various parts of the Empire. But all I could see was a Farfisa organ and a Ludwig drum kit floating down the Mekong Delta.

'Oh yes you do, Summers. You have arranged to play music in Vietnam. You calmly think that you, five British soldiers, can just poodle off to Vietnam. Do you realise, you idiot, what you're doing? This is an international incident: BRITISH SOLDIERS IN VIETNAM. We aren't in Vietnam, but you think you can just *poodle* off there and play "pop" music!'

'It wasn't confirmed, sir.'

'Thank God Sergeant Fuckwit intercepted this phonecall today. You are a blithering idiot, Summers. I wish you'd gone in some ways. I would have enjoyed throwing the book at you. You fools thought you could *poodle* off and sing songs in a war zone. March them out, Sergeant Major.'

As active British soldiers about to gig in Saigon, we'd been on the brink of taking Great Britain into the Vietnam War. In the days that followed, people were forever asking me what I'd been thinking. The truth was, I'd been thinking about getting some really good quality musical instruments and doing a good gig. Brigadier Niven's punishment was swift and meant the Shades of Blue were dust. I was posted to Penang.

TAPE #2

Conversation #2

Listen to that…Nirvana. Listen to Cobain's voice…he's not trying to be cool…not like fucking wispy, fucking, I don't know, what's his name, the lead singer of Radiohead? *This* is what we fucking need…this is what some of those DJs need. Voices!

DJs rule the roost at the moment, OK. Do you know why? Too many half-decent but essentially wimpy indie bands knocking around, like the Vaccines. Whereas, on the other hand, you've got three DJs like Magnetic Man going round with laptops and a light show and they're *really* getting people going. I saw Magnetic Man follow the Vaccines last year at a festival. It was frightening. They blew them away. They packed so much more punch. Although they played off laptops, they were much more raw and energetic. If rock bands are gonna survive, they've gotta compete with the likes of Magnetic Man. And you know what, if DJs are gonna become great, they've gotta harness the power and emotion of vocalists like Kurt Cobain. Find me a band like Nirvana…make a moment like punk…*listen* to that…Radiohead? I prefer 'Knights in White Satin' by the Moody Blues.

Nothing in life comes without thought. My thoughts have been changed considerably by what's happened to me. For most of my life I had a horrific skin disease all over my face. I'm going to tell you about it. I'm more thankful for having a spotty face and red nose than I am for anything else. Because having that forced me to change the way I thought about life. I've changed the way I see the world.

Thom Yorke. That's his name, Radiohead's guy. He cares about the environment. I respect that, his charity work. Maybe I'll email Scissor Sisters and tell them to listen to 'Thorn In My Side'. I think that might help. How d'ya spell 'Eurythmics'?

27

TAPE #3
(7TH JANUARY 2012)

How to Fake Your Own Death

I spoke to Scissor Sisters late last night. Someone's suggested they work with Brain Eno. I said to them, Eno'll throw a bunch of ideas at you and hope soundscapes wins. You'll end up sounding like, fucking, wispy disco. What they need to realise is how good *they* are. Take a song like 'Take Your Mama'. They wrote that when they had nothing, when they were living in New York, partying, buzzing off music. They had a gig the following night and needed an extra song. So they wrote one, bam, fearlessly, and it was an international hit.

I've not been with them long. They interviewed a lot of different managers – not just me. They picked me, they told me, because I was the only manager who talked about music. I was the only one that *confronted* Scissor Sisters. I told them they had to look insides themselves, not go around blaming others for the comparative commercial failure of their third album – there's some great songs on *Night Work*. Listen to 'Invisible Light', it's fucking great. They're wonderful people. But they don't need Brian Eno. They need each other. They need to banish the fear from themselves. False Evidence Appearing Real. I think we need some…I think we need some mint tea…where were we?

[Long pause]

Penang. *Penang*. In Penang, I became a corporal. Two stripes. I was actually a pretty good radiographer. People used to like me

28

because I could take good X-rays. Much better than the suck-up killjoy who stitched the Shades of Blue.

The good thing about Penang was a guy called Chester. He was a laboratory technician who wasn't really called Chester. He was called Michel because his mum was French, but you don't want to be called Michel in the army, so he changed his name. He was originally from Chesterfield. I smoked a lot of grass with Chester. It literally grew on the trees. For half a crown you could buy a quarter of a kilo. We were into *Sgt. Pepper's*. Me and Chester used to spend all day getting stoned and X-raying people. It was cushy. We'd do a bit of work and then skip off to the beach in Penang, which was beautiful. It's crap now because they've built a bunch of depressing hotels, but it was beautiful then and we'd sit on the beach smoking joints and talking about music.

Despite the efforts of Brigadier Niven, the Shades of Blue weren't quite finished. The people of Singapore loved us too much. I was able to get the promoters to put my air fare from Penang onto the gig fee. So I'd fly down in these little planes that sounded like motorbikes. I wasn't supposed to do it, but I didn't give a shit. If someone was really ill they could always take them to the local hospital and I'd get in the shit when I got back. I'd fly down for the odd weekend and I even got the band a gig in Penang; the promoter paid to fly the guys up from Malacca.

My friend Div. His name was Divney. Actually, his name was Patrick. He was the keyboard player in the Shades of Blue. He had three months to go before he could get out of the army and he planned to go to Perth and start a band with this brilliant singer we knew. I thought this was a fantastic idea – getting a band going in Australia. All I wanted was to play. Play music and not be a soldier.

I sat in Penang on my bed and I thought, what can I do? How can I get out of this army? Some ideas presented themselves to me:

the first was that Chester and I could apply to go back to England over land during our twelve weeks disembarkation leave. There was a tradition for doing this. The army encouraged it, said it made men of us. It was really the hippy route. You'd get a boat to Madras, go through India, Afghanistan, Iran, Iraq, Turkey, through Europe and back to England. Buses, trains. Chester wanted to do it for fun and, while conducting his research, he'd learned of a doctor in Madras who sold dodgy death certificates for five hundred quid. And you see, if you had typhoid or cholera, diseases you could pick up pretty easily in India, they had to bury you really quickly to prevent the disease spreading, which made faking your death a pretty plausible thing. Because the hardest thing about faking your own death is the absence of your corpse, OK. Five hundred quid was a lot of money in those days, but I had it. I hadn't been drawing on my army pay and I'd made quite a bit with the Shades of Blue, boot-legging Tiger Beer and, of course, my hand-modelling. We ran a couple of really big gigs in Malacca, too. They used to advertise Shades of Blue gigs at the local cinemas there. I also had gear I could sell. It was possible; me and Chester could go to Madras, and I'd get the death certificate. He'd then go back to England and report that Corporal Summers sadly got typhoid in Madras, died and was buried there. And that would be me, free. I could disappear, go to Perth, be in a band with Div.

He was in the signals and somehow he could call me for free on army telephones. We fixed everything. We didn't pay for anything. We ran an old Ford Mercury, a huge V12 with American diplomatic plates that hissed as it went along. We'd drive round Malaysia, smoking dope, drinking Tiger and talking about music, talking about the band we'd start in Perth. We ran the car on Avgas we stole from the helicopter base.

TAPE #3

As it happens, I couldn't go through with it. It was a lie and I don't like them. Faking my own death felt like tempting fate. I was fearful of the boat sinking on the way to Perth. I considered swallowing silver paper to fake a duodenal ulcer – I knew how to do that on a barium X-ray. But faking my death, and even faking illnesses, got me thinking about how I'd never see my mum again.

People's Arses

It's very easy to upset the military establishment. They get pissed off if you grow your hair too long or you don't wear your beret properly. It's so easy because there are so many rules and fascist sergeants.

In 1968, I made a conscious decision to misbehave and, within a few days, I'd pissed lots of people off. I'd been insubordinate, dressed scruffy. I'd sworn loudly at inappropriate moments. I was up before the local company commander. This was part of my plan. After he'd given me a severe reprimand, fined me fifteen pounds and was about to have me marched out, I declared I had a social problem.

'What is this *social problem*, Summers?'

'It's a personal problem, sir.'

'Explain yourself.'

'I'm homosexual, sir. And I'm finding it quite difficult.'

'Oh my god! We need to do something about that.'

'It started in military school, sir. But it's progressed. In Hong Kong, sir, I had an intense relationship with a Pan Am steward. Maybe it explains why I'm always in trouble…I'm living a lie.'

All my life I've had a lot of gay friends. I knew a lot about what they did. I knew they felt no differently about each other than heterosexuals did. A friend of mine had an affair with an English TV actor and had really confided in me. For my story, I turned the actor into a Pan Am steward. And the truth was, in Hong Kong, I was friendly with a gay Pan Am steward. His mother was a concert pianist and he was a great pianist, too, and he used to sit in with us sometimes when we played at the Ocean Terminal. He loved me and he was always trying to jump on me. He used to give me free flights to Manila. I took my Chinese girlfriend there.

Loads of the sergeants were gay in the army in those days. This was 1968, homosexuality had only been legalised outside the military the previous year. The sergeants were always trying to jump on you. You were always fighting for your virginity. But, officially, they maintained that being gay wasn't allowed.

'OK, Summers. This is extremely serious. Be reassured, we're taking this matter seriously. Return to the X-ray department and await further instruction.'

Within two hours, I was medically evacuated. Me, a homosexual, albeit a pretend one, was assigned a medical escort. We boarded an army plane to Singapore and, really, the truth is, my medical escort was gay. That's ironic, isn't it? He'd tried it on with me once or twice in the past and I'd rebuffed him – told him I was straight. I think he was a bit miffed that I was suddenly homosexual.

There was an ambulance waiting on the runway when we landed. I was admitted into the military hospital, the psychiatric ward, where it turned out all the homosexuals and alcoholics go. I was in the nuthouse again. I lay there in a bed for two days, pretending to be gay. In the bed beside mine was a seriously fucking downbeat alcoholic. Occasionally, a nurse would come along and take my temperature.

I had a meeting with a psychiatrist. I had my story straight: I'd had sex with men in Aldershot and Woolwich. I'd fallen in love with the Pan Am steward. I felt stressed, vulnerable and nervous all the time.

Usually, an army doctor wore a long white coat, but this psychiatrist was a Major, sitting there in full army uniform. He was obnoxious as hell, a real fucking fascist, furious-looking, eyes like a horrible dog.

'So, you're queer then, are you?'

'I beg your pardon, sir.'

'You're *queer*.'

'No, sir. I'm homosexual.'

'How did you find out that you were queer?'

'I've always known, sir. I had feelings for boys at the Gordon Boy's School. I fell in love with an American in Hong Kong. Since then, I don't feel I can be my true self. It's difficult.'

'What's difficult?'

'What's difficult is, I can't express myself. I can't be myself. I feel very nervous, because I know it's against army rules.'

'So, you're queer,' he said. 'Do you take it up the arse or do you shove it up the arse?'

I was prepared for this question. I thought, if I say I'm a receiver they're bound to inspect my anus. So I said I didn't receive.

'So, you *shove* your cock up people's arses, Summers?'

I was disgusted by the way he was treating me. This was a psychiatrist. I was thinking, Imagine how upsetting this would be if I *was* gay. I looked at him and I thought, Fuck you, fuck you, you big horrible bastard.

'So, do you suck cocks, Summers?'

I was upset and angry. I'd had enough.

'Actually, sir,' I said, 'yes, I do. I love sucking cocks. And actually, sir, if you unzip your fly now, sir, I'll suck yours.'

BIG LIFE

And of course he went absolutely mental, jumping up and down, screaming for the staff sergeant. 'Get this man out of here! Get this pervert out of here!' And I was thinking, 'You fucker. You horrible, rude fucker.'

I went back to the ward and lay on my bed, talking to the alcoholic on one side, the schizophrenic on the other, and occasionally having my temperature taken. Eventually, the staff sergeant came to see me and said, 'Look, it's pointless having you lying here for three months before we medivac you. We're low on radiographers.' And I thought, 'Fine.' It beats sitting on this bed having my temperature taken, and maybe I can get a few gigs going in Malaysia with the Shades of Blue.

Most people in the Singapore X-ray department had heard the rumours about me being gay. I had to be pretty careful because nurses were everywhere, you know, beautiful army nurses, and that was a bit of a temptation. There was a gorgeous nurse who kept flirting with me. I had to give her a wide berth because I was still gay. The good thing was I was able to get over to Malaysia and play with the band. They'd replaced me by then, but if I turned up, he'd have a drink, their new drummer.

It was saddening and tiring, pretending I was gay. My plans never seemed to quite work. The pretence ruined my social life and suspended the practice of heterosexual fornication, which I loved. Eventually, after some tricky and pretty sombre months, I was summoned into a room and on a blackboard was a list of all the medical evacuees.

Private Jones – fractured femur
Private Alice - P.I.D
Colonel Lancaster – Alzheimers
Corporal Summers – Homosexual

34

TAPE #3

I boarded a VC10 with a bunch of severely injured people, people with missing eyes and limbs and also, I remember, the alcoholic from the hospital. He was going home, too. And I was thinking: I don't have to pretend to be dead. I don't have to desert. I'm finally out the army. Finally.

We flew in to RAF Lineham in Wiltshire. I'd been abroad for two and half years. England looked so green from the air that day. It looked beautiful. All the really badly hurt people were taken off the plane first and put into ambulances. There were only three of us left. Me, the alcoholic, and a strange looking guy with a scarred head. We walked off the plane and were led to an ambulance. We didn't go through customs. If only I'd known – just imagine what I could have brought back from Singapore. As the double doors of the ambulance closed, I asked where we were going. I didn't quite catch the paramedic's reply. The doors slammed and the back of the ambulance became gloomy.

'Lads, what did he say?' I asked.

The guy beside me had a long red scab running across his shaved head and a ghastly look in his eye. The type of look where you wonder what the fuck they've had to see. He turned to me and tried to smile.

'They're taking us to Nettley,' he said.

I was on a big ward. About twenty beds. You'd lie there, you'd go and eat your meals, they'd take your temperature before you went to bed, you'd make a rug, you'd look at an inkblot test, you'd say it reminded you of a pelvis, you'd go to bed and, lying there, you'd think, 'Oh, fuck.' And you're nervous because you're back at Nettley, where you were almost sent to military prison three years previously. You're just sitting there, in limbo. You can't telephone anyone and you're wondering what the fuck is going to happen.

35

BIG LIFE

Some retired colonel came and did the rounds. And while he spoke to everyone else, like he chatted to the drunk about football, he looked at me and walked on. He was a homophobe. I disgusted him.

Those were long, horrid nights spent worrying about my future, longing for freedom and to be playing music somewhere, having a drink and talking to a girl. Out of the blue one afternoon, a medical orderly came in and issued me with a train ticket to Ash, near Aldershot. I was told to collect my papers from the Medical Corps Depot there. I knew what that meant. It meant I was out.

In Ash, they gave me a bed for the night and told me they'd issue me with my papers the following morning. That night, I bumped into this gay sergeant that I used to know and he asked me what I was up to. I couldn't tell him I was gay because that would be his dream come true. I said I was just staying over night and would be away in the morning. He invited me for a drink. I said I had to go to bed. I was knackered.

The following morning, I went to pick up my discharge papers from a pale, rawboned corporal. He looked old for his age. Lots of them did. He smoked a cigarette tenderly. 'This'll get you home to Yiewsley,' he said, exhaling a lungful of smoke and offering me the ticket. 'You've got ten weeks disembarkation leave, then report to the Military Hospital at Catterick on the 10th of June.'

My mind went blank. Catterick? 'Sorry, mate, but that's not right. I'm supposed to be discharged.'

'Not according to this, mate.'

'But I'm homosexual.'

'I don't give a fuck what you are. It says here you've been posted to Catterick. Get on with it.'

TAPE #3

The Cigarette

Posing as homosexual hadn't worked. I felt so low. I didn't wanna go to Catterick, in the middle of the Yorkshire Moors, in the arse-end of nowhere, for three years.

There was this guy in Malaysia called Colonel Tucker who really liked me. He loved my X-rays, but hated the fact I was always in the shit. 'Keep your nose clean, Corporal Summers,' he used to say. I called him up in Woolwich. We had this nice conversation about Penang and Malaysia. He took me for a pub lunch and I convinced him that I wanted to stay in London and work under him in his X-ray department. All I had to do was promise I wouldn't get in the shit any more and keep my nose clean. I'd resigned myself to the fact I had three more years left in the army. I'd tried everything and failed. But at least I'd be in London, where I could gig, rather than Catterick.

I'd arranged to smuggle a load of marijuana into the country via the army mail. I'd sent a letter to my partner in crime in Singapore and told him to stuff X-ray boxes with a bit of lead and a lot of marijuana wrapped in silver paper, as though they were X-rays. He was on his way back from Singapore so it was a good time for the scam.

I started collecting the mail at work, looking out for the name Staff Sergeant C. Hall (we'd used Chester's name). I signed for these boxes, took them to the X-ray department, told no one to touch them and, for two days, I just left them there to check no one suspected anything. When I finally opened them they were absolutely chock full of marijuana. We got eight hundred quid each for it, which in 1968 was a stack of money. That was July. In August, all my papers arrived from Singapore and I had to go for an interview with the company commander. These were the guys who really used to upset me. All I really wanted was to be a radiographer and do a few gigs. But these fucking brainwashed idiots were always on at you about your haircut or whether your stripes were pinned on your white coat properly. They had nothing better to do. I marched in to see this guy and he's sitting there looking at my papers, which are full of all my indiscretions, a litany of infamy, all the stuff I'd done in Hong Kong, Penang, Malaysia. My charge sheet was epic, biblical – more fucking pernickety charges about hair, uniform, driving sports cars, insubordinate behaviour, schizophrenia, drunkenness, trying to tour Vietnam, lateness, homosexuality etc. And he's looking at all this, and I'm standing there.

'I've no idea how you've got two stripes on your arm, Summers. It's disgusting. We don't like people like you in our unit, do we, Sergeant Major?'

'No, sir. We don't.'

'Watch this man, Sergeant Major. If he steps out of line, throw the book at him.'

The next day, I was a minute late. The sergeant major charged me. I got another charge for dust under my bed, then another for not wearing my stripes on my white coat. It was purgatory. On the upside, I'd already got myself a few gigs, including a nice little jazz gig on Sunday afternoons.

We always used to steal Dexys from the hospital, most of which we'd use ourselves, but some we'd flog to dealers in Wapping, down the East End, who'd then flog them to Russian sailors. I was able to shift the Singaporean weed onto the Wapping dealers, too, and I bought a dark blue Mini Cooper with half of the money. Really, I'd have liked a red one, but I couldn't find one.

Army crap had come into my life again. I went to see old Jim Swain, the head of army radiography. He offered to send me to

TAPE #3

Bahrain. It wasn't too good there in the sixties, so I declined. Next, he offered to show me my confidential report, which he wasn't supposed to do really. He was good guy, Jim Swain. He was trying to help me. On one hand, the report said I was a gifted radiographer. On the other, it said I was a pain in the arse who didn't turn up for the sergeant major's parade, who was cheeky, who was scruffy and had long hair, who was always late and was too interested in music. Jim Swain explained to me that it was my efforts as a radiographer that was keeping me in the army. 'Mess radiography up,' he said, 'then they'll drop you.'

The staff sergeant in the X-ray department was an Indian guy, a really nice guy. I think he was probably Kenyan-Asian, I don't know, but he could get a little bit hot under the collar with me because I was so annoying and because he'd been told to keep an eye on me. I used to accuse him of siding with the wankers, which was true, but it probably hurt his feelings a bit.

The Universe lines up when you want it to, you know. I think it lines up all the time. But when you really want it to line up, it does. The Indian guy was in the darkroom and I was in the office. Patients came in and I'd take their ID numbers, names etc. I started deliberately making mistakes with the admin. I jiggled around with established protocol. I was taking all the correct information down, but I was putting it in the wrong order. The army hates those kinds of tiny deviations.

Within twenty minutes, the Indian guy bursts out of the darkroom and lambasts me for fucking up. He knew I knew how to do it. I gave him a bit of lip and told him I'd sort it out. It was harmless really, the mistake I kept making, but the army hate all mistakes with equal passion. Once he was back in the darkroom I got back to work. I started really labeling the X-rays arse about face, all the information in the wrong order. Before long, he came steaming down the corridor, accusing me of all sorts. I sat there at my desk. I told him to cool down and to hold his horses. I asked why he was getting so upset. He got extremely angry and I got pretty sarcastic. He went back into the darkroom and I labeled the next X-ray correctly, then on the next I made a small mistake. Then I did one completely fucking wrong and out he came again, livid, beyond livid. He went all red in the face and this was a terrible thing that I did, I didn't like doing it, but as he got more angry his accent became very thick. I told him I couldn't understand him and asked if he wouldn't mind speaking English. It was an awful thing to say. He hit the roof, as you might imagine. He marched me down to Colonel Tucker's office, pointed at me and said there was no way he could continue to work with 'this'. Tucker snapped. He'd warned me to keep my nose clean and I hadn't. '*Get out!*' He was outraged. 'Get out of this X-ray department. You promised me! I never want to see you again.'

They put me in the stationery department. I counted pencils, rulers and rubbers for two days and distributed them to people in need of them. I made a drum kit out of plastic tubs and tins and played it for hours using a couple of rulers for sticks. I was playing it when the orderly sergeant came to see me. There were no windows in the stationery store and I'd taken to switching the lights off and drumming in the dark. 'Summers?' he said. 'Is that you? The colonel wants to see you.'

Everyone smoked in those days. I smoked eighty a day. The colonel was sat behind a wide mahogany desk, calmly smoking a cigarette. He did something quite strange. He dismissed the sergeant major, the bane of my life, and offered me a seat and a fag.

'Thank you, sir.'

TAPE #3

'Summers,' he said. 'I've talked to Warrant Officer Swain, I've talked to Colonel Tucker, I've talked to Staff Sergeant Pereira. They all tell me the same thing. They tell me you're a brilliant radiographer. They say when given responsibility you rise to the challenge. They say with the corners rounded off you wouldn't make a bad soldier. I've decided to promote you to sergeant, Summers. I've decided to put you in charge of the X-ray department up in Chester.'

I stood, approached his desk, leant towards him and stubbed out the cigarette in an ashtray near his hand. 'Listen,' I said. And here I did something unexpected. I slapped his desk hard with both hands and said, 'Sir, I'm a round peg. I'm a round peg, sir, in a very square hole. I've been incarcerated in the military since I was twelve, sir. I don't *want* to be here, sir. I don't want to be a sergeant, sir. I don't want to go to Chester.'

I emphasised this last remark with more slaps on his desk.

'Would you like another cigarette?' he asked. 'Sit down, for Christ's sake.'

'I'm a round peg, sir. I've been a round peg for so many years.'

'Would you be prepared to give up your stripes?'

'*Yes,*' I said. 'Give me a razor blade and I'll cut these stripes off my arm now!'

I was panting from all the desk slapping, but the colonel was calm. He let smoke plume from his mouth and then he blew it forcefully into the air between us. Through the smoke, he looked at me. 'I don't promise anything,' he said, 'But one thing's for certain. I'm not going to pass you on like everyone else has. I'm going to deal with you.'

That was a Thursday or a Friday or something. I left his office with no answers. What did any of it mean? It was definitely Friday. I skipped my duties at the stationery store – they wouldn't miss me. I went home to see Mum for the weekend. I suppose I spent the weekend pissed. Mum ran an off licence there in Yeiwsley. She'd give me a bottle of Scotch or I'd go down the pub. I didn't really know anyone round there except Mum. I went to see this really good blues band play. On Monday morning, I couldn't face the hospital. I got Mum to telephone and say I had chronic diarrhoea. She was cool with stuff like that. Later that day, a sergeant called and asked me to confirm my address for the ambulance.

'What ambulance?'

'You're sick, aren't you? We need to get you to the brigadier's office at nine tomorrow morning.'

'Forget the ambulance,' I said. 'I'll be there.'

I put down the phone and turned to my mum. She wiped her hands on her apron and asked to know what was happening. I gave her a kiss on her cheek and said I didn't know.

Breakfast

I jumped on the train to Woolwich that night. At half past seven the following morning I ate bacon and eggs and toast and then, at half past eight, I met with the colonel. He drove me in silence to this huge Victorian building in Woolwich, full of arches, towers, bulbous colonial features, flags and a massive parade square. It was everything I'd been trying to escape. Fucking Victorian nonsense. Everything glistened. Outside the brigadier's office, an anal sergeant major, all sashed and squeaky, marched me around, *left, right, left, right*, into the brigadier's office, *mark time, halt, left turn*.

This brigadier's sitting behind a ludicrous desk with gold braid all over his hat and a firing squad of officers behind him, maybe eight of them, all of them covered in gold braid and giving me deadly serious eyes. You don't see eyes like that much any more.

TAPE #3

'I don't like these kinds of things,' began the brigadier. 'We've looked at your records. You've bucked authority in the military and you'll buck authority on Civvy Street. With effect from the 9th of September 1968, 23544654, Corporal J Summers RAMC, you are discharged from her majesty's service – Services No Longer Required. March him out Sergeant Major.'

'*Left turn. By the front. Quick march. Left, right, left, right, left, right, left wheel, right wheel. Halt!*'

I didn't halt. As I left the brigadier's office I found myself marching into a long corridor, at the end of which, a door opened onto the sunlit parade ground. '*Halt!*' I was marching towards the open door and that sunshine. '*Halt!*' I didn't halt. '*Come back here! You're still under military discipline!*' I ran down the corridor and out into the centre of the deserted parade ground. I removed my beret and flung it as hard as I could towards the sky and I stood, all alone, the cries of the sergeant major distant now as he clung to the shadows of that Victorian nightmare. 'I'm out,' I shouted. 'I'm out the fucking army. I'm out!'

I picked up my beret, walked back to the hospital, picked up my drum kit and loaded up my Mini Cooper. I loaded it up with drums and some clothes that I kept in the hospital and I drove away.

Free. Finally. After nine years, six days and a breakfast. Since then, I've always subtracted nine years off my age. I'd missed the sixties, the birth of pop culture. I lost nine years of my musical life.

I've been trying to get them back.

PART TWO

TAPE #4
(8TH JANUARY 2012)

Conversation #3

Can you get 'em to choose three pieces of merchandise for the Gaga tour? Yeah, we're only allowed three. Yeh, obviously a T-shirt, but also, I don't know, a hat, a scarf or whatever. A mug. And get Ana to email all the Lady Gaga fans. We need to try and steal them. A bag? Do people buy Scissor Sisters bags? I would. Yeah, I think I would…a tote bag. Exactly. They're in. At some point today I need to phone Klaxons, Richard Ashcroft, Youth and La Roux. And also, I need to eat some sprouts, OK.

Fat Deiter

I slept a lot in 1968 and I also read the newspaper. I was numb. I listened to music and did fuck all. Suddenly, there was no system to fight against. It was strange.

I went to every drum audition going. Every night I'd play somewhere. Where? Oh, I don't know…the Pied Bull in Islington… the Bridgehouse in Canning Town. Then sometimes the band got going and we'd do a tour or make a single. Most bands earned a living from the road in those days. I'd play in Manchester, Newcastle, Leeds, Plymouth, Exeter, Sheffield, Glasgow, Liverpool. Every college had a good gig. England had gone through the mid-sixties pop thing with the Beatles, Freddie and the Dreamers and what have you. We'd gone into progressive bands, bluesy, funky, rocky type stuff. It was a mish-mash, exciting, Jethro Tull were coming up, Ten Years After, Cream had just split up, sadly, but great rock bands were buzzing up and having big gigs. Bands played exceptionally well because they were gigging six or seven nights a week in the clubs.

In the daytime, I worked part time at Poplar Hospital, taking X-rays. In the night time I played in blues bands or jazz bands or Top 40 bands, but what I really wanted, *all* I ever really wanted, was to be in a real band. My boss at Poplar Hospital was trying to persuade me to go full-time, but I wasn't interested. She said she'd make me Superintendent Radiographer. She was really trying to tempt me. I actually met my first wife at Poplar Hospital.

I started drumming in this band called Blue Hurricane. The singer's girlfriend came up with the name so we were stuck with it. Ten years had passed since I'd drummed with that band in Newcastle and almost gone to play in Hamburg. Then suddenly I got a second chance. And Blue Hurricane were a real band. Blues-rock. We did a few Top 40 songs – you had to, but we also did our own stuff. We had a Hammond organ and two lead singers. We sailed from Harwich to the Hook of Holland and did a gig in Belgium, another on the Dutch border, and then we drove into Germany in our Ford Transit. It was winter 1969. It was freezing.

Crooked agents ruled the roost because there were so many gigs. DJs weren't a big deal. They'd just spin between the bands. You'd play for four hours a night, so you had to have a load of material, or you'd jam or I'd do a drum solo. Hammond organ solos were good because they could just keep going forever. We travelled across Germany, starving, hungover, and hardly getting paid. Whenever we asked to be paid we got told not to worry: 'Wait until Frankfurt. Deiter, the agent, is based there. You'll get your money.'

TAPE #4

We get to Frankfurt and, sure enough, the German agent's there. In fact, we're playing his club. He had us down for three one-and-a-half-hour sets. We were owed, I don't know, we were owed about three hundred quid by Frankfurt. There were no roadies in those days, you did it all yourself. There were no guitar-techs or drum-techs; you lugged it all into the venue yourself. So we're sitting in the van, which, by Frankfurt, was like sitting in a dead man's underpants, and I said, 'They're taking the piss. We gotta get paid.' We had another thirty shows to go. I think we had one in Italy. That's why people could sing so well in those days. That's why they had those International voices - because you played so much your voice became incredibly strong. 'Fuck this,' I said. 'I'll go see Deiter. I'll say unless we get eighteen hundred Marks we won't play his club. If we don't play his club, he's fucked, right?'

I walked into the guy's office at the side of the club. He was a fat guy with long blond greasy hair, smoking a cigar, posters all over his walls and massive fucking medallion rings on his fat fingers. He looked like a woebegone European porn star, but he was more like a malevolent pimp.

'Are you Deiter?'

'Yah.'

'I'm the drummer in the band. We're playing your club tonight. If you don't mind, we need to be paid.'

'You've been paid.'

'No, we ain't. You owe us eighteen hundred Marks. How much commission you taking?'

'Who are you?'

'The drummer.'

'*Who?*'

49

BIG LIFE

'I'm the fucking drummer in the band. I'm not leaving till you pay me some money.'

He was a real obese geezer, Deiter. He really could have thrown me round the ring.

'If you're taking ten percent, you owe us sixteen hundred Marks. And I wanna know when we're gonna get it.'

'We take fifteen percent here.'

'All right, so you owe us fifteen hundred Marks.'

'Are you the manager?'

'No, I'm the fucking drummer.'

'Are you trying to be the manager?'

'*No*. I'm the drummer.'

Fat Deiter leaned back in his chair. It looked like he was slowly inflating, getting bigger and bigger, puffing on his cigar and looking at me.

'How much do you want?'

'I want at least fourteen hundred Marks tonight because we want to eat. We want to do something.'

'I haven't got the money, man.'

'Let me put it to you straight,' I said. 'We're playing your club tonight. We're playing three sets. I want a third of the money now. I want a third before we play the second set and a third before we play the third, OK.'

'No one ever refuses to play my club.'

'Well,' I said. 'Get used to it, mate.'

And so he goes to his safe and he pulls out five hundred Marks and, with a rather rude sigh, he chucks it at my feet. I pick it all up and go to shake his hand. He just looks at me. Later, before we played the second set, I went up to the bar and got the second installment, and the same before the third set. We had him by the short and curlies.

50

TAPE #4

Beautiful German ladies danced to our music that night. I met a divine Frankfurter – actually, she was the bar girl. We danced and she introduced me to schnapps. We downed shots and I charmed her a bit, paid her compliments. She admired the fact I'd stood up to Fat Deiter. I was so happy to be there, to be out of the army. I had money in my pocket and felt free. She was blonde and looked like Julie Christie, who I'd fantasised about quite a lot. I packed my Ludwig drum kit away and there she was, waiting for me in the snow, under the streetlights, outside the venue. We went to a tiny late night bar and then to her home, which she shared with her brother. We smoked a spliff and went to bed and that was magical. This was it – living. I'd played and got paid and made love and was touring Europe.

The following morning, I walked back to the venue through deep snow, still drunk and daydreaming about the night. I wore a scruffy old army coat, a navy one actually, and I'd grown my hair by that time. We were due to leave for Mannheim at 9am. I got there about quarter to and found all the guys busy loading up the Transit.

In those days, you had college bands and you had bands who formed locally or from adverts in *Melody Maker*. Blue Hurricane were working class, south London boys. They hadn't been to college. They had the same dream as me. To be musicians and to make it.

'Why's my kit on the pavement, guys?'

I stood beside my bass drum, which was collecting snow, and I watched them load the Hammond organ into the van.

'What's going on?'

The guitarist came close to me.

'We have to ask you to leave the band, Jazz.'

51

BIG LIFE

'Leave? But we've only just fucking started.'

'We had no choice.'

'What?'

'He's told us to kick you out, or the tour's cancelled.'

'Who has?'

'Deiter.'

'That fat git,' I said. 'But what will you do for a drummer?'

'He's found us a German one. He's waiting in Mannheim.'

'You bunch of cunts,' I said. 'You bunch of fucking cunts.' I stood beside my drum kit. They slammed the back doors and started up the van. I was pretty friendly with the bass player. He came over to me, said he was sorry, said there was nothing he could do. 'Fuck you,' I said. 'Fuck the lot of you. I got you paid.' One by one, they climbed into the Transit and looked at me through the frozen windows. I gave them the finger. It was knackered and covered in shit, that old blue Transit; it sort of smoked off round the corner. I stood with my drum kit, alone on that Frankfurt street, watching the snow fall. I sold the kit to pay for the flight home.

TAPE #5
(26TH MARCH 2012)

Wife #1

I was broke, freezing cold, twenty-five and fucking miserable. I was living with Mum and had to sell my Mini to make ends meet. I phoned a mate called Peter Curtis, a keyboard player. 'I've got a vision, Peter,' I said. 'I want to own a house, what do you want to do?' Peter said he wanted a fuck-off car. 'All right,' I said. 'Well let's start our *own* band.'

I saw this nurse a lot. She got pregnant. She had an abortion. She got pregnant again. She said I had to marry her. I did. She had a miscarriage. She hated me being in a band. She liked the idea of me being a radiographer, which I pretty much despised. She liked me a lot, but she was crazy. We were drunk. We got married when we were drunk. Her name was Eilish.

I had a terrible job in a Mass Mini Truck. I drove round London with these two old guys, taking X-rays of East End factory workers. We were based out of East Ham. I was spraying working class people with radiation all day long. I'd go to Bryant and May, the match factory, X-raying hundreds and hundreds of tired, thin people. But the banter was always good.

Peter Curtis could sing, play keyboards and he could also play bass with his feet, as you can with a Hammond organ. We didn't have a Hammond, we had like a Vox Continental or a Farfisa, but Peter could play those with his feet, too.

Up and down the Old Kent Road, in fact anywhere in the East End, there were bands in pubs, earning a living playing Top 40 songs. It was what musicians did. In your spare time you'd work on your own material, but your bread and butter was playing the Top 40. When new songs came along, you'd get together and learn them. I'd wander up and down the Holloway Road and talk to the governors of the pubs. I'd tell them our band was called something like the Holloway Road Boys, and I'd wangle a Wednesday night or a Tuesday, we'd play well, play the Top 40, tell a few jokes and then, all being well, we'd get a gig on a Friday or a Saturday. I got us a gig on Balls Pond Road under the name the Balls Pond Explosion. I had my own little jazz gig going in Sidcup, too, on a Sunday lunchtime, with Bernie from the Shades of Blue.

It was a shotgun wedding, me and Eilish. We had an addictive sex life, which caused all the pregnancy. We split up for a bit, but our addictions got the better of us. So we got more drunk and more sexually addicted. We got married at Poplar Town Hall during her afternoon break. We had chicken and chips in a paper bag. Eilish didn't want me being in some 'scrudgy band', as she used to call it.

Peter Curtis and me played in a pub on the Hackney Road where the stage was six-foot high. We called the band Hackney Racket. I remember when we first played that place, I said to the governor, 'Why's your stage so high?' 'You'll see,' he said.

From Thursday through to Sunday night the fights were almost constant. The only way to keep the band safe was to heighten the stage. You'd be playing, watching everyone kick the shit out of each other, bottles and glasses shattering on people's heads and blood spurting upwards and splattering down. One night Eilish came, I remember, and she sat at the bar all night drinking brandy and Babysham and putting them on our slate. When I went to collect the money, there was nothing left – she'd drunk our earnings. She got groped as we were packing the gear up, too, and so everything got heated and, of course, in those days, you drove drunk. Pissed out of your head, you'd drive.

After flogging my Mini I'd bought an old Rover 105s. Eilish and I drove back to Poplar. She was furious. It wasn't so much the groping as the fact I was in a band. 'This *stupid* band, Jazz,' she kept saying. 'This stupid, *scrudgy* band. Lower-class people watching you and fighting.' As I drove along, pissed as a sad old duke, Eilish grabbed my long hair and dragged me down and battered me round the head. I rammed on the brakes, leant across the car, opened her door and pushed her out onto the road. No one wore seatbelts. I set off home. I hadn't got far when Eilish suddenly leapt onto the bonnet of the Rover 105s, brought her hammered face close to the windscreen and screamed. She hung onto the windscreen wipers as I steered from side to side, trying to shake her off. Then I heard a siren.

I pulled over. I wound the window down and let my face droop out of it. Eilish, looking windswept and pretty disheveled, was climbing off the bonnet. This cop comes over absolutely apoplectic.

'What the fuck are you doing? What the fuck are you doing, driving with her on the bonnet?'

'She's my wife,' I said.

Maybe breathalisers weren't out yet. I don't know. The cop told Eilish to get back in the car and that was that. We were lucky, I suppose, but I think that incident ended our marriage. We had a glass-fronted alarm clock to get us up for work each morning. And I remember calling her a mad bitch when we got home. The next thing I knew she was smashing the alarm clock over my head. I was picking glass out of my scalp for days. I left a few weeks later. I left a big trunk of records round her house. Eilish went down Chrisp Street Market and sold them all for a fiver.

BIG LIFE

We did a DIY divorce two years later. I tracked her down to a small flat in Mile End. I loved her, really, Eilish, because she was funny, wild and sexy, incredibly sexy, but crazy. And however wild she was, she had this idea that musicians were scrudgy – the lowest of the low. That would never change. We went out round Mile End and got really drunk together. We talked about our brief marriage. We were both twenty-seven by then. After the pub, we went back to her flat, signed the divorce papers, both of us drunk as hell, and then we went to bed and consummated the divorce.

I keep a photo of her. I always will. And I smile when I look at it, remembering the times she beat me up, all the windows she smashed and how much I lusted after her and adored her, too. I left her flat in Mile End the next morning and filed our divorce papers on the Strand. And that was the end of it. I never saw her again.

It was around this time that I noticed a red lump growing between my eyes. It was like a big boil and it wouldn't go away. I'd quit the Mass Mini Truck and was working as a radiographer at Old Church Hospital. I'd wander round those corridors like a hippy in a white coat. People used to ask about my face and I'd pass it off as some kind of short-term infection. Every night, I was somewhere in London, sitting at the drums, making music.

24hrs

I started going out with a Go-Go Dancer called Tracey. She used to dance beside the band and I chatted her up one night and took her out to a gig. We moved into a house in Romford. We had a room to rent and we heard that Richard Digance, a local folk singer, was having trouble with his dad. We invited him over. He didn't pay any fucking rent.

TAPE #5

A tall, timid, skint, skinny guy, Richard Digance had an afro – a folky afro. He slinked into my bedroom one day wearing flared jeans and a tight checked shirt with the sleeves rolled up. 'Here, Jazz …' He had to roll his sleeves up on account of his long arms. 'Here, Jazz,' Richard said. 'I think I've got a record deal with Transatlantic Records.'

I was pleased for him. He had a manager called Kevin Wyatt Lown and he'd been to Transatlantic, who were a folk label with acts like Pentangle, Bert Jansch and Ralph McTell. Before they signed Richard, they wanted to hear him play with a full band.

'Chappell Music'll give us their studio on Bond Street to make a demo,' Richard said. 'Can you drum and put a band together?'

We rehearsed at the house, in the conservatory, much to the annoyance of our neighbours. We went up to Chappell studios and when we were done, once the songs were mixed, we went to celebrate at a pub on Bond Street. Two or three drinks in, Richard told me that Kevin Wyatt Lown was off to live in Los Angeles.

'Oh, really,' I said. 'That'll be ok. You'll get another manager. And Transatlantic will definitely sign you – these demos sound like finished records.'

'I want you to do it, Jazz.'

'Do what?'

'Manage me.'

'Richard, I'm a fucking drummer, I'm not a manager.'

'Come on, Jazz. I know you're a drummer, but you fix things. You run three bands in god knows how many pubs. You're playing seven nights a week, you're playing on *Top of the Pops* albums. Everyone knows it. You fix stuff.'

Since Fat Deiter fucked me over and Eilish and me broke up, I'd been playing non-stop. I'd been working in the day at Old

BIG LIFE

Church Hospital, gigging seven nights a week with Peter Curtis at the Wheatley Taverns, and playing jazz with Bernie on Sunday afternoons in Sidcup. And I was fixing bands all over East London, putting bands together, subbing drummers and guitarists and singers from one pub to another. I was spending my nights on Dexys, recording *Top of the Pops* albums in a studio near Marble Arch. They were big in the seventies, the *Top of the Pops* albums; they contained covers of Top 40 songs and had models on the sleeves. We recorded them; me, Peter Curtis and others; they were debauched sessions, those, spliff and rum as well as Dexys, chips and lots of kebabs and women, too, in miniskirts and fishnet tights, smoking fags and off their heads and us, in the middle of it all, imitating Top 40 songs till dawn. But that wasn't the point. I couldn't manage Richard. Couldn't handle the responsibility that comes from looking after someone's career.

'I can't, Richard,' I said. 'I'm sorry, but I can't.'

In the weeks that followed, Richard stalked me round the house. I'd be waiting for the bathroom, half-asleep, in my dressing gown, and he'd be badgering me to manage him. I'd be waiting for the toast to pop, and he'd be lecturing me on the pros and cons of being a folk manager. He wouldn't let it lie.

In 1973, aged twenty-nine, I became Superintendant Radiographer at North Middlesex Hospital. They showed me into my office and I couldn't believe it was all mine. I wasn't sharing it with anyone. There was a lovely old desk in there, bookshelves and a nice comfy chair. I lowered all the blinds, sat down in that chair and thought about my life. It was probably possible, I thought, to organise the X-ray department in the morning. In theory, that left the afternoon free. The first telephone call I made as Superintendent Radiographer was to Richard Digance. 'I'll do it, Rich,' I said. 'I'll

58

manage you.' I could manage Richard in the afternoon and then, in the evening, I could go down and play in Walthamstow with Peter Curtis – I'd found us a gig at the Lorne Arms. It was a life-changing decision: I knew absolutely nothing about managing an artist.

It was a villain's pub, by the way, the Lorne Arms. I'd never have played a police pub. The landlord was a guy called Danny. We became drinking companions. He loved me, for some reason, Danny. He never made me pay. Many were the nights when we'd sit among the villains and drop ten bottles of Pils and ten double gins and tonics. They were nights of booze and bugger all, Chinese restaurants, bottles of wine, slurred conversations over Irish coffee, dreamless nights, interrupted by harshly lit fucking days of headaches and office work and yearning to play drums.

When you go into a record company, it's easy to be overwhelmed. Don't be. Stay calm, OK. You meet the head of press and think, 'Wow, fucking hell, this is the head of press!' I was lucky – there were some great people at Transatlantic in 1973. I met a guy called Martin Lewis, a brilliant young marketer who had his sights set on Hollywood. And in those days, labels had people called Van Salesmen - guys who drove round all the record shops in vans selling the music. They formed close relationships with the owners of the shops and that was a smart idea. Transatlantic had this guy called Ray Cooper, a hippy, gentle, laid back guy. He ended up running Virgin Records in America. There was a girl called Vivien Goldman, who went on to be a really successful journalist for *NME*. The place was full of talent.

Most men in the folk industry grew beards. I grew one. I grew one because of my face. The redness had spread down from the big boil between my eyes and it was all over me. All over my face –

mostly my chin. A big bushy beard helped to camouflage this. Not completely. But it was something. I didn't know what to do.

I knew nothing about management either. I knew fuck all. But I was serious and passionate about Richard and his music. I went up to Cecil Sharp House, the centre of the English Folk and Dance Society, and I placed a full-page advert in the folk directory. It included a photograph of Richard – that cost me a lot. And it was extravagant, a full page for an unheard of guy. But I was going for it. The advert read like this:

> *Richard Digance – Folk Singer*
> *Contact: Manager – Jazz Summers*
> *(24hrs)*

Slabbering Pugs

I was living with Tracey the Go-Go Dancer. I started really bugging the folk clubs about Richard. And it was all, like, Richard Who? So I made some little packs and used to talk to everyone about how fucking great he was and how he was signed to Transatlantic. Meanwhile, we had him in Chipping Norton studios, making his first record. He came to me one day and said we had to do a press release.

'What's a press release?' I said.

'It's like a letter that we send to folk journalists.'

'Oh,' I said.

'People at *Melody Maker* and *NME*.'

'Don't the record company do that?'

'No,' Richard said. 'Not at first.'

Every afternoon, I'd lock myself in my office at the hospital and I'd dig out my list of folk clubs and bug them for a while, then I'd draft press releases and then, if I wasn't playing at the Lorne Arms, I'd go home and carry on phoning folk clubs. I'd take a half-day on a Wednesday and go down to Marylebone High Street for meetings with Transatlantic. I never let on to them I was a radiographer. I made out I was a full-time manager.

The key to success as a folk artist, I'd figured out, was playing at the Cambridge Folk Festival. Me and Richard had gone to the festival the previous year because Richard said there were loads of girls there. I convinced them to put Richard on the main stage there. I bugged them about it and they took a shine to me. I think because I was so passionate. I was. I was passionate about Richard. I knew he'd make everybody laugh and get everyone singing along. He just needed the opportunity.

In those days, you'd make a record and, bam, the label would release it. No six-month set up, like now. You had people like Ray Cooper driving round England in his little van, talking passionately to record shop owners about the music. And of course there were thousands of record shops. People bought records like nowadays people buy clothes. The people in the shops knew a lot about music. There were no supermarkets. You'd never hear folk on Radio 1, unless John Peel played it, but the record shops did the job for you. They introduced people to the new folk acts.

Richard's debut album was called *England's Green and Pleasant Land*. I leant him my clapped-out Hillman Imp and set tours up for him around the country. He used to get £15 a night. We had articles in *Melody Maker* and *NME* and sent the clippings to the venues, too, with photographs of Richard, to really get them going. As a manager, you have to hustle. It's not glamorous. You have to act. Do things!

Steeleye Span had a huge hit with 'All Around My Hat'. I had this idea to get Richard to support them. Steeleye were managed by an American guy called Joe Lustig. Joe's dead now. I think he was an ex-boxer. He had a long-standing feud with Nat Joseph, who ran Transatlantic.

I went round Joe Lustig's house to try and negotiate Richard onto the Steeleye tour. Joe was in bed with some sickness, so I sat in the living room and had a cup of tea with his wife. She was lovely. She's still alive actually. They had two pug-dogs, running round, I remember, and Joe strode out in his silk dressing gown. He looked quite the ex-boxer – bit of a flat nose. The only thing he was missing were his boxing gloves. He was coming into the ring to fight!

'You want Digance on the Steeleye Span tour?'

'That's right,' I said. 'And Richard's great, Joe. And he's on his own. So he's cheap - no fuss.'

'I want Nat Joseph to pay for full page adverts in *NME* and *Melody Maker*. If he doesn't, Richard isn't coming, OK?'

'Nat's not going to do that,' I said.

Lustig lay on his sofa with his two slabbering pugs. I bit the bullet and phoned Nat Joseph there and then. 'Where's Joe,' Nat said, 'I heard he was ill. He's not in bed with the fucking pugs, is he?'

'No,' I said. 'He's here. He's willing to negotiate.'

I cut a deal between the two of them. I got Richard on the Steeleye Span tour. I think Nat agreed to half-page ads in *NME* and *Melody Maker*. That was the compromise. Performing on that tour, along with his appearance on the main stage at the Cambridge folk festival and all the gigs we'd done, really elevated Richard. In a year or so, he'd become the biggest new act on the folk scene.

He wrote a wonderful song for his second album, I remember. It was called 'Working-Class Millionaire'. Everywhere we went people would be singing it. It was my first encounter with that heavenly scent that a hit song gives off. It's like clean clothes on a countryside washing line. Cut grass in early summer! I love that smell.

We took it to radio, but they didn't play it. I called up the producer of *The Old Grey Whistle Test* from my hospital office. I really bugged him. Luckily, Whispering Bob Harris saw Richard play at Cambridge. He let Richard on the programme and he played great – record sales went up, gigs got bigger. I'm always looking for opportunities, OK. If you want something done, do it yourself. You can't leave it to the record label – Transatlantic probably had five acts that they wanted on *Whistle Test*. I only had one.

[Pause]

It's like tomorrow – I'm gonna call up Glastonbury and make sure they put Culture Club on next year. You've gotta do it yourself. I'm gonna bug the Brits to give them a lifetime achievement award, too.

I thought Richard could play the Albert Hall. I thought he could be as big as Ralph McTell. 'Working-Class Millionaire' could be Richard's 'Streets of London'.

Coke Can

Richard spent time in Canada in the early seventies. He had a brother there. When he returned he'd really gone on about these restaurants he'd eaten at. 'They're fantastic,' he'd said. 'Oh, Jazz, you've got to try them. The chips are great. The drinks are great.'

We toured America in 1974. In New York, he and I were staying at the St Moritz near Central Park and we had a day off. I wanted to look around – I remember Richard was a bit fearful of getting mugged, but I reassured him. I persuaded him to go round Times

BIG LIFE

Square at two in the morning. I was a bit pissed because I nearly always was. Times Square was a bit hairy in the seventies. There were transvestites with big bushy beards, people completely out of it, people selling drugs on every corner. In that little triangular bit in the middle there was a trannie with a big ginger beard and thick smudged black eyeliner and bright red lips. She was dressed in half a skirt and high heels and she was dancing round a Coke can, dancing and dancing and singing and Richard was a bit timid, but I wasn't; I wanted to look at everything. So we stood for ages and watched the trannie dance round the Coke can.

The next morning we hailed a taxi outside the St Moritz. Most of the cab drivers in those days were American; guys in checked shirts and baseball caps, smoking fags and sitting low in their yellow cars. Richard and me jumped into a cab, feeling like a couple of pretty cool guys, free in America, living it up in New York, although I was massively hungover. We jumped in this cab and the cabby was thinking, Lovely, tourists, probably hoping we wanted a tour of the city or a ride to Wall Street. But the truth was, I was really hungry, and so once again Richard starts waxing lyrical about these lovely restaurants he'd eaten at in Canada.

'Here, Jazz. Maybe there's one in New York! Do you have a McDonald's here, mate?'

'McDonald's?'

The cabby shifted round in his seat and looked at us. He looked at us like we were a pair of Limey idiots. We were. I think he thought we were taking the piss. We weren't.

'You two wanna go to McDonald's?'

'Yeh,' said Richard. 'Where abouts is it?'

'Which one you want? The one on *this* corner or the one on *that* corner?'

TAPE #5

'There's more than one!'

The cabby didn't dignify that with a response. He pulled round the corner with one burst of the accelerator, hit the brakes and charged us three dollars.

A Strange Period for Taxi Drivers in New York

In 1974, a lot of the taxi drivers in New York looked like John Denver. I remember once Richard and I asked one to take us to Central Park South. And I think he was on acid, this John Denver, because he didn't seem to know the way. We ended up driving the wrong way up Broadway. We abandoned that cab and got in another one. And this second cabby, who also looked like John Denver, didn't know where Central Park was either. It was a strange period for taxi drivers in New York.

Once, after a gig at the Bottom Line, we hailed a cab, loaded the guitars in the boot and this cabby, who was the spitting image of John Denver, asked if we were musicians. And, of course, Richard was a lovely, warm, obliging man.

'Hey, man,' he said. 'You should come to my gig tomorrow. I'll get you tickets.'

I was sitting beside him thinking that this was an awful idea, inviting one of these mad, John Denvers, most of whom were completely out of their box and weren't the type of guy you particularly wanted turning up at a gig.

'Can I bring along my wife?'

'Of course! Pick us up at six and we'll all go together.'

Six the next day, the cabby didn't show. Richard and I went to the venue and then, as we're sitting in the dressing room and Richard's tuning his guitar, the manager of the Bottom Line came

65

in, I think his name was Alan Pepper, anyway he comes in and says there's a guy outside with his wife claiming to be on our guest list.

'Oh, right,' Richard said. 'Jazz, could you …'

I went out and there was the cabby, looking like a shampooed John Denver, standing with his arm round his wife, who was sort of trashy, naughty-looking and smelt a little tipsy. In those days, at a venue like the Bottom Line, you'd sit down at a table and watch the acts. I can't remember who was headlining, maybe John Prine. No, it wasn't him…it was Tom Rush.

The four of us sat together after Richard's gig: Richard, me, John Denver and his wife. Out of the blue, perhaps because he was bored, John Denver says, 'Hey, you guys wanna go to a club?'

Richard was worried about his guitars. But I persuaded him the club was a great idea. The place we went to was packed, really quite happening, and I'm sitting with a girl and, across the table, I see Richard deep in conversation with John Denver's wife. John Denver's off talking to someone else entirely and, suddenly, Richard starts throwing me these really rather petrified glances. He looked timid as hell. I tried to pacify him with my calmest, most reassuring smile, but it didn't work. The next moment, Richard starts nodding in a strange manner and I realised John Denver's wife had got hold of his penis! John Denver sits down next to me and I sip my drink as calmly as I can.

'My wife wants to fuck Richard, Jazz.' John Denver was really out of it. He was on everything. He was probably on acid. His eyes were blinkless and absolutely massive and freaky, like they were sticking out on stalks. 'And that's fine by me,' he said. 'Fine by me.'

From across the table, Richard gives me a coy grin. And then he and John's wife get up to leave. As they leave, John Denver, who had his arms wrapped around a couple of girls, he shouts, 'Hey, Richard, have a good fuck!'

I'd heard America was like this, but you never really expect to encounter the fun stuff, do you? All around our table people were raising colourful cocktails up and toasting the departure of Richard and John Denver's wife, all smiling and saying, 'Yeh, guys, you two have a fabulous fuck!'

I stayed at the club. I ended up making progress with a girl. After a few more drinks, me, the girl and John Denver jumped in the cab and drove to the St Moritz. We walk into the room, which was my room, too, and there's Richard sitting up in bed, sheet pulled over his chest and arms over the covers while, beside him, John Denver's wife is half-dressed and all sprawled and disheveled.

'Guys! How was it? Richard, did you have a good time?'

Richard smiled like only an Englishman can smile in such a situation, reluctantly and between flushed cheeks. The minibar opened and the whole lot of us drank for hours. At the peak of the party, the girl, whose name I didn't know, jumped into my bed and wriggled out of her clothes. She tossed her bra onto the floor.

Richard and I took the train to Washington the following day. He was worried and maybe a little ashamed, too, but mostly he was hungover and convinced he'd contracted some kind of sexual disease from John Denver's wife. He stared out of the window, watching the suburbs of New York come and go. The truth was, he was fine. I was unlucky; I'd got scabies.

After New York, we did four nights at the Cellar Door club in Washington supporting the comedian Steve Martin. He's a great banjo player. He used to walk round our dressing room playing banjo. He'd burst in and say, 'Hey, Richard, can you make a folk song out of this...' And then he'd play a riff on his banjo. He was fresh, Steve Martin. He'd walk out on stage in Washington and say, 'You know, I love Washington. You wanna know the thing I love about Washington? The surf.'

I used to drink every lunchtime. Every day I would drink, and of course I was smoking eighty cigarettes a day. We used to smoke in the hospital. Hard to imagine, that. I'd go out at lunchtime with my colleagues. They might have a gin and tonic because they were girls and I'd have a sausage sandwich and a few pints. Even remembering it worries me. If I was playing at night I'd drink five large gin and tonics, eight bottles of Pils lager, a pint of Guinness, a brandy before I went on, then several Scotches before I went home.

One lunchtime, I drank three cans of Special Brew and returned to the hospital. I was pissed. There was a cardiac angiogram going on. A cardiac angiogram is when you put a catheter into the femoral artery, put it up into the heart, inject iodine dye and take pictures of the dye going through the arteries to see if the patient needs a heart bypass. And as you can imagine, the dye needs to be pumped in at quite a high pressure. So I'm fiddling with the pump because it wasn't working and there was a nurse, I remember, who had her foot on the pump and, because I was drunk, because I was pissed and slow, I gave her the go-ahead and the pressure pump's plunger went straight through my hand. It cut the tendon in my finger. It still doesn't bend, that finger. There was talk of a skin-graft. There was talk of them permanently bending the end of my finger. The orthopedic surgeon said my whole hand might end up not working. He said the best thing was to try and live with it, which is what I did.

The scabies was more curable. The thing about scabies is, whoever lives with the sufferer has got to get treated, too. By the time I was diagnosed, I'd given it to Tracey the Go-Go Dancer and the woman who lived next door to us in Romford. We all had to treat our scabies with this pink powder. For weeks the air round ours was pink.

After America, I really began to feel the pressure of managing Richard, running the X-ray department and playing in a band. In life, if you're doing a bunch of different stuff, it's hard to concentrate. I firmly believe now that there's no accidents in life. You create stuff. I created a fucking pump blowing my hand to bits. I created that, OK.

After my hand healed, I still played the odd jazz gig with Bernie on those slow south London 1970s Sundays. I joined another pub band, too. I kept trying. I remember sitting at the kit one night, listening to the singer, who couldn't sing, listening to the bass player, who had no rhythm, listening to the keyboard player, who played with no heart, and I thought, What am I doing here?

I'd sunk pretty low. After all, I was a founding member of the Shades of Blue. I'd nearly taken the British into Vietnam. I couldn't see me reaching those heights again. That war was over. My hand hurt when I played. Since the age of five, I'd played drums and dreamed of playing drums forever. I sold my kit to a shop on Denmark Street.

TAPE #6
(27TH MARCH 2012)

All Artists are Serious

After Richard's third album, Nat Joseph took me for a ham sandwich. He told me Richard wasn't selling enough records. Transatlantic were terminating the deal. I was a bit disappointed, but it's never the end of the world when you leave a label, OK. I thanked Nat for his sandwich.

The bigger problem was between Richard and me. Richard didn't want to be a funny man any more. He didn't want to be telling jokes in between the songs any more. He wanted to get a load of new musicians involved and to be a 'proper band', a 'serious artist'.

'Richard,' I said. The two of us sipped pints of ale, smoking fags in a smoky stinky pub in Romford. Locals played darts while some drunk slurred a shanty. 'Richard, you haven't got a good enough voice for that,' I said. 'You're not Rod Stewart. You've got a folk voice. Your appeal is you're really fucking funny. That's your career.'

He'd met a girl, Richard, and moved out of Romford. He phoned me one day and told me Joe Lustig, the ex-boxer and pug-owner, was going to manage him. A month later, Joe had got Richard a deal with Chrysalis Records, which, if I'm honest, was a lot better than I could ever have got him. Lustig was big. He managed Steeleye Span. I was a radiographer who drank in his lunch hours.

I'd kept Richard, fed him, chatted up girls for him, taken him from playing at the back of a bus in East Ham to playing New York City. I'd got him on *The Old Grey Whistle Test*, got him on the

70

main stage at the Cambridge Folk Festival. But, really, I'd made the fatal mistake most managers make with the first artist they manage. I'd failed to be objective. I'd got too close. I'd been present for everything. My girlfriend, Tracey the Go-Go Dancer, cooked Richard's dinner and washed his clothes. I loved him.

Lustig probably bullshitted him, promising Richard he'd turn him into Rod Stewart. My heart was broken. Richard's deal with Chrysalis didn't go too well. He split with Lustig and was managed by London Management and they managed him as a DJ on Capital Radio and a comedian. He got a TV show called *Richard Digance Presents*, which was a comedy show, and he wrote some great books and, I love Richard still; he makes a living today going round telling funny stories and playing wonderful songs.

Punching People

Mum voted Tory. I think she probably fancied Ted Heath. Dad died before we could really discuss political issues. I was raised in a racist, homophobic, aggressive household. I remember punching Dad's raised palms, left, right, left, right.

I was eating shit and being pissed out of my head, OK. This was the mid seventies. I was keeping late hours, taking Dexys and drinking multiple pots of black coffee. Oh, and I was fornicating. There was a lot of women in X-ray departments in the seventies. Anger was in me like a…like a…I don't know…like a *skeleton*. Richard went round telling people I'd threatened to kill him. I loved him. I couldn't believe he'd left me. I delved deep into drink, drugs and fornicating.

We ran a folk club in Ilford, Tracey the Go-Go Dancer and me. We'd pack it out with five hundred people. We put on Long

BIG LIFE

John Bawrdy, John Martin, Anna and Kate McGarrigle, Rufus Wainright's mum, Jasper Carrott, Fred Wedlock. They used to stay at our house – that was how folk clubs worked. Peter Sarstedt played – he wrote, 'Where Do You Go To My Lovely?' What a beautiful song. Mark Knopfler used to come down and do floor-spots, but I don't really remember him. A floor-spot was an invitation for members of the audience to get up and perform. It was a good way of getting punters into your club. Not all the people who came down were as nifty as Mark Knopfler and, the truth is, some of those floor-spotters were awful. One guy, I forget his name, he used to come down every single week and play absolutely appalling songs about how broken his heart was. The situation with this guy became so unbearable that, one evening, when I encountered him at the entrance, I explained that, since he'd done so many floor-spots in the past, it was probably time for him to let others play.

He *demanded* a floor-spot. I was horribly pissed. Tracey tried to reason with him and this guy told her to fuck off and grabbed hold of her mackintosh collar. I went for him. I picked him up and threw him down a steep flight of stairs. I still remember the silence after I did that.

The previous year, I punched someone at the Cambridge Folk Festival. It was July 1975 and Richard was playing. Transatlantic were there in force. They'd signed a guy called Harvey Andrews and it was quite a big deal. I was trying to get them to go and see Richard, but by then Transatlantic were going a bit cold on us. It was the first time I'd ever experienced a record company losing interest in their own artist. It made me incredibly angry. I suppose he wasn't selling enough records but, as far as I was concerned, that wasn't the point. The point was he was good. Every time I bumped into someone from Transatlantic I'd ask, 'Did you see Richard?' And they'd reply, 'No, but did you see Harvey Andrews? Wasn't he great!' And I'd say, 'Fuck Harvey Andrews, why didn't you come and support your other fucking artist?' And this kept happening. And after maybe the fourth time, I said, 'If someone fucking asks me if I've seen Harvey Andrews I'm going to smack them in the mouth.' Not long after, a little promotions guy came up to me.

'Hey,' I said. 'Did you see Richard?'

'No, but did you see Harvey Andrews? He's amazing!'

It was the drink and the drugs perhaps. The violence. Maybe it was the fact I'd been trapped in the army for the sixties, when I should have been playing music. I'd missed that decade, as far as I was concerned. Richard gave a great performance at the Cambridge Folk Festival in 1975. He got the crowd singing. But I certainly shouldn't have punched that promotions guy. He burst into tears. I stormed off to the bar feeling wretched.

Those two acts of violence trouble me. After I'd thrown that bloke down the stairs, Tracey the Go-Go Dancer grabbed me and said, 'You could have *killed* him! Look at yourself. You're *dangerous*.' And there was so much fear in her voice. Because I was abusing myself, I was punching people. I made a vow of non-violence. I gave up drinking spirits. I told myself spirits were the cause.

Marxist-Leninist Jumble Sale

I got one O-level. Which subject was it in?

[Pause]

I don't remember.

[Pause]

Yes, I do, it was biology.

BIG LIFE

I used to watch party political broadcasts and feel perplexed. There was a lot of political upheaval in the seventies and there was this girl who worked at the X-ray department. She was political. She overheard me talking in the staff-room about the National Front and the Tories and, God knows what I was saying, but she invited me to a meeting of the Workers Revolutionary Party.

I guess I was looking for answers. My mind was militarised somehow, but reading helped demilitarise me. I wasn't playing drums or managing. I had time to read those books and people like Marx and Hegel were like radiographers. They X-rayed reality and showed me the bones, the structure, the class struggle, how the world ticks, how capitalism ticks.

At the meeting, a woman made a speech, accusing the Labour government of conspiring against the working class. I was given a book: *Ten Days That Shook the World* by John Read. I read it from cover to cover. I was like a sponge. I read Trotsky. I went to hear a speech by Gerry Healey, who seemed to me to be a maniac with a squeaky voice and I wasn't too impressed. But then I read a book called *The State and Revolution* by Lenin. I read it lying on my bed listening to John Lennon's 'Imagine', which is probably my favourite song of all time. The lyrics in 'Imagine' were what I'd started to believe in. Imagine no fucking countries. No religion. No crap possessions. I read Marx. I joined the Worker's Revolutionary Party and became a Communist.

I'd been raised as a racist and yet I wasn't a racist – I had black friends and lovers. It genuinely confused me why things like racism and homophobia existed, why my mother, who I loved, was racist and homophobic. And I had time to think. I didn't have anything to do that year apart from drink, take drugs and chat some girls up in the Worker's Revolutionary Party. There were a lot of actors in there, out of work, and I was the new guy in the North London branch. And of course I ran an X-ray department and so the revolutionaries and I were keen to radicalise the whole of North Middlesex Hospital. I started wearing a red shirt to work. It made sense to me, being a revolutionary.

At six in the morning one day, the doorbell went. It was freezing and barely light. There were no buzzers to let people in, so I got out of bed and opened the icy window. Standing beneath me on the frosted pavement was a girl – one of the out of work actor revolutionaries who looked a little like Karen Carpenter.

'Good morning, comrade!'

'Morning,' I said. 'What's happening?'

'Comrade, there's a crisis!' That made sense, given she'd woken me up at six o'clock on a winter's morning. 'We haven't got enough jumble for the jumble sale. You need to help gather some, comrade!'

I couldn't imagine Marx waking Engels up at six to gather chipped crockery and old clothes. I liked reading the books, and I liked selling the paper – the *News Line* – because that was educational, but all that jumble crisis stuff left me cold.

Really and truly, Marx had quite a bit wrong. But he was right about the class war. It's rich against poor. Reading made me see what the Tory party stood for, what the Labour party *should* stand for. I read huge amounts on Mao Tse-tung. I wanted to make a film about The Long March. But although I'd changed my mind, some things I couldn't change. I drank more. I shagged more. I abused myself more and my face got redder and redder. The boil between my eyes became bigger and bigger.

Gerry Healey was the squat, supreme leader of the WRP. Everyone feared him because of his squeaky voice. He used to shout and thump the table. He'd met Trotsky, or so they said, and he'd been imprisoned and was, really, a left-wing legend at the time. He was ferocious. Every meeting was about the revolution and about the taking of the power and, of course, everyone up there on the stage with Gerry believed they were the future leaders of Britain.

I went down to the centre in Brixton for a meeting one time. Healey, the glorious leader, was chairing it. I took my seat and did my best to follow the debate. I was a good worker. I was great at selling *News Line* and I was great at accusing people of being revisionists, too. I put my hand up during one of the discussions – we were probably debating how best to seize control of the means of production. I kept my hand up for a while, but I was completely ignored and the issue went to the vote.

'Excuse me.' I stood up and waved my hand. 'I had my hand up,' I said. 'I've got something to say.'

'Sit down,' Healey said. 'We've moved on.'

'But I disagree. I had my hand up.'

'Shut up!' Healey screamed from up on the stage. 'Shut up and sit down. Don't you realise that the Party is the highest form? Shut up. There's no room for these individual outbursts!'

'But I wanna have my say.'

Gerry Healey's face turned red and seemed to twist violently. He screamed even louder. 'Shut up, shut up!' I thought, 'Fuck this, why is this fat little shit screaming at me?' I spent nine years in the army with people screaming like that. I got to my feet and told him, 'Fuck you. *Fuck you.* Don't you fucking scream at me you squeaky voiced little fat shit! Who the *fuck* do you think *you* are?' I really lost it with him. Two men restrained me. Although, looking back, I think I was saying what a lot of people in that room were thinking.

'*Get him out,*' screamed Healey. He sounded like a whipped piglet. '*Get him out! Anarchist! Anarchist!*'

TAPE #6

That whole party was based on fear really. Healey led people into fear, attained and sustained power by making people fear him. I'll tell you what fear is. Just as I tell La Roux and Scissor Sisters what it is. It's False Evidence Appearing Real, OK.

[Pause]

Now, let's have some lunch. On the terrace. I need to call Tim Parry. Then we'll do…then we'll do punk.

New Man/Numan

I went to the Cambridge Folk Festival in 1977. Why shouldn't I? I went with my drinking friend Danny. Danny was a soul boy. He rolled around in an old Rolls Royce. We drove it up to Cambridge with a snooty Don Maclean sitting on the backseat with his guitar. We'd picked him up from Heathrow and Danny played his soul songs on the stereo all the way. Halfway to Cambridge, Don Maclean leant forwards and said, 'Jazz, could you ask the driver to change the music?' Danny smiled at me and turned the music up a notch.

At Cambridge that year, I spoke to a bloke who ran a club called the Vortex. He came up to me and said, 'Jazz, you've gotta come and hear this punk thing.'

'Punk?'

'Punk.'

'What's it like?'

'There's a band called Tanya Hide and the Vibrators!'

I liked the sound of it. Back in London, I went down the Vortex and it was all pogoing and spitting and people wearing plastic bags and nobody could play and everyone had lots of energy. It was a total revolution against prog-rock. We were going from people sitting on the floor at the Marquee swaying their heads to twenty-five minute drum solos, which I personally hated, to this, to punk. It was 1977 and I was thirty-three. But take away the nine army years and I was twenty-four. I went down the Vortex feeling eighteen in my head and I was thinking, Fucking hell, I wanna be up there behind those drums, banging them as hard as I possibly can and spiking my hair up. I can't, I thought. I knew I couldn't. But I loved punk. I was head over heels with the noise and the spectacle.

I started a punk night on a Monday at the Cock in Palmers Green. I put an ad in the paper: 'Any punk bands want to play North London, contact Jazz Summers.' In some small way, I was back in the music industry. Punk had spurred me to do something. I received a call off Gary Numan's dad: 'Mr. Summers, you wanna put my son's band on. They're called Tubeway Army.' He sent me the music and I really liked it. It wasn't punk, but I liked it. I phoned him back and said so.

A band called the Stukas played my punk night. They used RnB chords and didn't make angry punk rock, as such, but they had this wonderful, deadpan singer and they were gigging all over, people were writing about them, John Peel played them; they were buzzing up. I started to manage them. We put out a single called 'Clean Living Kids'. The Stukas were primed for a proper record deal. They played the circuit – all the colleges, the Nashville, the Hope and Anchor. I went round the major record labels trying to get them a deal.

The singer was a problem. Because he was a bit different to the normal punk singers, the major labels wouldn't go for it. They wanted Johnny Rotten, basically. I was of the opinion that if one guy in a band is no good then you chuck him out. Simple. So I convinced the rest of the band to replace the singer. And sure enough, with a new, better looking singer, who had a more conventional punk attitude, I was able to sign the Stukas to Mickey Most, the legend behind people like Jeff Beck, Donovan, Herman's Hermits. Mickey was the guy who produced *The House of the Rising Sun*.

Did it work? Answer: not really. In fact, it didn't work in any way. Messing with the Stukas' line-up might have earned us a record deal, but it altered the core DNA of the band. I fucked with the chemistry. We chased the money. We acted heartlessly towards the dead-pan guy. And the results were awful.

I should have taken them on, *with* the dead-pan singer, and I should have believed in what they *were*, not what they weren't. I was so concerned with landing the big advance I'd become blind to the beautiful chemistry from which great music is born, OK. I'd meddled when I should have had faith.

I took record after record to Mickey Most's office. It was full of gold-discs; it was like an altar to the hit record. Not once did Mickey smile and say, 'Jazz, we have a hit!' He'd grimace and suggest some song we should cover or rip-off. After a year of that, everyone was fed up. The band was done. I was done. Mickey dropped us. The lesson is simple: don't fuck with the line-up. Trust the people that make music you love. If something's not right for you, don't get involved. Walk away.

Tim and the Strawberry Nose

I split with Tracey the Go-Go Dancer after she went to Japan. She went there to dance in Tokyo. The truth is, we'd cheated on each other something rotten. I was having sex with half of Romford at the time. After a while, Tracey returned to London to have her gall bladder removed. I let her live with me. She couldn't dance so she started working for me, answering my phone at home while I was at the X-ray department.

I put on rock and punk nights at the Pegasus and the Greyhound on Fulham Palace Road. I put the Vibrators on at the Pegasus and packed it out. The punk night at the Cock came to an abrupt end, by the way, because I put on Slaughter and the Dogs. Three hundred punks came down and smashed the place to pieces and that was the end of my punk night.

It was a fast fucking life, promoting bands: deafening nights and derelict mornings, driving my aching head to the hospital.

Tracey the Go-Go Dancer told me about a mod band called the Crooks. I gave them a support slot at the Pegasus and, to be honest, I wasn't altogether sure they had it. But they played a song called 'Making Love To You Is Like Banging My Head, Banging My Head, Banging My Head Against A Brick Wall'. I enjoyed it so much I barged into their little dressing room after the show.

'Who wrote that song?'

'Which?'

'That one that went, *making love to you is like banging my head, banging my head, banging my head against a brick wall*!'

A slim, pallid young man sat quietly in the corner of the room, fastidiously restringing his guitar. He looked up from his work, nodded and said, 'I did.'

'What's your name?'

'Tim…Tim Parry.'

'Anyone who can write a song like that, I've got to manage.'

I'd already broken my golden rule. I was managing a band and I didn't much like the singer. But, the fact was, I had no intention of meddling with the line-up and, the truth is, I was managing them because of this guy Tim Parry, who'd written a wonderful pop song, 'Making Love To You Is Like Banging My Head, Banging My Head, Banging My Head Against A Brick Wall'.

The Crooks had a song called 'The Modern Boys'. We made a video for it at the Hope and Anchor in which I took on the role of a bouncer. I marched around, man-handling fans, looking stern with my big mullet haircut. I think that was the first video I was ever involved with. It was made by the Moving Picture Company, who are a big film company these days – they make the Harry Potter films. I remember they were really fucking around making 'The Modern Boys' video. The crowd was getting angsty while they fiddled with the lights and stuff. I walked up to the producer and asked if he was from the Moving Picture Company. He nodded and I said to get fucking moving then. I thought that was funny. It was a strange time for me. I was mad slightly and doing a lot of Dexys. I was a bit out of it most of the time. I stopped smoking and it felt like giving up breathing.

The Crooks didn't work out. Tim Parry kicked the singer out and formed a new band called Modern Jazz, with a singer called Andy O. I put Modern Jazz on at the Pegasus and they were great. I put them on at the Greyhound on Fulham's Palace Road, which was a pretty big rock gig at the time. Both gigs got smash reviews and so the labels came sniffing. In 1979, Michael Levy signed Modern Jazz to Magnet Records and insisted they change their name. We were fine with that. Tim Parry's band became known as Blue Zoo. *Blue Zoo*…have you heard of them?

[Pause]

I managed a band called the Late Show, too. I signed them to Decca and managed to get them on tour with Darts. I introduced them to Tommy Boyce and Richard Hartley and, with them, the Late Show recorded a cover of a song called 'The Bristol Stomp'.

BIG LIFE

I remember I was getting calls from other managers asking how the hell I was getting Decca to spend so much money. The answer was pretty simple. I was really passionate about the Late Show and I was really passionate about 'The Bristol Stomp'. It was clear to me that the song would be my first proper hit. A couple of weeks before it was released I got a call from the guitarist. I was sitting in my flat on my own, having a drink of Barley wine.

'Jazz?'

'Yeh?'

'We know you're not a proper manager.'

'Sorry?'

'We know about your job, Jazz. At the hospital. We know you're not a proper manager. It's over.'

They were a strange bunch, really, on reflection, the Late Show. I think they were a bit concerned about 'The Bristol Stomp'. I think maybe they didn't like me very much. 'The Bristol Stomp' went into the Top 40. It wasn't a massive record, but it would have been nice to be involved.

The administrators of North Middlesex Hospital brought me in to discuss my consistent absence from work during the afternoons. They accused me of disappearing quite a lot, and that was true; I did disappear. I disappeared every day.

Stopping fags made life unpleasant and strange. I'd been smoking eighty a day and it was a melancholy year, the year I gave up. I got acupuncture in my ears. I started eating more. I started drinking more, too. My nose was getting really red and my face was covered in spots. I arrived at a Blue Zoo gig once and, as I entered their dressing room, Andy O, who was very handsome, said, 'Oh look, Rudolph's here!' And although it was only a piss-take, that

TAPE #6

remark really affected me. I lay awake that night, thinking about it, watching my bedroom ceiling spin and spin.

I'd look in the mirror every day and think, 'My God, my face looks fucking terrible.' I went to see a skin specialist at North Middlesex. This was in 1978. I didn't have to say anything; he could see as soon as I entered his office I was in serious trouble.

'It's acne rosacea, Jazz.'

'What's that?'

'It effects the centre of the face, normally, though in chronic cases the whole face becomes enflamed. As it has here…I'm afraid, Jazz, there's no cure.'

'No cure?'

'I mean you could drink less, lay off spicy food, but you can only hope to control it, I'm afraid. I can give you antibiotics, but the worst thing is, you're going to end up with a strawberry nose, like the old guys you see. I'm afraid that's what it leads to.'

He prescribed me antibiotics and I took them. I took them religiously. I'd put on a pile of weight since stopping smoking. I had a tendency to lose my temper, too. In fact, I'd lose my temper a lot. In fact, really, I screamed at people every fifteen minutes. I'd scream at Tracey the Go-Go Dancer, at colleagues at the hospital, at record companies, A&R men, promoters, members of bands. I very rarely stopped screaming for long. I was angry. I drank Scotch in the middle of the night.

TAPE #7
(28TH MARCH 2012)

Heart

I was driving up to Cambridge on a June day in 1981. It was hot and I couldn't breathe. I had a tight feeling in my throat, a pain down my left arm. I swerved into a lay-by, opened the door and crawled from the car. I lay down on my back, watching tiny black birds flying in the white sky, blinking between the darkness and the light.

Beer, steak, chips, Chinese, Indian, whiskey, gin; I'd put anything inside me in the seventies. Every time I stopped taking antibiotics, the acne rosacea came back worse, so I kept on with the drugs. I was a screaming nightmare lunatic. There was a lot of sex in this period, I think. If there's different partners all over the place, that can confuse a man. I was thirteen-stone since quitting fags; thirteen stone as the eighties began.

I used to nip home from the X-ray department to check in on Tracey the Go-Go Dancer. I'd take the piss a bit, of course, leaving the hospital about midday and not returning much before three. I was driving back one day and the same thing happened: I couldn't breathe, pain down my left arm, the clammy sensation. I walked into the X-ray ward and the nurses there looked terrified. They forced me into a wheelchair and wheeled me through the hospital for an ECG scan. But the scan revealed nothing. The doctors told me I was fine.

TAPE #7

Wife #2

I met Angela in California one Christmas. She was intelligent and beautiful and, most of all, she was straight-laced – the complete opposite of Eilish. I was drawn to Angela's tranquility. I felt, I think, like maybe I was too old for fashionable clothes and wild nights and endless fornication; so I decided to settle down.

When I got back to England I wrote to Angela every day. That's what you did, OK. You wrote love letters, including your feelings, ambitions, your intimate thoughts and desires. You seduced women with words and it was a slow process that gave hope and lovely thrills to otherwise normal days.

Angela wasn't the only important relationship in my life. I'd become very close to Tim Parry. I managed him, but I was also his friend. We'd go for dinner together. I got on well with his girlfriend, Mel, because we used to drink together. Rather than the manager carrying the artist home, it was Tim, the artist, carrying his wife and his manager home.

I went to Tim and Mel's wedding with Angela. She'd moved to London to be with me. We went to the lunch and then, that evening, the plan was to have a nice get together in a West End club. Me and Angela were walking up the stairs to my flat, intending to have a rest before we went out again, and the pain returned. It happened again.

'You've gone grey. Jazz, Christ, you've gone grey. What's your 911? What do I dial for 911?'

'Water. I'm fine. Just fetch me some water.'

I crawled into my bed like an old man who'd just had a heart attack. Angela came through and helped me to sip some water.

'Angela, I don't want to die.'

'Don't even say that.'

'I'm thirty-seven. I've got things to do.'

'Please, my darling –'

'I've never had a hit. I want a baby.'

'Jazz, stay calm. Lie down.'

I went up to North Middlesex to see my friend Dick the Doctor. He took out his stethoscope and listened to my heart. He took some blood. I went and got an ECG, a chest X-ray and, an hour and a half later, he told me I was completely normal. He removed his glasses and asked if he could be candid.

'I know you're in the music business, Jazz, as well as working here. What drugs are you taking?'

'I'm not taking anything, Dick. I've not had a spliff for six months. I've cut down on my drinking. I'm with an American woman.'

'Are you taking *anything*? Aspirin? Headache tablets?'

'Well, I'm on some antibiotics.'

'What for?'

'*This*.'

'Of course. How long for?'

'Off and on … three years.'

'*Three years*!'

He sat me in a chair, held my tongue down with a spatula and made me swallow.

'Jazz, tell me, are you constipated?'

'Yes.'

'How constipated are you?'

'Very.'

'When did you last…?'

'Six weeks ago.'

'The lining of your oesophagus is red raw. Your digestive system has been eaten away by the antibiotics, which has made your oesophagus go into spasm, which will give you the same symptoms as a heart attack. You've gotta get off the antibiotics *now*.'

I walked out of the surgery, found a bottle of laxative and downed it. I went home, to the bathroom, took a screwdriver and removed the medicine chest from the wall. 'Fuck the medical profession,' I told Angela. 'Fuck them.' The cabinet was full of every kind of tablet you can imagine: paracetamol, anti-histamine, all my various antibiotics. I opened the window and flung the whole thing down into the disused canal that lay stagnant at the back of our flat.

I was disillusioned with modern medicine and with X-raying people. I was desperate to work in the music industry. I went to see the consultant radiologist and I told him I was leaving. 'I'm gonna go into the music business,' I said. I remember him looking at me like I was mad. 'It's so insecure, Jazz. Are you sure? You've got a job here till you're sixty-five.'

Hearing those words confirmed to me that I was doing the right thing. I didn't want to be sixty-five and still X-raying people. I loved music too much. Music stirred me up and I want to be stirred up by things. I began renting a small office on Fink Street. An office to manage bands from.

I found a book about alternative medicine and I read about water treatment, acupuncture, mud treatment, homeopathy, herbalism and allergies. I didn't care what modern medicine said about there being no cure. I wasn't going to have a strawberry nose.

I heard about a guy called Dr Brolley. He'd treated James Coburn, the actor, for rheumatoid arthritis. Coburn had gone from being in a wheelchair to happily swimming in his pool in the Hollywood hills.

My nose was so red and so sore it was impossible to even touch it. I put Tracey the Go-Go Dancer in charge and went to LA to meet Dr Brolley. Tracey wasn't a dancer any more. She was my assistant, but we weren't having an affair. She worked at the office on Fink Street and Tim Parry started hanging around there more and more.

Dr Brolley never discussed what was wrong with you. He had a holistic approach, not that I knew what a holistic approach was, I just knew my nose was getting redder and redder. Dr Brolley showed me a chart that showed my allergies. Milk, cream, yoghurt, ice cream – anything to do with cows, I was chronically allergic to. There were meats I was allergic to, too, but nothing as bad as dairy. Brolley said people go through life, eating away, and sometimes the body creates antibodies to deal with that food. It's a bit like when you first smoke and you feel sick. A lot of the food you eat a lot can become dangerous; your body becomes addicted, reliant, then it can't take any more and you become allergic. Brolley was telling me to eat pears and walnuts one morning, apples and brasil nuts the next; he was telling me to quit dairy and totally overhaul my diet. He wanted me to rotate what I ate so my body didn't become allergic to any one foodstuff.

I was determined to change my diet. I threw myself into it and lost an enormous amount of weight. I felt light, light-headed; I was a complete beanpole. Everyone lost weight on the Dr Brolley diet. I think it sends you a little bit crazy, too; I was hyperactive, cranky and went around ranting and being boring about my rotating diet. I never shut up about pears and brasil nuts.

I was in some London office, bugging people about Blue Zoo and Danse Society (another band I'd started managing) when suddenly, mid-sentence, I fell silent. Across the room, a woman was sitting at her desk, listening to a song. It was strange. It sounded like the Sugar Hill Gang, but it had an English accent. The singer was singing about DHSS.

'Hey, who is this?'

'This?' The woman looked up from her work. 'I think they're called Wham!'

'Wham!' I said. 'What a fucking great name.'

'They're signed to Mark Dean at Innervision.'

I knew Mark Dean vaguely. He worked with Brian Morrison. I knew Brian because he'd signed Danse Society's publishing (he saw them in Leeds and thought they were the next Pink Floyd). Mark Dean had signed Wham! for about five hundred quid. What I heard that day in the office was a white label release called 'Wham! Rap'.

I went to Deano's office in South Molton Street and asked, straight up, 'Who's managing this band?'

'No one,' Deano said. 'They're coming in in a minute. Hey, listen to this…'

He played a new demo he'd just received from the band. It was called 'Careless Whisper'.

'Who wrote that?' I said.

'Wham did.'

'How old are they?'

'Eighteen.'

'Play it again.'

A door opened. George Michael and Andrew Ridgeley strolled into Mark Dean's office. They were handsome, particularly Andrew; they were luminous.

'I'm Jazz. I'm Jazz Summers. I've heard your songs. I'm Jazz Summers. Hello! These songs, they're fucking…well, they're fucking…'

BIG LIFE

They said hi but, really, they weren't interested in me. It was a little awkward for them, I think, having to shake my hand and listen to me. I managed to tell them how much I liked 'Careless Whisper', but they were already much too big for someone like me to manage. I think they were wondering who the fuck this red-faced guy was.

PART THREE

TAPE #8
(9TH APRIL 2012)

The Importance of Being Big

If you're a manager and you haven't had a hit, you're a wanker. If you're a manager and your bands are starting to have hits, you're a genius. If you're a manager and you come through a second time with *more* hits, you're a crook. That's the way it works. In 1982, I was a wanker.

In November 1983, Wham! had a hit with 'Young Guns'. It was nothing to do with me – I couldn't get near them. But at the same time, as 'Young Guns' was at number three, Blue Zoo were at number thirteen with a song Tim Parry wrote called 'Cry Boy Cry'. And as Blue Zoo played *Top of the Pops*, I had Danse Society at number one in the indie chart, too. Briefly, I was a genius.

I'd heard a rumour that Simon Napier-Bell was deeply bored. Napier-Bell, of course, had managed the Yard Birds, Marc Bolan and Japan. He was already a legend of the management world. He could even write songs. He wrote that beautiful song, 'You Don't Have To Say You Love Me'. If I could team up with a man like that, I might be able to get Wham!

A sky blue Bentley was parked outside his flat in Bryanstone Square. Inside, a wide staircase led nowhere. I crossed his white, shag pile carpet, passed under a huge chandelier. His living room was dominated by two cocaine-white leather sofas. A pink, porcelain Dalmation sat in the corner by a leather-fronted cocktail bar. Simon Napier-Bell himself looked like a pleasant man, podgy and gleaming. He watched me with the grim satisfaction of a man watching a strip-tease; I took a seat on the sofa and crossed my legs.

'So.' His voice was suave and warm. 'Do you want to work for me?'

'Not really.'

'Champagne?'

'I need your clout,' I said, sitting forwards, my shoes buried deep in his shag pile. 'I want to manage Wham! Nobody thinks I'm big enough. I've heard a ballad they've written that's out of this world.'

'Wham…' Napier-Bell handed me a flute of bubbling champagne. 'Yes, I saw them on *Top of the Pops*.'

'And there's another band we could go for called Eurythmics.'

'What's that?'

'It's a girl and a guy.'

'No,' said Napier-Bell, sharply. 'I don't want to manage *a girl and a guy*. But Wham, I accept, look rather good.'

Simon Napier-Bell was part of the sixties establishment. Listen to 'You Don't Have To Say You Love Me'. It's a wonderful song.

'If we get to manage Wham,' I said, 'I'll do all the work.'

'I should hope so.'

Napier-Bell talks about this meeting in his book *I'm Coming To Take You To Lunch*. He makes a comment about my face. How red it was. He also describes how he fucked off to Thailand as soon as we went into business. But Napier-Bell was up for it. He had a company called NOMIS Management. I walked into my office there as the manager of Blue Zoo and Danse Society. The first thing I did was phone Morrison and Leahey, Wham!'s publishers. I said I was coming over.

'Jazz,' said Brian Morrison, in a sympathetic voice, 'it's great you're working with Napier-Bell, but Wham are managed by their lawyer. That'll be the case until Michael Jackson's people take over, Weisener and DeMann.'

'Really, Brian? You think? Weisener and DeMann themselves?'

I knew Ron Weisener and Freddy DeMann ain't gonna be interested in some English pop duo who'd done fuck all in America.

'I'm gonna bug you about this, Brian.'

'Jazz, why don't you calm down? Relax, for Christ's sake.'

'I'm gonna *bug* you about this! Listen to me!'

It was in me. There was something in the Universe pushing me; I could feel it. I hadn't even bothered to argue with Napier-Bell about the Eurythmics. I needed to manage Wham!

Katie

I stood outside the hospital in the rain, looking at the grey sky and feeling full of love. I'd just met my first child. She was a beautiful little baby called Katie. I was shivering and thinking and my heart was really bursting. I was a father. I'd always wanted to be one. I called up Tracey the Go-Go Dancer to tell her the news.

'I'm walking on fucking air,' I said.

'Brian Morrison wants you and Simon to meet with Wham!'

'He does? Fuck…fuck. *Fantastic*…I'm a dad, Tracey!'

Here it was. A chance. The Universe was aligning. I contacted Andrew Ridgeley and gave him the address of Napier-Bell's flat. It was best to meet there, I thought. It was an impressive place, or at least it seemed so, in those days. In the hour before the meeting, I combed my hair continuously, looking out the window, drinking red wine. Napier-Bell sat in silence on his huge white sofa, reading a newspaper. We were waiting for Wham! For destiny. After an hour, when it was clear they weren't coming, Simon sighed, folded his paper and made cocktails.

Morrison and Leahey had given me George Michael's phone number. I called his house on Napier-Bell's ivory telephone. It went to the answering machine: 'Look,' I said. 'My wife's just had a baby. She's four days old. I've left her to have a meeting with you and you haven't shown up. I don't think that's very good.' I put the phone down thinking, well, that's probably the end of that. But, in actual fact, the phonecall worked. We met with George and Andrew a couple of days later.

When I saw George, and I heard him speak, I knew he was something very special. He was nineteen and had an air of complete confidence. He strode into Napier-Bell's lush living room and smiled. He was much taller than I'd expected. Andrew was even better looking than he was on TV. It was obvious how strong the bond between them was. I knew straight away all my passion was justified.

'You can manage us for the world excluding America.' This was George. 'We've got Michael Jackson's manager in America, and they want Japan, too.'

'That's not right,' I said.

'Weisner and DeMann are strong in Japan.'

'This guy.' I clenched the shoulder-pad of Napier-Bell's blazer. '*This* guy's strong in Japan. He managed fucking Japan in Japan! *We* do Japan.'

'The thing you've really got to do is fix our record deal. We're broke.'

Wham!'s record deal with Innervision was one of the most notoriously awful, unfair fucking record deals that ever got signed in the whole torrid history of pop music. They'd got about £500 each advance. They'd sold thousands of twelve inches, but the deal stipulated they weren't entitled to royalties on twelve inches. They'd been on *Top of the Pops*. They'd had hits and the label, CBS, who owned Innervision, were absolutely screaming for the album. But George had taken the tapes home and put them in his mum's shed. He was protesting, and rightly so.

Andrew was a beautiful young man. George was a beautiful genius. He was the prince of fucking heaven as far as I was concerned. He knew exactly where he was headed. And I knew how to help him. And I wanted to help. I understood his music, how it would work in clubs, what mixes to go for, where they should be placed in the press. Napier-Bell was a bit out of the loop, to be honest, but I understood the destiny of Wham! I was so impressed with George's foresight at those early meetings. His determination. A lot of people write-off Andrew Ridgeley, but he was important. He was vital. Vital to the magic and the chemistry, to the DNA of the band. This wasn't like Richard Digance coming to me and mumbling about management. I love Richard, but this was different. These two young men knew where Wham! was headed. They were clever. They knew they had to put two women in the group, Dee and Shirlie, a black girl and a white girl. Two guys and two girls, like an exclusive club, something kids would want to be part of. Andrew looked like a popstar. George hadn't quite found his style, but, when you looked into his eyes, you knew he was looking at his future. He was the most focused artist I've ever met. He knew that 'Careless Whisper' would be a massive hit. He knew 'Bad Boys' wasn't so good, was a bit throwaway. He had visions for videos. He wanted to make it in America.

BIG LIFE

After that first meeting at Simon's flat, I got home to find Angela asleep on the sofa. Katie asleep in her arms. I kissed them both and opened a bottle of wine.

A Meeting with Innervision's Mark Dean in a Gloomy Restaurant

The first song we worked on was 'Club Tropicana'. Napier-Bell went to the video shoot in Ibiza. I stayed in the office doing the hard work. George and Andrew were on the front cover of *NME* that month, July 1983. They wore leather jackets.

We'd hired a legal firm called Russells to help renegotiate the record deal. Tony Russell was a man-eater, not in the sense that Napier-Bell was; Tony Russell might literally eat a man, if that man stood in the way of legal victory. He had ball-breaker hands, viper eyes and I think he was a big Bruce Springsteen fan.

I wanted to speak to Mark Dean before these lawyers got involved. He deserved the chance to change his mind and volunteer to renegotiate Wham!'s record deal. I took him to lunch at a funny little place. I wanted to try to help him before things got ugly. Deano had dark hair, dark eyes, was tightly wound and paranoid. Everything he touched was turning to gold. He'd transitioned from wanker to genius with rare ease. The restaurant was called the Little Chef, not too salubrious, somewhere behind Marble Arch. Low lighting. Weird food. I ordered a bottle of wine.

'Deano, to be frank, this record deal is shit. It's completely unfair. The boys have sold hundreds and thousands of records and hardly seen a penny. They're skint. The royalty rates are ridiculous. You're backed by CBS. We're willing to go to court with you over this. I probably shouldn't say this, Deano, but we're gonna try and walk out of this contract. You know what litigation brings.

98

TAPE #8

It brings heartache, Deano. So why don't we, hand in hand, go to Maurice Oberstein and get a better deal for Wham and a better deal for you?'

'Absolutely not.' Deano folded his arms, looking as intense as ever. 'We knew you and Napier-Bell would do this. I've spoken to Oberstein. We're ready for you. The fact of the matter is, I've got a signed contract. George and Andrew *signed*, Jazz.'

'They were eighteen, Deano. They were kids.'

'It doesn't matter.'

'Let me tell you something, Deano…heartache. That's what's coming here. Heartache for you, for me, for the boys. Heartache for us and cash for the lawyers. And when we're all fucking heartbroken and when the music inevitably doesn't get made, doesn't get recorded, doesn't get delivered, and when everyone's coming to you saying, Mark, where the fuck is the new Wham album, let me tell you something: CBS, Oberstein, they're gonna *shit* on you from the top of Soho Square. You'll be fucked. Wham will sign to CBS. I don't want to see that happen. Your youthful spirit has got Wham here. But, believe me, CBS are going to *shit* on you.'

'Have you finished?'

'Believe me, Deano. Heartache.'

'CBS are backing me up. Fuck you, Jazz, coming here. The boys signed the contract!'

'Deano, I like you. It's gonna hurt my feelings to have to watch you get fucked and shit on. I'm sitting here because I like you.'

'Fuck you.'

'You're being naïve.'

'I'm not going to talk about this. I'll talk to you about the next Wham record.'

'Deano,' I said. 'There ain't gonna be one.'

99

BIG LIFE

Money is the Law

I walked away from the Little Chef saddened. I hadn't taken Dick Leahey or Napier-Bell with me because I didn't want Deano to feel too pressured. When I told our lawyer, Tony Russell, that I'd failed to convince Mark Dean to renegotiate the deal, he just smiled. It was one of those smiles only lawyers know how to do; his lips barely moved.

The thing about litigation is it's fucking expensive and the problem we had was we had no money. Wham! didn't have any either, of course. We needed hundreds and thousands of pounds to pay Tony Russell to eat Mark Dean's lawyer. We needed ideas. You always need ideas in the music industry. A day without ideas is like a song without a chorus. It's frustrating.

Kaz Utsunomiya is a huge Japanese personality in the music industry and one of my best friends in the business these days. He signed the Clash and Nirvana before anyone else. He's a genius. He signed Tears for Fears and the Pet Shop Boys. He worked in Simon's basement with me, helping to sort Wham! out in Japan. He'd recently returned from Tokyo with a proposal that we'd declined at first. It was something that, according to Kaz, could make Wham! huge in Japan and make us some money to pay the legal fees. Maxell, a blank tape manufacturer, had asked Wham! to appear in a television commercial. They wanted Wham! to dance around on camera holding Maxell blank tapes. They were willing to pay us sixty thousand pounds for that.

'What a brilliant idea,' said Napier-Bell.

'It's not very cool, Simon.'

'It's in Japan, Jazz. Everything's cool in Japan! Anyway, it doesn't matter.'

Whether it was cool or not was really a side issue, as it happens, because in order to do the advert CBS had to agree to let Wham!

appear in it. The head of CBS, Maurice Oberstein, whose decision it would be, was, at the time, chairman of the BPI, an organisation which was spearheading a furious campaign against the sale and use of blank tapes. Blank tapes were hurting record sales, see, or so Maurice Oberstein feared. He was unlikely to sign off on it.

I took him to lunch at Langan's on Marylebone. I'd stopped talking to Mark Dean by this stage and, in any case, the copyright issues weren't his side of things. Maurice Oberstein was tall, thin, American, pretty squeaky and a complete hoot. But he was serious, too. He wore a large cowboy hat and ordered a Langan's hamburger.

'I don't like blank tapes either, Maurice. But Kaz says we'll break Japan.'

'I'm the head of the BPI, Jazz.' He sounded a little like Mickey Mouse – a high-pitched, slurring, accent. 'How the fuck can I sign off on this? Blank tapes? *Blank fucking tapes*!'

'Turn a blind eye?'

'That's your suggestion, Jazz, a blind eye? Are you serious?'

The following day he called me to Soho Square. He'd spoken to the Japanese. 'OK,' he said. 'The Japs are saying we could sell hundreds of thousands of records off the back of this! In light of that, I've changed the contract. The contract now says I don't have copyright jurisdiction in Japan. OK? So *you* sign off on it. Now let's never talk about blank tapes ever again.'

Napier-Bell took the boys to Tokyo. It was a pretty awful advert, as I recall. In it, George and Andrew appeared to be flying very slowly across some kind of desert. Still, it worked in its way. Seems funny now, talking about blank tapes…

[Pause]

Poor old Maurice Oberstein, thinking blank tapes were hurting music. He was dead by the time the Internet came round. And you couldn't do an ad like that these days. It'd be on the Internet twenty minutes after it aired in Japan and you'd be a laughing stock. As it is, the Maxell advert is on YouTube. But we weren't to know about YouTube in 1983.

Two years later, when we toured Japan, we started with four sold out shows at the Budokan in Tokyo. The ad broke Wham! in Japan, as Kaz had predicted. There's no doubt, Wham!'s success in Japan was down to Kaz. He's a great guy. Wham! were the first English act to be number one in the domestic and international charts since the Beatles. Kaz wept in a West London wine bar the day he told me that.

More importantly, the ad gave us a start on our legal fees, but it wasn't enough to pay the lot. We decided to do a UK tour. A tour would bring in some more money and would radically raise the band's profile – that would put CBS and Deano in an even more desperate position.

We approached a famous promoter named Harvey Goldsmith, who'd probably never heard of Wham! Harvey was Mr Bruce Springsteen, Mr Stevie Wonder, Mr Michael Jackson. He was a pillar of the promotional community. We met at Napier-Bell's flat. Harvey Goldsmith, I remember, always looked on the brink of loud laughter. It was like he was being tickled quite discretely with a feather.

I pitched the idea of the tour to him.

'The thing is, Harvey, we need a hundred and ten thousand pounds up front.'

Harvey really did laugh when I said that.

'This band has never sold a ticket, Jazz. And you want *how* much?'

'They're good live, Harvey.'

'They've never *played* live!'

'They were good on *Top of the Pops*,' Napier-Bell chipped in.

'True,' I said. 'They were great on *Top of the Pops*. They're a great live band. We need a hundred and ten grand, Harvey.'

'I'll give you seventy.'

'No. A hundred and ten.'

'Fellas, this is ridiculous.'

'They'll be very good live, Harvey. A hundred and ten.'

We needed all that money because we were so broke. We had no royalty money flowing in because of our awful as hell record deal. We needed to put on a dazzling fucking spectacle to show CBS just how big Wham! were – to show them they were fucking around with a band that was rising and rising. And the truth was, I believed in George and Andrew. I believed they could comfortably work off that advance. I believed they could do a sell-out tour. Harvey gave us most of the hundred and ten grand that very day.

You win litigation by how much money you spend and how much you can bluff. I remember Mark Dean came up for the first gig of the tour in Aberdeen. It was just before the Wham! trial. Napier-Bell was pretty off with him. In fact, Simon and me were both a bit out of control. Pissed as a puppet, I said things to Deano that I shouldn't have; things about court and about how we were going to fuck him, had evidence against him etc. That was a mistake, saying those things. Tony Russell gave me the biggest bollocking of my life for that. I guess he thought I was a bit of a red-faced idiot. I've never had such a bollocking, even when I was in the army.

In the courts, Round 1 went to Mark Dean. He successfully got an injunction to prevent us walking out on the record deal. We were in limbo. But there was no way we could work with Mark

Dean again. The situation was irreversible. All we could do was keep going with the tour and hold our breath. The money from Japan came through and the tour sold out. Wham! *were* great live. As our legal fees soared we landed a good deal on a Wham! calendar, too. We got fifty grand; Christmas was coming up and the calendar man was so desperate.

Tony Russell called in January 1984 to say that Maurice Oberstein wanted a meeting. I knew what that meant. We'd won. It was agreed we'd walk away from Innervision. We got a decent royalty and they agreed to pay us on twelve inches. We got a forty-five thousand pound advance, too. George and Andrew finally had some money to show for their success.

Mark Dean wasn't given an over-rider on Wham!, the band he had found and signed. An over-rider would have given him a royalty on anything Wham! ever released. He deserved one. It would have made him a rich man. But I'd warned him in the Little Chef about how these things work. Once you enter litigation, you've lost the act. Avoid it at all costs, OK. CBS shat on Mark from the top of Soho Square.

George was relieved the whole thing was settled, relieved to finally earn the money he deserved, but he was sorry, too, for Deano. George enjoyed the tour, I think, although he oversang and overdanced, so he got a bit hoarse and tired. But that was youth and enthusiasm. We had fun. He put a shuttle-cock down his trousers and played badminton at the Hammersmith Odeon.

Yazz

Napier-Bell called me up and said his boyfriend, Donovan Nelson, had found a good band. Donovan was totally over the top, kind of

TAPE #8

bitchy, I thought. He didn't know much about the music industry; he ran hair fashion shows normally. The band were called the Biz. A trio. There was a bloke called Austin Howard, who I'm still friendly with today, a girl called Suzette, who I haven't seen for years, and there was a girl called Yazz. Yasmin.

They were signed to Magnet Records, of Blue Zoo fame, and Napier-Bell asked if I'd give Donovan a hand managing them. He showed me a picture of them.

'OK,' I said. 'Let's organise a meeting today.'

She didn't turn up to that first meeting. Only Suzette and Austin Howard did. It was Donovan's fault, I told him; he'd made a classic management error. He'd told Yazz about the meeting a week ago and failed to remind her. With some artists, if you want them to attend a meeting, you've got to remind them daily for about a week and then hourly on the day of the meeting and then, with half an hour to go, call them and book them a cab from wherever they happen to be; that's how it works.

The first time we met was round at Napier-Bell's. Simon sat in the corner on a white leather throne. Donovan stood with his hand resting on the snout of the porcelain Dalmatian. Sitting there, on one of the huge white sofas, was Yazz. I sat next to her.

She kept laughing at everything I said. She was tactile, too. I don't know. I think I fell in love with her there and then. I could hardly breathe and my heart hurt. I'd seen her in pictures and thought she looked good, but, in person, Yazz was something very divine. Tall, beautiful figure, long legs, an electric smile and flashing eyes. Slender hands and long arms. She was funny, Amazonian, Jamaican/English. I don't know what she thought about me.

I managed the Biz and got to know her a little. And then one day Donovan wouldn't let them into our office on Gosfield Street.

BIG LIFE

He was hanging his head out the window for some reason, calling them slags and sluts and whores. Yazz phoned me from the pub round the corner and I went to meet them. They were shaken, as you would be, getting a barrage from Donovan. The band was falling apart; that was clear. And every time I looked at Yazz I fell a little bit more in love. And every time I looked at her I thought of my wife and baby.

TAPE #9
(10TH APRIL 2012)

Go

In January 1984, George and Andrew went to Italy and I went with them. We were doing some press, some television and radio. We flew to Rome. That morning, George picked up Andrew to take him to the airport. He'd seen a note on the kitchen table that Andrew had written to his mum, drunk, the previous night. He'd written, 'Wake me up before you go.' But he'd written 'go' twice, George explained, as we sat together on the plane. He'd written, 'Wake me up before you go go.'

I didn't bother George and Andrew with my problems. I was their manager. I thought they were both fantastic, but they didn't need to hear about my personal life. I was cut up. I was tense and torn. For months I'd been engaged in a hot-blooded and totally electrifying love affair with Yazz. I was delirious with love and lust and pain. I had a nine month old daughter I would have died for. But I'd met a woman who made my heart sing. The things you do…I don't know.

[Pause]

The things you do.

Angela discovered a love letter Yazz had written to me. That must have hurt. I betrayed her, didn't I, yes, I did; I betrayed her. After spending time in Italy with the band, I returned to our flat in Acton. It was empty. All her belongings and all my daughter's little belongings were gone. When you split with someone, it's equally

107

painful for both parties, I think, don't you. I felt I could still be a father to Katie, albeit from a distance. They returned to America.

[Pause]

To hurt people is painful.

A month or two later, Yazz and I were officially together. It was around this time I went down to Sarm Studio and found George laying down a monitor mix of a new song. He gave me a tape and I played it many, many times that night. He was such a fearless guy, George Michael. He was working in the studio on his own, no producer, just his talent.

'George, I think this is a smash. I think this is number one all over the world.'

'Who should we get to mix it?'

'I think it sounds great as it is.'

'I was thinking that exact same thing!'

And so that was it. Wham!'s single, 'Wake Me Up Before You Go-Go', was a monitor mix that George did on his own. I rushed down to Hyde Park Corner and played it to Dick Leahey, to Brian Morrison, and everyone knew it. Epic Records went crazy for it. It was obvious. We had a smash on our hands.

Doomed Fun

Nine weeks into my relationship with Yazz, we went to Munich. She modelled out there a lot, was part of a fashion scene. It was all very exotic and eighties, I guess, looking back at the spectacular glitz and all the wine and schnitzel and the towering European models in wild clothes, all the beautiful legs and eyes and lips, sipping weird drinks, sniffing cocaine from long painted fingernails. I didn't really fit in, in some ways – my face was red as hell and I was too drunk, I think, to take cocaine. I was thrilled and full of love. Yazz took me dancing, doing things, you know, drinking. She wrote 'Ich lieb dich' on the bathroom mirror in red lipstick.

At Munich airport, she hugged and kissed me passionately and begged me to stay, even though she was due back in London at the weekend.

'Ich lieb dich,' I said. 'I'll see you Friday.'

Early on Friday evening she left a garbled message on my answering machine, saying she'd missed her flight. On the Tuesday of the following week she arrived back in London. She returned to our flat in Acton, but something was different. She wasn't interested in speaking to me or kissing me. Her voice had changed. It had flattened, deadened; sounded horribly apathetic. She didn't want anything to do with me. On her second night back, I overheard her talking to another man on our phone.

I upped my alcohol intake. I hit the bottle very hard. I drank a heck of a lot of wine. One night, I took Yazz out for dinner and I guzzled three or four bottles. I argued with her about the other man. I was angry and hurt – they were speaking constantly on the phone. I was out of control. We were down in Earl's Court and I tried to get Yazz into my Ford Fiesta, but she refused. She walked away and I pursued her and I almost ran her down. I very nearly did. I abandoned the Fiesta and chased her through the street. I held her in my arms and told her I was sorry.

He was a German model. They made plans to travel round Europe on their modelling earnings that summer. My skin was really bad. My skin was really shitty, very red. The more I thought about the German model, the more red and swollen my face seemed to become.

We got hammered one night on tequila in a bar in Covent Garden. It was Yazz and me and some other girls, I remember, and a guy who'd produced Pink Floyd. We all got paralytic and Yazz and me raced home and made sensational and intense and wild love. But mostly we made no love at all in this period. I just delighted in her beautiful company and, apart from that night, and apart from trying to run her over, we had some fun. Doomed fun, perhaps, but fun.

Yazz came in one day and said, 'That face! It looks awful, come here.' She put make-up on me. She had to do it with great tenderness. My face was almost raw. I remember I had a meeting at Napier-Bell's that evening. I slinked into his living room, slid gracefully onto his leather sofa, feeling really good about my face for once.

'Notice anything different about me, Simon?'

'Yes, Jazzbo, you've got make-up on. And you've done it really badly!'

A guy at MTV once said my face looked like someone had taken a blowtorch to it. It gets to you, that kind of comment. Yazz and me worked really hard on getting my make-up just right. We discovered a brand called Kinebo – an expensive, Japanese, powdered foundation. She taught me to apply it myself. I maybe looked a little tanned, but I felt more confident. And it was the eighties, so tans were fine – Napier-Bell slept on a sun-bed, I think.

I drove Yazz down to Notting Hill that spring. She left for her travels with the German model. I wound down my window and blew her a kiss. She waved quickly, looked both ways, and then negotiated the traffic on Queensway and disappeared into the crowd.

WHAM! MANIA!

After reading several video treatments, George Michael decided that in the video for 'Wake Me Up Before You Go-Go' everyone ought to wear white and pink and that the band should play for a crowd of dancing kids.

We put it out on Capital Radio, in the *Sun* and the *Mirror*, that Wham! were making a video for their new single on Friday morning at Brixton Academy. Anyone wishing to attend should come along dressed in white and pink. Connie Filipeno, our press officer, was in her element.

'Thousands,' said Napier-Bell. 'We're gonna have thousands and thousands of kids. We'll get the press down and hey presto!'

Our tour manager was a phenomenal Scottish tough guy called Jake Duncan. He'd do anything. Impossibilities hardly inconvenienced Jake at all. He'd level mountains to get to soundcheck on time. That's useful in the music industry; you need strong soldiers – roadies who can lift all day, drivers who can drive all night. Jake was around on the day of the 'Go-Go' shoot and I'm glad he was.

I arrived at Brixton Academy at around half eight in the morning. It was pissing down with rain. Round the back of the venue, a very thin line of shivering girls in pink and white were waiting to be let in. They were wet, bedraggled, mud-splashed, most of them clutching damaged umbrellas. We let them in, hoping they'd be the first of many. They gathered in three small lines at the foot of Brixton's high stage, on which was the rostrum where George wanted the band to play.

It looked like Wham! Whimpia! We decided to get the girls on stage, around the rostrums, and once they were up there it looked a little better. Providing you filmed the performance close-up, there was no way of telling quite how few girls had attended the shoot.

'Jazz.' This was Jake Duncan. 'The paparazzi's arrived. Shall I let them in?'

BIG LIFE

'Lock 'em out.'

'What do you mean? There's a guest list.'

'Fuck the guest list, Jake. Lock 'em out.'

Outside, sure enough, a gaggle of papparazzis were jostling in the pissing rain, demanding access. Among them, I recognised a young bloke I'd met once or twice. He was new to the scene and so I took him to one side.

'I'm going to let you in, OK, and you're going to take a photo. But irrespective of what you see inside this building, you are going to report scenes of wonder and frightening fanaticism, OK? You're going to crop your photo very carefully. You're gonna say there's thousands and thousands of kids in this building all going mad for Wham! Is that clear? I'm giving you an exclusive.'

He shook my hand and in he went, leaving all the other paps outraged and banging on the door or calling Connie Filipeno from the phone box round the corner.

George, Andrew, Pepsi and Shirlie, they all danced around on the rostrum, cheered on by a handful of cold, muddy London schoolgirls. '*Closer*,' the director kept saying. 'We're gonna have to zoom in *much* closer.' Weaving his way among the girls, cameras and wires was my little friend, the green paparazzi, twisting the lens of his camera over and over.

The following day, I was on a plane heading to New York. A hostess handed me copy of the Star and there, across the middle pages, was a huge picture of young girls dancing in a frenzy at the Brixton Academy. Above the picture was the headline *WHAM! MANIA!*

Sometimes, it's all about timing, a locked door, and lying. It's more about how you avert catastrophes than it is about orchestrating success.

TAPE #9

In April, 'Go-Go' went to radio and I insisted we use our own radio plugger, rather than the no-hoper at the record label. We hired a fellow called Gary Farrow. He's still George Michael's plugger today. Russell's are still George's lawyer and Connie's probably still handling his press. He's a loyal man, George.

I watched it recently; it's a very camp video, although I didn't think that at the time. I just thought it was brilliant. 'Wake Me Up Before You Go-Go' went to number four, which was big time in those days. Only the Jam went straight in at number one. A couple of weeks later, Wham! climbed to number one.

TAPE #10
(11TH APRIL 2012)

How to Break America

A lot of people in England don't know how America and Japan work. They don't take their eyes off the Thames long enough to figure it out. I'd been to America a couple of times to talk with Weisner and DeMann, Michael Jackson's managers. I liked Freddy DeMann, he was a kind guy, but Ron Weissner was a bit of a cock. He acted very big time with me, sitting in his LA office, surrounded by platinum discs. He'd talk on the phone the entire fucking time. I'd sit there while he gossiped with Diana Ross or counseled Michael Jackson. It was all tinsel town nonsense. It was rude. He'd just started managing Madonna.

I couldn't help thinking that they didn't give a shit about George and Andrew. I thought I could do better myself. An English A&R guy reported a conversation between Freddy DeMann and some marketing guy at Columbia Records, during which Freddy was told, 'If you think you're going to get Michael Jackson treatment for Wham you've got another thing coming.'

Any time we tried to communicate, they fucking ignored us. I didn't know much about America, but I was drawn to it as a market. I studied it. I'd got my head around the fact that it was a vast fucking place and breaking it wasn't as simple as doing a few shows in New York and LA. There was more to it than that.

In January 1984, Freddy DeMann came to London. Ahead of his visit, I tried to explain to George that I'd found them pretty

114

incommunicative. I reminded him how little contact he himself had had with Weisner and DeMann. We'd done more to get Wham! going in America than Weisner or DeMann had, to be truthful. We'd been sending press cuttings over to Columbia Records in New York already, trying to vibe them up about the boys. 'George,' I said, 'I don't think these guys are very passionate.'

Freddy DeMann came for a meeting in Napier-Bell's front room and I was pretty frank. I told him that I knew Columbia had told him not to expect 'Michael Jackson treatment'. I accused him of being hard to get hold of and work-shy.

'What are you *really* going to do for Wham in America, Freddy? I don't think you give a shit. I think Madonna's keeping you busy.'

He didn't have the answers.

I went to see George that evening: 'Let *me* manage you in America. Let me have a go, George. They might do Michael Jackson, but I'm passionate about your songs.'

He gave me one of his beautiful, piercing looks. He knew how important America is for an artist. He knew how difficult it was and how many big acts had failed to even come close to being successful there.

'I promise you, George. I'll break you in America.'

'You better.'

You'll Get Used to It

The first thing about America was they weren't bothered about singles. They wouldn't start releasing singles unless they'd heard the album. George had to get cracking on the record. Of course, you couldn't tell George what to do. He lived at his own pace and made his own decisions. He wasn't even sure whether he wanted to put

BIG LIFE

'Careless Whisper' on the second Wham! album. He considered it a George Michael solo song.

I sat down with Andrew in a Mexican Restaurant in New York, bought him a gigantic margarita and smiled:

'You know, Andrew, George is under a lot of pressure to finish this album. You need to help him.'

'George writes the songs, Jazz. The trick is to let him get on with it.'

He was a cool guy, Andrew Ridgeley. He understood his role. Remember, he co-wrote 'Careless Whisper' with George. I don't know how much or how little he did. Maybe he just kept George company, made him laugh, gave him confidence. I just know he was vital. They were school friends. It was chemistry.

Just before Christmas 1983, I came up with the idea of Jerry Wexler producing 'Careless Whisper'. Do you know who Jerry Wexler is? He founded Atlantic Records with Ahmet Ertegun. He produced all those amazing Muscle Shoals songs: Aretha Franklin, Ray Charles. With his soul background, I though he'd be perfect for 'Careless Whisper'. I mentioned it to Napier-Bell and, in true Simon fashion, it quickly became *his* idea. George thought Wexler was perfect. He and Napier-Bell went off to Muscle Shoals to record. I didn't mind, really, because at the end of the day, we know what we do, right?

Everyone raved about the recording. Dick Leahey raved about it, Napier-Bell raved about it; everyone thought it was amazing. George was beside himself because he'd made a record with Aretha Franklin's producer. To me, it sounded old fashioned.

'George, I've been in love with *Careless Whisper* since the moment I heard it. I think it's a global smash. But the Wexler version won't work. This is 1984. It sounds 1964.'

TAPE #10

'You'll get used to it, Jazz. Trust me.'

That's what he always used to say when people disagreed with him. 'You'll get used to it.' George wasn't arrogant. He just had so much self-belief. So much faith in what he did.

'I won't. I'm gonna bug you about this, George. I won't get used to it. It's not right.'

I bugged him about it for the next few weeks until one day he turned round and said, 'Stop bugging me about this, Jazz. You'll get used to it. I'm not changing it!' Then one day, in May or June '84, I heard that George was recording in the Advision Studio opposite our office on Gosfield Street. I decided I'd go and see what he was up to.

The studio was George's element. I never saw him unhappy when he was recording music. They were laying down the sax solo as I arrived and George had a big smile on his face. He never said I was right about the Wexler version, that wasn't George's way, but that day in Advision he recorded and produced the most sublime version of 'Careless Whisper'. The version everybody knows.

I Wore Very Baggy Suits in the Eighties

I had to convince Columbia Records to release 'Wake Me Up Before You Go-Go' without them having heard the Wham! album. To do this, I lied a lot. I told them the album was very, very nearly finished. I told them that by the time they had 'Go-Go' moving up the charts, the album would be with them.

Wham!'s debut album hadn't done too badly in America. Without any co-ordination, *Club Fantastic* had sold a hundred thousand copies, mostly in little pockets like Miami, San Francisco, New York, Boston, Los Angeles. There were more independent radio stations then. They used to play acts that were doing well in England. Believe it or not, KROQ in LA used to play Wham! I remember in the nineties, when I was managing the Verve, I went for a meeting there and said, 'Last time I was at KROQ, you were based in Pasadena and you were playing Wham!' That put them on the back-foot! They knew I was right, those denim jacketed KROQ hipsters, but they didn't like admitting it.

I've seen fashions come and go and come and go. Baggy suits, denim jackets, flares and tight jeans. I love fashion. I love clothes. But I don't get bogged down in fashion when it comes to music. I love music when music moves me. I like Elgar, Mozart, Bach and the Futureheads. Beethoven was a rock star. Wagner's music comes from Mars. They move me. Muse don't, for some reason – they're one of the biggest bands in the world and yet they leave me cold. Lately, I like...I like 'Video Games' by Lana Del Rey...'Time To Pretend' by MGMT.

[Long pause]

A song that lingers inside my head is 'Love Will Tear Us Apart'.

We went to America – George, Andrew, Napier-Bell and me.

I was back in New York, back where me and Richard got scabies in the seventies. Times Square wasn't quite so crazy, but it was still pretty mad. You couldn't go to the East Village without fear of being mugged. We went to a fashion party. It was all very eighties; cocktails, hair spray, yellow suits and tans. The following day, jet-lagged and mildly hungover, Napier-Bell and I went to meet the people at Columbia Records for the first time.

Columbia Records was based in the CBS building, a big black thing on Fifty-Second Street known as the Black Rock. We took two breezeblocks of press cuttings, including the *WHAM! MANIA!* article and also 'Wake Me Up Before You Go-Go' and a video we'd

My first gig, aged ten, Handcross, Sussex, November 1954

Gordon Boys' School Band (front row, second from right),
aged twelve, January 1957

Bandsman Summers, Royal Army Medical Corps – sweet sixteen!

Hong Kong, 1966. With Jennette, my lovely Chinese girlfriend

Drumming with the Shades of Blue,
Singapore, 1967

The Shades of Blue promo flyer,
Malaysia, 1967

January 1974, I officially became a manager. Ad in *Melody Maker*
© *IPC Media*

Left: 1983 with Katie, three months old.
A bad case of acne rosacea

Below: Again with Katie, sixteen years later
in 1999 – clear skin!
And no make-up…

With Yazz, Tiananmen Square, 1985. Wham!'s trip to China

George and Andrew of Wham!
at the Great Wall of China, 1985
© *Owen Franken / CORBIS*

My marriage to Yazz,
Montego Bay, Jamaica,
December 1985

Receiving a BPI Award for going to China from Norman Tebbit MP,
with Andrew and George, February 1986
© *Richard Young / Rex Features*

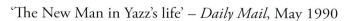

'The New Man in Yazz's life' – *Daily Mail*, May 1990

With Jazzie B at a Soul II Soul reception for Gamble and Huff, 1994

Receiving the Strat Award at the Music Awards, presented by Lisa Stansfield, 2007

The Verve on stage at Glastonbury, 2008. The best gig I have ever been to
© *Getty Images*

With Richard Ashcroft at my recent wedding to Dianna, 2013
© *Bruce Fleming*

recently made. We'd timed our visit perfectly; 'Go-Go' was at number one in the UK.

The meeting took place in a vast boardroom, glitzy and swish. We sat in beige leather swivel chairs round a huge onyx-plated table. A wall of windows looked out into downtown New York and the Hilton Hotel. CBS was so powerful; you name it, they had it: Jackson, Springsteen, Bob Dylan, Cyndi Lauper, Sade. All the power people of the Black Rock were at that meeting - Head of Radio, numerous marketing guys, Product Managers, Senior Product Managers. There wasn't one woman in the room. It was a pandemonium of penises – testosterone hell. You gotta picture it. A dozen straight-faced American men watched as Napier-Bell and I waddled in with our Wham! press cuttings. They all wore bright blue jeans and pale-coloured loafers and had their shirts tucked in tight over bulging beer and steak bellies.

Napier-Bell and I sat opposite each other. We presented Wham! We talked about what we'd been up to in England and the rest of the world and about the success of 'Wake Me Up Before You Go-Go'.

'Yeah, sounds great,' someone interrupted. 'So where's the album?'

In anticipation of this question, I'd hired the designer Peter Saville. I loved what Peter Saville had done. I loved all his Factory Records stuff, his sleeve for 'Love Will Tear Us Apart'. He was the best in the country. I didn't know him from Adam, but I phoned him up and said, 'Peter, would you like to do a Wham! sleeve?' And he said, 'Yeah, why not?' I feared he'd be a bit indie schmindie, Saville, but he wasn't, well, he *was*, in a sense, but he was also cool and interested in all sorts of different things. Before I went to America I'd handed him a pop portrait of George and Andrew and asked him to put a Wham! logo on it and to print it on a twelve-inch card. So when all these Americans started asking me where the album was, I stood up and held aloft the piece of card Saville had made.

'Here is the artwork!' They all looked impressed. 'The album, gentlemen, will be finished in the next four weeks.' This was total bullshit, but I had to say it. There was no point telling George that the album had to be done in four weeks. He wouldn't give a shit. Bullshit the Americans with the fake sleeve and, later, carry on bugging George to finish the album; that was the plan.

The meeting seemed to be going OK. The lack of album was the main problem and Saville's sleeve had created a helpful illusion. Napier-Bell started hyping up the hype we'd created in England, saying Wham! were the biggest thing since the Beatles. I suppose he went a little too far because halfway through his speech, Al Teller, the head of the label, started banging on the onyx table with his fist.

Al Teller had the best comb-over I'd ever seen. A swathe of tawny brown hair went from one ear to the other. Al 'comb-over' Teller – the most powerful man in the room. I don't know what had upset him. Maybe it was Simon being over the top, or maybe it was just that there was so much bullshit getting shovelled round his boardroom, or maybe he was high on something or coming down. Whatever it was, out of the blue, he started beating his fist against the table, shouting at me and Napier-Bell, shouting, 'What the *fuck* do you want? Who the fuck *are* you two? Why the fuck do you come in here and talk about fucking Wham Mania? What the fuck do you think you're *doing*?'

Everyone was a little bit shocked.

'Look at the figures!' Al Teller was flushed. His comb-over was coming unstuck. 'You sold a hundred thousand albums last time,' he said. 'Fuck. All. I don't give a fuck what you did round the rest of the world. You're fuck all here. What are these demands for special treatment for some English pop band? This is America. There's no Wham mania here.'

Napier-Bell was teetering about on the brink of a hissy fit. I gave him a warning look, trying to calm him.

'I know we haven't sold many records here.' I spoke as calmly as I could. 'And I know you don't really get this. But look at this, right, let's watch this video.'

A shitty little nine-inch monitor hung from the ceiling. I handed the video over. A lot of artists didn't make videos in those days; MTV was just coming in. This was the eighties; I was praying the video would work in their video-player.

'Watch this,' I said. '*Look* at George Michael.'

Halfway though the video, a guy called Ray Anderson, who's dead now, who had a large, back-combed auburn bouffant, he turned to me and frowned. He hadn't even bothered to turn to look at the screen.

'Yeh, Al,' Ray said. 'You're dead right about this. How the hell am I supposed to get *that* on American radio?'

That was 'Careless Whisper'. All around the room, people were shaking their heads, grimacing at the floor, looking out the fucking window.

'Listen,' I said, 'you've got to listen to that song again! That song's a smash! That song's beautiful! Listen to it again!'

It didn't matter what I said. The meeting ended and Napier-Bell and I stood by the elevator in the foyer of the Black Rock. I was tired and shocked. Napier-Bell was hyperactive and irate. 'How could they, Jazzbo? What the *fuck* was that all about? I'm going to speak to Oberstein about this.'

'This is America, Simon. These guys aren't scared of Maurice Oberstein. They don't give a shit about England.'

BIG LIFE

'What are we gonna do?'

'I'm gonna stay here. I'm not gonna leave. I'm gonna bug them, Simon. I'll hassle this whole building, this whole fucking country.'

Ray of Light at the Black Rock

George's songs were fucking fabulous and yet the Americans could care less, as they say. Why? Why do they say that?

[Pause]

I returned to the Black Rock the next day in search of people who might believe. I'd heard there was a guy who had helped to get radio play on Wham!'s first album.

I walked down a long corridor till I found a glass door labeled 'Mr John Faggot'. It was slightly ajar. I could see a man striding around in front of a chaotic desk, wearing a headset and shouting. He beckoned me in without looking at me and then continued berating whoever it was. The argument developed and Faggot seemed to win it. He said goodbye emphatically, tore his headphones from his head and smiled at me. 'John Faggot!' He shook my hand with real vigour and guided me to a swivel chair. 'You're Wham's guy, right? I love those guys.'

I later learned that John had been advised to change his name, but had refused. He refused to let his children change their name either. Anyone called John Faggot has to have balls, I thought. He sat at his desk, took a bite from his cheeseburger and swung a pair of baby blue moccasins up onto the desk. Years later, I met his daughter. She worked for Geffen when I managed Embrace. I don't remember her exact name, but it was Something Faggot. John once hand-cuffed himself to a radio programmer's desk to get him to listen to a song. 'Jazz, I love Wham!' He threw some fries in his mouth and wiped his lips with the back of his hand. 'It was me who got them on the radio last time. I recommended them to independents. I got them what little they got. I loved that 'Bad Boys' record. I got them on in Atlanta, in Miami. And that 'Young Guns' record, what a song, 'Wham! Rap'. We got pockets of play. And I love this 'Wake Me Up Before You Go-Go.''

'Would you be willing to work it with me? No one else is interested.'

Really, people could only work on the records they were told to work on. John Faggot's boss was Ray Anderson ('How the hell am I supposed to get *that* on American radio?') Faggot swung his moccassins off the desk, stood up proudly and said, '*Of course* I'll work it!' You don't find many people like John Faggot at American labels these days. In fact, there's no one like John in America now. John would work on a record whether the corporation instructed him to or not. He would work on a record simply because he loved it. It wasn't conglomerate radio stations being dictated to by idiots at the top. There was independent stations, who thought independently. Of course they took bribes – money, bags of cocaine, but there were significant pockets of independent thought in American radio. There were passionate pluggers like John Faggot; people who cultivated real relationships with DJs and chained themselves to the desks of radio station programmers. Relationships based on love of music. It was still rock 'n' roll.

A ray of light came through the window and I squinted.

'Thank you, John. I'm gonna be back in a couple of weeks.'

'Great, man. Come see me.'

I had an insider at the Black Rock. Somebody who believed.

BIG LIFE

Lolly

When Wham! left Innervision and went to Epic, there was a party. There, in the aftermath of my relationship with Yazz, I met a girl called Lorraine Trent, who was commonly known as Lolly.

She was cute and very lovely and ended up being Wham!'s Product Manager in England. We had to keep it secret, of course, because you couldn't have a band's manager and a band's product manager going out. It wasn't ethical. She was a special person, Lolly, and I managed to seduce her, thanks in part to Yazz having taught me to apply make-up so well.

When I returned to America, George had written a couple more songs. That happened with him. Nothing would happen, then suddenly he'd give you a wonderful song like 'Freedom'. I had 'Freedom', 'Go-Go', 'Careless Whisper' and a couple more. My aim in America was to work the floor, to motivate CBS, to bug them. The first thing I did was go and see John Faggot. We were trying to get a release date for 'Go-Go'.

There are many ways of breaking an act. You have to try more than one, OK. Clubs is one way. It may seem funny, the idea that you could break a song like 'Wake Me Up Before You Go-Go' in a club. But in America, in the eighties, you could. 'Young Guns' and 'Wham! Rap' had done well in the clubs. Working the clubs is perfect for when radio stations don't wanna play your songs. In 2008, we only really got La Roux's 'In For The Kill' buzzing up off the back of a club remix.

Back in 1984, I knew this promoter on the West coast called Ken Freedman. He had all sorts of ideas for 'Go-Go'. First thing, he wanted to stimulate the market by importing three thousand UK twelve-inch copies of 'Go-Go' into LA. It was a great way to

TAPE #10

get a story going about the song. I could tell people it was doing well in the club charts on imports alone, that they were selling like hot cakes. You have to make things happen, OK. Songs don't just break themselves. You have to work hard, get involved, make sacrifices, go sleepless.

East Coast Hitman

I was lying on my hotel bed, pretty stupefied and drunk and sulky and maybe lonely, I suppose. This was New York. I was thinking about Lolly. It took a while to realise the phone was ringing. I answered it without saying hello.

'Mr Summers? Are you there?'

'What is this?'

'My name's Mark. I'm calling from Philadelphia. I love Danse Society. I want to bring them over for a tour of America.'

'Right.'

It was the last thing I needed – some guy asking me about Danse Society. I lay there, sick and shaky and thinking about Lolly, pining for her a little. I lay my head on the pillow, let go of the receiver and let it drift from my ear. I took some deep breaths to try and soothe the horrid nausea. And it was then that the little crackly voice inside the telephone mentioned the name Fred DiSipio. I grabbed the receiver and sat up in bed.

'You know Fred DiSipio?'

'That's what I'm saying, Mr. Summers. I'm working with him.'

'*The* Fred DiSipio?'

'Sure.'

In those days, American radio was controlled by a couple of people. There was a fella on the West coast and a fella on the East.

BIG LIFE

The Hit Man of the East coast was Fred DiSipio. His name was so legendary some people doubted he even existed. It was said that he could break a record with total ease. But getting to him was impossible. Especially for someone like me. I was down at John Faggot's level, and that was fine, but if the Universe offers to take you out for a cup of tea and a sandwich, you accept, OK.

'Listen, Mark, I've got a few new Danse Society records with me here. I'm gonna come and see you tomorrow, OK?'

'Wow! That's great.'

'The thing is, I'd really like to meet Fred.'

'Sure.'

'I don't wanna come down and not see him, you know.'

I leapt out of bed, ran to the bathroom and splashed my face with water. I wasn't wearing any make-up and my hands were shaking. It was like my eyes were staring out from a red mask. They looked sad, my eyes, so I splashed some more water on them. I poured myself a drink and paced up and down, thinking about how to impress Fred DiSipio.

The following day in Philadelphia, I was greeted by Mark, who, it quickly became clear, was a kid they'd got in on work experience to find new bands and learn the ropes. He was sweet. He made me a coffee and we talked about Danse Society – the whole Barnsley goth thing. 'Listen,' I said. 'I'd really like to see Fred, if possible.' I was anxious. I knew this was my only chance. 'Is Fred around?'

[Pause]

Fred was around. I pushed open his office door and blinked. It was startling. Fred DiSipio slowly turned the pages of *Playboy* magazine, sitting behind a huge desk in the middle of a room as gold as the sun – framed discs all over every wall. He wore a brown and beige suit, beige brogues and a pair of horn-rimmed shades.

126

TAPE #10

His hair was dyed black and swept back. When he stood, I saw he was twitchy, perky, wired; one of the most well-connected men in American music.

'Hello,' I said. 'I'm Jazz.'

'*Jazz*? *Really*? Your name's *Jazz*? Wow! Do you wanna drink, Jazz? It's good to meet you, Jazz. Have a seat, Jazz. Jazz, what can I do for you?'

'I've got a band I'd like to play you.'

'You have? Oh, well, I really wanna hear this, Jazz. I really wanna hear this band, man. Did you happen to see a cup of coffee anywhere?'

'This record.' I held up the vinyl. 'This is number one in England at the moment. A group called Wham!'

'Wow, Wham! I never heard of Wham! Let's hear it, Jazz. Play me The Wham. I'm excited.'

I put 'Wake Me Up Before You Go-Go' on. When it was finished, I insisted that, before we discuss it, we listen again.

'That sounds like a smash.' DiSipio was dancing around. He paused by his desk and fanned his flushed face with *Playboy*. 'What label's it on?'

'Columbia'

'Columbia? Does Walter know about this?'

'I don't know. Al Teller doesn't think it's a hit.'

'Fuck Al Teller, Jazz. Go to the top. You need Walter.'

I knew who Walter was. Walter Yetnikoff. Not the head of Columbia, but the head of CBS – a hit-maker supreme who breakfasted on vodka and cocaine each morning at the summit of the Black Rock. DiSipio was taking me high up above Al Teller's comb-over. He pressed a button on his phone: 'Get me Walter!'

'Listen to the song again, Fred,' I said.

127

BIG LIFE

'Are you kidding me?'

'Let's listen to *Go-Go* again.'

'Really? *Again*?'

'It's a smash.'

'I already heard it twice.'

God knows how I did it, but he listened to it again and he danced again and he got even more excited, by which time, his secretary was phoning through the news that Walter Yetnikoff was on the line. I couldn't have got a meeting with Walter in a million years. But Fred DiSipio was a Hit Man. He'd broken Walter's acts – Jackson, Springsteen, Pink Floyd. He had him on the phone in minutes.

'I've got this guy Jazz in my office, Walter. He's got this English band, the Wham! It's a smash, we gotta work it! Do you hear me? We're gonna work this record, all right. All right? All right!' He smashed down the phone, danced over and shook my hand. He smelt of fried chicken. 'It's a deal, Jazz. What a song! The Wham! Great to meet you, Jazz. Have you seen my cup of coffee?'

I had no idea what the situation was, really. But I'd got him to play the song three times. I'd put Wham! on the radar of two of the most powerful men in the American music industry. I left a bunch of copies of the song on Fred's desk. I'd never have got to speak to him if I hadn't been manager of Danse Society. And they did the tour, Danse Society, a few months later. They toured the East coast and did some pretty decent shows.

Bugging People

I went into the Black Rock day in, day out and I badgered them. John Faggot said I had some balls, going to meet Fred DiSipio. But John was doing great work, too – getting 'Go-Go' some plays on independent stations in places like Miami and Fort Lauderdale. I sat at people's desk all around the Black Rock, playing them 'Go-Go' over and over until Wham! were wedged in their minds. I didn't speak to Al Teller or Ray Anderson. They were upstairs in offices the size of tennis courts. I worked the ground level. I bugged them. I followed people up and down corridors, talking about George and Andrew.

The thing I couldn't seem to figure out was how to get Ken Freedman his import copies of 'Go-Go'. As it was, Napier-Bell and I had had to pay Ken out of our own money – the Americans refused to pay him, and so did Wham!'s publishers, Morrison and Leahey. They didn't believe. But I knew Ken was right to want import copies. In those days, music fans *loved* them. Owning an import copy meant you were ahead of the curve. You were cool before your friends. The trouble was, Ken wanted to import three thousand twelve inches. I didn't see how that was possible.

I lay in bed with Lolly in Acton one morning, staring at the ceiling. I was thinking about three thousand fucking twelve inches. Lolly lay beside me, snoozing. We'd eaten out in Earl's Court at a Thai restaurant the transvestites adored. We liked it, too, and we'd eat and drink with lorry drivers who were dressed in yellow feather boas, lipstick and leopard skin miniskirts. We'd drunk too much, or I had at least. I woke up tipsy and downed the pint of water I kept beside my bed. Then I lay there longing for tea.

'Lolly?'

She groaned in her sleep.

'Lolly, we need cups of tea. And it's your turn.'

'Right.'

'And are there any *Go-Go* twelve inches in the London warehouse?'

'Eugh! Probably. Why?'

'You need to wake up. I need three thousand twelve inches to export to America. Any chance?'

'*Three thousand?*'

'Yeah.'

'No chance.'

We drifted back to silence. Lolly got up and went to make tea. When she returned, I was standing on the bed, completely naked, bouncing slightly and batting the lampshade a bit.

'We're building up a fan club, right?'

'Right.'

Lolly was patient and totally lovely. I can see her, as I speak… standing there clutching her tea in a purple satin dressing gown. 'I'm gonna telex you asking for three thousand *Go-Go* twelve inches, OK.' I was still bouncing on the bed and batting the lampshade. 'I'm gonna say they're for the members of the fan club. What do you think of that?'

'Please sit down, Jazz. You're gonna break the bed.'

'Whadayathink? And then I'll export them to America instead!'

'I suppose it's worth a try.'

I don't know how she did it, but Lolly not only managed to get the records from CBS for nothing, but she even managed to ship them to Ken Freedman in LA at the label's expense. She was a star.

Ken sent three hundred copies to Miami, two hundred to San Francisco and kept two and half thousand in LA. He took it to KROQ and they started playing it. He drove round all the independent record shops in Malibu, Pasadena, West Hollywood, Santa Monica, in his car, giving away these import twelve inches. *That's* why Napier-Bell and I paid him ourselves, when the label and the publishers wouldn't. Because Ken was a guy willing to drive round in his car lugging heavy imported twelve inches into record shops. He believed. He worked hard. He did the dirty work.

At the Black Rock, I bugged this TV woman big time about MTV. I kept playing her the video and nudging her, saying, 'Imagine this. Imagine *this* on MTV. Just imagine it! Look how lovely these boys are.' I kept moving back and forth to America, keeping close with Faggot and Freedman. KROQ kept playing the song. It was playing in the clubs in Miami, LA and San Francisco. We managed to get some plays on MTV, too, and then, finally, Ken Freedman loaded up his car with the last thousand of the twelve inches and took them down to Tower Records on Sunset Boulevard. It took him two trips, but they bit his hand off. Those thousand records sold out in one morning. They flew out of the door like hot fucking hotcakes. The next day, I walked into the Black Rock to see John Faggot, as usual. I was walking down the corridor to John's office, when Ray Anderson stepped into my path. Ray Anderson, Head of Promotion, one of the crown princes of the Black Rock. Ray Anderson, who months earlier had asked me, in front of all his steak-bellied colleagues, how the hell am I supposed to get *that* on American radio? Ray held me firmly by both shoulders and said, 'Mr Summers, your record is blowin up!'

'It is?'

'They've sold a thousand imports at Tower on Sunset! Your record is blowin up!'

TAPE #11
(11TH APRIL 2012)

Torquay

Since Angela left, and Yazz dumped me for a German model, I'd gone back to wearing pretty cool clothes. I'd really re-immersed myself in fashion, drugs and fornication. I still wasn't drinking spirits. I was a wino. I loved wine. I became an expert. I knew where all the different grapes grew. But after a bottle or two, I'd drink anything, any old plonk. I went to the wine bar in Gosfield Street every single evening at seven. By eight-thirty, I'd be pissed and slurring things about Wham! to strangers. I remember one night, Lolly joined me. She kissed me hello and commented quietly about how pissed I was.

'How long have you been here, Jazz?'

I'd been there less than an hour.

My hair was getting thin on top. The idea of an Al Teller comb-over appalled me. I got in the bath one day and swept all my hair back, as you can when it's wet. It looked pretty good, I thought, particularly once I'd had my long, flowing mullet trimmed to the collar. That became my style – the swept back look.

I lived alone in Acton. Lolly and I spent a lot of our spare time together. She was a complete relief from the trauma of my time with Yazz. Over the summer, I'd had a few postcards from her, Yazz, saying things like, 'Hi, I'm in San Tropez and Wham are all over the radio!' Then, around the beginning of August, she phoned.

'I'm back in London. Do you wanna get together?'

TAPE #11

We met for breakfast in Notting Hill. I took her the twelve inch of 'Careless Whisper', which I thought was pretty apt, really, because the song's about unrequited love. I didn't do badly at breakfast. I still loved her, but I wasn't too needy.

News of my efforts in America had got back to the UK. CBS invited the Americans, the Columbia hierarchy, to come to their Annual Sales Conference. The aim was to consolidate Wham! in the minds of the Americans. The sales conference was in Torquay that year.

In the eighties, in the land of plenty, CDs were coming up and back catalogues were being re-released. Records were selling in their zillions. All the record companies had sales conferences around September, where they presented their new releases to the retail sector.

They were bloated, decadent affairs. Savage, immoral piss-ups that culminated in a dinner and a dance on the Friday in the banqueting hall of a huge hotel. I hadn't seen Lolly all week. I was excited ahead of the Friday meal, where we'd be on the same table. We still couldn't interact romantically in public. It would have meant the chop for her.

Napier-Bell didn't come because he'd fallen over and twisted his ankle – I think in a sex-romp. It was important for me to go because of all my American work; we needed to consolidate their belief in the band. As well as Lolly, I sat with George and Andrew. They'd flown into Torquay by helicopter. And the Americans were at our table – Al 'comb-over' Teller, Ray ('Your record is blowin up!') Anderson. There were drinks before the dinner and I drank as much as possible. I was wearing plenty of make-up. George got incredibly drunk, too, I remember, and he disappeared. He had to give a speech, so I went looking for him in the toilets. I went

133

round shouting 'Yog', which was what his family and close friends called him. He often didn't answer to George when he was drunk. I found him in the toilet, throwing up. I was rat-arsed, but was able to splash George's face with water and guide him out into the main hall. To his credit, George made a good job of slurring through his speech. He thanked the Americans for their belief and hard work.

Meanwhile, Ray Anderson leaned in to me and asked about Lolly, saying what a fine woman he thought she was, and how, you know, he'd like to fuck her brains out. He didn't know I was in a relationship with her. I felt a huge, horrible anger towards him. He'd been such a prat when Napier-Bell and me first presented Wham! at the Black Rock. Ray was totally macho and sexist and he was whispering rude comments in my ear as though I should slap him on the back in congratulations. I wanted to punch his lights out, but I'd been committed to non-violence for years. And I knew it was a poor idea to punch the head of promotion at a major American record label. I drank to deal with the anger. And as I drank my vision blurred and my brain blanked and all I really remember is telling Lolly how shit and unbalanced the food was, and how much I missed Richard Digance, hated my red face and wanted to manage Prince.

I don't remember anything after that, but the thousand people who attended the Torquay conference do. They describe how I accosted Lolly on the dance floor and demanded that she come to bed with me. She told me to fuck off and that I was a terrible person. Of course, people came to her rescue and pushed me around. I have a flash of a memory where I'm lying in a lift and, as I look up, a man is holding a wine bottle above his head and he's about to hit me with it. Apparently, the hotel manager and his wife tried to calm me down and, in response, I pushed them both and threatened to set fire to the building. The police got called, I'm told, and they arrested me. A guy called Gerry Turner, the head of marketing at Epic, who's dead now, too, persuaded the police to let me go. They're all dead, aren't they. So many of these people.

[Long pause]

I woke up the next day covered in bruises. All over my body. My face was a mixture of smudged make-up and red spots. I have vague remembrances of wandering round the hotel in the middle of the night, trying to kick doors down, shouting Lorraine's name. But they're like memories of dreams; they're blurry and all fragmented, you know. I had to catch the early train. I phoned Lorraine's room from Torquay train station.

'Fuck off, Jazz, you fucking bastard. I *never* want to see or hear you again.'

I sat on the train, feeling scared and thinking dreadful thoughts. A guy called Larkin Arnold, an American A&R man, sat opposite me. It was Larkin Arnold who, in 1983, went to Belgium, found Marvin Gaye, and encouraged him to make music. They'd made 'Sexual Healing' together. Healing was what I wanted. Not sexual. Just healing. Although Larkin was happy to speak to me, everyone else from CBS on that train completely blanked me. Larkin, you see, had gone to bed early.

I got off the train at Paddington with a miserable hangover. People I talked to every day were blanking me. Someone approached, but only to tell me that Lolly had resigned from Epic records, which was pretty dodgy for me, because it was all my fault. It put me in a precarious position with Wham! 'I'm sorry,' I said, but the person had already fucked off.

I did something I'd never done before: I got a taxi home and phoned in to work sick. I went to bed and slept till the next morning. I slept for nearly a whole day. I woke to the ring of the bedside phone.

'Hello, darling, how are you?'

'Yazz?'

'How are you?'

'I got drunk…I'm very bruised. Yazz, I think I was arrested.'

'It's in the newspaper.'

'It is? Oh, dear.'

'When you're drunk, Jazz,' Yazz said, 'I've got to say…you're ugly.'

Those words – *you're ugly* – stayed with me. I knew I had to stop drinking.

'Can I see you, Yazz?'

'I'll call you later. To see how you are.'

It would have been so easy for Simon Napier-Bell to have me sacked. One word to George was all it would have taken. But Simon was brilliant. He called Lolly and convinced her not to quit CBS. He phoned up everyone concerned and explained that I'd had a very heavy night and made a few mistakes, but that was all. And he told George and Andrew that they should support me at this difficult time. He was a true partner and a genuine guy. Simon had his flamboyant, bullshit ways, but he was so supportive in that moment. I'll always be grateful.

[Pause]

Where does it all go?

[Pause]

I should call Tim. I think I should call Richard Ashcroft. See how he's…

[Long pause]

OK. So Yazz called that evening and invited me to a musical. Afterwards, we went for a drink. I drank Perrier. For the next week, we went out every night, Yazz and me. We went to clubs and danced and I drank coffee or orange juice or Perrier.

After two weeks, she said she was proud of me. We kissed gently outside her house one night. When she went back to Germany, she called from Heathrow. She said she loved me. She said, 'I love you.' And I said it, too.

A few weeks later, we were shooting the video for 'Last Christmas'. We couldn't find any snow. In the end, we found a place called Sas Fe in Switzerland, where snow was forecast for the next day, and we all travelled there. The snow fell, we shot the video and then, out of the blue, Yazz arrived. She'd got our whereabouts from Pepsi in the band. That was it, really. We were together again.

The day after the CBS sales conference, the *Daily Express* ran an article. The headline read: *WHAM! MANAGER RUNS AMOK AT MUSIC CONFERENCE*

When was this? When did all this happen?

[Pause]

George did 'Last Christmas' in 1984…the plan was to get Christmas number one. But, as it happens, the song was the biggest-selling number *two* single of all time. Number one that year was 'Do They Know It's Christmas?' which George sang on, too.

'Wake Me Up Before You Go-Go' was a number one record in America. CBS pressed the button and Wham! blew up on MTV. In the UK, 'Careless Whisper' (by Wham! featuring George Michael) went to number one, too. The album, *Make It Big*, followed. There was only about eight tracks on it, but still, it was great. 'Freedom' is a great song. 'Everything She Wants' is fantastic.

Wham! were huge. We did a UK arena tour. Wham! were also huge in Japan, of course, thanks to Kaz and the blank tape ad. We sold over a million records there. We did a huge gig in Osaka. We did four nights at the Budokan in Tokyo. That was unheard of.

In Australia, George lost his voice at the first Melbourne show. It was in an old swimming pool, I remember. The acoustics were awful. The fans screamed from beginning to end and George fucked his voice trying to hear himself. He couldn't do the second Melbourne gig. The insurance company wouldn't cover us because George had a history of vocal problems. We stood to lose a hundred thousand pounds from having to refund the tickets ourselves. A doctor told George not to even talk for a while, which was a problem for the press conference, because Andrew refused to do it alone.

In the end, it was me who faced that swarm of Australian journalists. Everyone was there: magazines, daily papers, ABC News. I was so nervous. That night, lying on my hotel bed, I switched on the television to see how I'd performed. I honestly didn't notice what the man on the television was saying. All I could see was the horrific condition of his skin, how red it was, how awful it looked. Because of all the chaos and the stress, I'd forgotten to apply my make-up.

I went to the bathroom and looked in the mirror. I hadn't drunk any alcohol for three months, but I wanted to tear my face from my skull. 'Why me?' I thought. 'Why couldn't the spots be on my arse?'

TAPE #12
(12TH APRIL 2012)

Simon Gets Drunk and is a Genius

If you have a number one record in the UK, everyone knows who you are. But if you have a number one record in America, people know the song, sure, but they don't really know the artist – not properly.

I was over visiting my daughter Katie in LA in 1984. There was a family gathering and everyone was asking what I was up to. When I told people I was managing Wham!, they all looked at me blankly. No one had heard of them. But when I sang [sings] *wake me up before you go-go*, everyone suddenly knew what I was talking about and told me how the song was all over their radio.

'To truly break America,' I told George and Andrew, 'you need to do the whole thing. You need to be *real* to people. To get the press, the television, the sales, you need to go *everywhere* and play for your fans. That's how the Stones and Zeppelin did it. It's how Culture Club and Duran Duran are doing it now. You need more than radio to truly break America. People need to see you.'

'I'm not up for doing a long tour, Jazz.'

'George, you need to do it all. And you could do at least two arena gigs a night in twenty towns. Even four gigs in some places. You have to do the local papers, radio stations, the local record stores. You have to make yourself *real* to people, George. You'll have a career here for life.'

'I'll do six shows. At the most, Jazz. I don't like it. A long tour just isn't for me.'

139

BIG LIFE

Napier-Bell and me went clubbing a lot in this period. In Japan, it had mostly been gay clubs. I was getting a bit sick of them. I'd packed up drinking, of course, but Napier-Bell drank, and in fact, he got very pissed one night in a San Francisco club. We'd played the Kaiser Hall in Berkeley the previous night. The promoter there, a guy called Bill Graham, had told me I had the fastest-selling act since the Beatles. But that meant nothing if George didn't want to do a long arena tour.

'Fuck George, Jazzbo,' Napier-Bell slurred. 'These fucking *artists*. You've worked your fucking butt off over here. And he won't fucking tour properly. I'm bored, Jazzbo. We should be doing fucking stadiums. And I wanna go to China, Jazzbo. That's how fucking bored I am. I'm bored of the whole of Western fucking civilisation.'

'Simon,' I said – I was having to hold him up straight. We were walking down a quiet San Franciscan street, away from the club. 'What you've just said is very, very clever, you know.'

'Fuck George. Fuck everywhere except China. Fuck Western morality. Dreary fucking boring bollocks. This industry is so fucking *shitty*. Know that, Jazzbo? It's so fucking *shitty... You don't have to say you love me...just be close at hand...*'

As Simon sang that beautiful song he'd written back in 1964, I started thinking: MTV is really blowing up in certain parts of America. If we target those areas, places like Miami and New York, then maybe Wham! *could* play stadiums in America.

'Simon. Fuck arenas. Let's do a *stadium* tour. Seriously, this is a new era. Let's play stadiums where MTV is taking off!'

'I want to go to China, Jazzbo. I despise pop culture. It's dull, dull, dull. George should be bigger than Prince!'

'We *will* go to China, Simon.' I was really struggling to hold him up straight. 'You've had a fucking brilliant idea. If we're the first pop band in China, we'll get an avalanche of publicity in America. We won't have to go round all the fucking local radio stations and record stores. We'll get all the publicity in one fell swoop. You go to China, Simon. I'll stay here and get a stadium tour organised.'

'I'm tired, you know, Jazzbo. I'm so, so tired. Hold me.'

Simon wrapped his arm round me and I supported him back to our hotel. It was pissing with rain and he was singing.

'You don't have to say you love me…'

The plan was simple. I would fly to New York and try to organise a stadium tour. Simon would fly to Communist China and try to get two pop concerts organised.

Wham! had the biggest agent in the music industry. Her name was Barbara Skydel. She worked at Premier Talent. She was the first person I met in New York. My face looked pretty awful, I think. Barbara winced as I entered her office. She asked me if my nose hurt. Since the Australian press conference I'd been applying more make-up than ever. I looked like something from Madame Tussauds, but the redness still showed through.

Barbara was a hugely influential woman, elegant and stern. She booked gigs for Tom Petty, U2, the Who, the Pretenders. She looked after Bruce Springsteen, who had toured tirelessly for many years before finally being big enough to play stadiums. If anyone was powerful enough to get a Wham! stadium tour off the ground, it was Barbara Skydel.

'We could do twenty cities, Jazz. Multiple nights at arenas.' Barbara's soul was rock 'n' roll, but her image was uptown Manhattan. She had a Louis Vuitton handbag. She ran a hand through her loosely permed hair and smiled. 'This is gonna be huge. All the promoters are on the phone. Bill says you can do four nights at the Cow Palace. Brian says you could do four nights in LA at the Forum.'

'Barbara, stop,' I said. 'It's not gonna work. George says he'll do six shows.'

'Six shows? Jazz, darling, you can't break America with six shows.'

'Yes, you can, Barbara. We can do six stadium shows.'

'*Stadiums*, Jazz? No. Bruce has only just got to that level. The boys have only just arrived here. You can't be serious.'

'I think this is a different era, Barbara. I don't wanna do Cow Palace, I wanna do the Alameda County Stadium. I don't wanna do four nights at the Forum, I wanna do the Rose Bowl. I don't wanna do fucking Flushing Meadows, I wanna do Shea Stadium. We can play stadiums in LA, New York, maybe Miami or Boston. Look to where the MTV audience is big, Barbara. I think we can play stadiums there.'

Barbara said nothing. She wasn't listening. She picked up the phone and dialed.

'Oh, hi, Brian,' she said, cheerfully and pretty artificially. 'It's Barbara here.' She leant back in her chair and winked at me, really patronising. 'I've got Jazz Summers in front of me...he wants Wham to play the Rose Bowl this summer...that's right, the Rose Bowl...I told him that...no, he doesn't want to do four nights at the Forum...yes, he does think he's got the Beatles, doesn't he? I know, he's new, he'll learn...yes, I know that Brian, I told him, but he thinks he's got the Beatles...yes, he's sitting right here...yeah, I'll tell him, Brian...bye.' Barbara put down the phone, gave me a totally charmless, counterfeit smile, and said, 'See?'

I was agitated. I squirmed in my chair, thinking, thinking about all sorts of things. Thinking about the Shades of Blue. About our aborted tour to Vietnam, the Ludvig drum kit I'd never got to play on, and the horrid, patronising way in which Brigadier Niven had turned that dream to dust. It all came back to me as I sat there, looking out a window down into Manhattan ('You think you can just poodle off and play Vietnam'). I looked at Barbara Skydel. Her smile was fading now. She looked down her nose at me, thinking I was mad for wanting to poodle off and play stadiums.

'Barbara,' I said. 'You're fired.'

If ...

The music industry winced when I sacked Barbara Skydel. All except these two guys, John Marx and Rob Kahane, who called me and offered to act as Wham!'s new agent. I don't think they were completely sold on the stadium tour idea, but they really wanted to represent Wham!, so I guess they felt it was worth the risk.

Barbara immediately took to the press and claimed I was an English idiot who didn't understand how touring America worked. I felt lonely. She even began putting stadiums on hold for Bruce Springsteen in order to sabotage my idea. It was awful really, but I had a one-track mind. I truly believed Wham! could be a stadium band. Rob Kahane and I spent days making phonecalls to promoters across America. Plenty hung up when we mentioned stadiums, but some were intrigued. I guess some people had nothing to lose and thought it might be worth the risk. We found a guy in Toronto and San Francisco, then a guy in Miami. I found a guy in LA who couldn't book the Rose Bowl, but could get Hollywood Park, a racecourse out by LAX. The Police had played there the previous year.

I hired a big burgundy Chevrolet Caprice and drove out to Hollywood Park one smoggy day. The woman who owned the course was slightly strange. She was elderly, rode on a white pony, wore a violet velvet dress, hobnail boots and smoked a large pipe. She said there was a world war coming and I nodded and asked how the Police had gone down. 'Well,' she said. 'They played well…I ain't heard of your band…the Wham…' She made me walk right the way round the racecourse, even though I was only interested in the middle of it. At the finish line, she climbed off her pony and swigged from a silver hip-flask. When I told her I didn't drink alcohol, she took a bottle of the most disgusting root beer from her saddle-bag. I drank it and said it was delicious.

Standing on that racecourse, looking at the huge area we intended to fill with Wham! fans, I recalled how I'd booked the Pegasus in London and spent years traipsing up and down the Holloway Road, trying to get gigs. I felt a long way away from those days.

New York was impossible. I couldn't find anyone who believed that Wham! could sell out a stadium there. What's more, Shea Stadium was closed for the summer, so we couldn't play where the Beatles played. And Barbara Skydel had blackened my name among all the promoters. No one would take my calls. It was a fight. Every day was a fight. I found this promoter in Philadelphia who believed we could play the Vets Stadium. I thought maybe we could get AMTRAK, the trainline, to put on special trains for a day to carry fans from New York to Philadelphia. That would mean another fight.

It was during those days of fighting and arguing and desperation to do stadiums, that Napier-Bell called on a crackly line and said, 'Jazzbo, I've got China!' He'd been in deep and lengthy negotiations with the Chinese government.

The truth is, we wouldn't be the first band to go to China. Jean Michel Jarre had done it. But Jean Michel Jarre was managed by a guy called Francis Dreyfus, who was related to Captain Dreyfus of the 1896 Dreyfus Affair. I knew Dreyfus. He was Mr fucking Bourgeois. He thought Jean Michel Jarre was what he called 'an artiste'. So I knew if we went round telling the world that Wham! were the first 'pop' band to play China, there was no way Dreyfus would pipe up and say, 'But Jean Michel played Tiananmen Square!' There was no way he'd admit Jean Michel Jarre was a pop act.

To finance the trip to China, we decided to make a film. Video-cassettes were selling like mad in 1984. We didn't wanna make some poptastic nonsense. We wanted to make a proper film. To do that, we'd need a proper director.

I sought the advice of Martin Lewis, who used to market Richard Digance at Transatlantic. He came to see me in New York, where I was trying to solve the stadium problem. 'I don't wanna make pop promo goes to China, OK, Martin?' We ate sushi in downtown Manhattan. Martin was a movie producer these days. 'I don't wanna make anything too tacky, you know?'

'I've got a great idea, Jazz.'

'Go on.'

'How about Lindsay Anderson?'

I *loved* Lindsay Anderson. Here was a man, a radical, the man who'd made completely fantastic films like *If...* and *O Lucky Man!*

'Do you think we could get Lindsay Anderson to make a Wham movie?'

Lindsay was doing a play in New York at the time. He agreed to come and meet the band in London, providing we pay for him to fly on Concorde. Welcome to the film business, I thought. All of a sudden I was a movie producer.

Napier-Bell and I took George and Andrew to lunch to discuss the film. George wasn't keen. Napier-Bell told him he didn't have to be in it, which was quite a fantastic lie to tell a popstar. I never like lying to artists like that. I always try and negotiate with them and agree on a way forward. But Simon was stressed, I think. He'd spent a long time negotiating with the Chinese government and he was anxious that the trip go ahead. That was the difference between Simon and I. I liked to plan and negotiate. He didn't.

The upside was, George knew all about Lindsay Anderson. He came to meet him at Langan's. No one could quite believe how posh Lindsay was. 'And so, Mr Michael.' He had this incredibly trebly voice, with really received pronunciation. 'Are you excited about this Chinese adventure?'

The Answering Machine

We could call the trains 'WHAMTRAKS' – the trains that took the New Yorkers to Philly for the Vetts Stadium gig. I was proud of that idea. Things were slowly coming together. I'd got some decent supports acts sorted for the stadium tour. That was vital. We had Katrina and the Waves – 'Walkin' on Sunshine' was a big hit at the time. Then we had the Pointer Sisters and Chaka Kahn. I tried to get Stevie Wonder, but it didn't work out, probably because Barbara Skydel was shoveling so much shit on me in the press, saying I was ridiculous and didn't know what I was doing. Barbara knew Wham!'s publishers, Morrison and Leahey. She knew Morrison from the Pink Floyd days. After I sacked her, she warned him I was making big mistakes, said I was fucking up and being a dumb ass. She told him the stadium tour would ruin Wham! in America.

Towards the end of May 1985, Dick Leahey called me over and suggested we all get together and talk – me, Napier-Bell, the band

and the publishers. 'We'll meet tomorrow,' he said, 'and, Jazz, I'm really gonna grill you in the meeting, about the stadium tour, just so there's two sides for George and Andrew. Don't hold it against me. I'll be convinced by your arguments and then, as a result, I think George and Andrew will understand.'

We were yet to put tickets on sale. Every gig we'd ever done had sold out. But I had five forty-to-sixty-thousand-seater stadiums on hold, plus two outdoor arenas in Chicago.

Andrew Ridgeley always went with what George thought was best. Simon Napier-Bell, if he walked into a room thinking one way, and found that everyone in the room disagreed, he'd change his mind immediately and completely. I was really in the hot-seat at the meeting. Dick Leahey, as promised, grilled me. He mentioned that Barbara Skydel thought I was mad.

'This could fuck Wham up in America, Jazz. Be honest, it *could*.'

'We're in a new era, Dick. MTV is *incredibly* powerful. The record is selling in areas where MTV is big. I'm not going into Orlando or Austin or fucking Bumfuck Idaho, Dick. I'm going into big metropolitan areas where MTV is massive. Look at the stats, Dick. We can do it.'

'I'm sorry, Jazz, I don't agree.'

'I don't agree either,' said Napier-Bell.

'We shouldn't do this,' said George.

'Agreed,' said Andrew.

'Well, what shall we do?' I said. 'You want me to cancel the stadiums?'

'That's right,' said Dick.

'I've worked really hard on this, guys. I've fired Barbara Skydel. She's roasted me in the press. I've got four promoters out there who think this can happen. I've been on this for months.'

BIG LIFE

It was a Friday afternoon. I went home dejected. I didn't blame George. It was his career, after all. It was his name on those tickets, not mine. If they didn't sell, it was his livelihood and reputation that would suffer. I could see how, when confronted with the arguments of Dick Leahey, George didn't want to risk it. But we were the biggest pop band in the world. I'd told George we'd break America and we had. We'd done eight million records worldwide.

Nevertheless, I telephoned Rob Kahane and told him to cancel the stadiums and to let the promoters know not to put the tickets on sale. I told him Barbara had won. Rob sounded relieved, to be honest, which didn't make me feel any better. He started talking about booking twenty arenas, minimum, as replacement venues. I told him we'd discuss it some other time.

I'd stopped drinking, of course, so I couldn't get pissed. I picked up Yazz from some studio and took her to dinner. She was still trying to write songs, even though the Biz had ended. She was making poppy soul stuff on her breaks from modelling. She could see how fucking miserable I was. I felt vaguely humiliated, too, having shown so much enthusiasm for something that other people thought was stupid. And now I'd failed. We ate at Puccis on the King's Road, which was small, lively and trendy. I needed that sense of hope that a good restaurant restores, you know.

We had answering machines in those days. When Yazz and me came in about eleven, the red light was flashing. Seven messages. They'd been coming in at fifteen minute intervals for the previous couple of hours.

'*Jazz, call me. It's Rob Kahane. It's urgent. Thanks, bye.*'

'*Jazz, Rob. Miami's on fire. Call me.*'

'*Jazz, call me now, wouldya? You got that? Call me.*'

'*Hi, Jazz, it's Rob. Could you call me when you get this, please?*'

TAPE #12

'*Jazz? Jazz? Are you there? Jazz? Pick up if you're there.*'

'*Jazz Summers, you fucking prick, there's a riot going on in Miami. Call me as soon as you get this.*'

'*Where the fucking hell are you, you motherfucker? Call me. Call me the second you get this fucking message.*'

I called Rob.

'Jazz, we *have* to put these tickets on sale in Miami. The local radio have been talking about the gig.' (Good old John Faggot had done his job!) 'Kids are bombarding box offices all over the city. They're saying we could sell it out. There's eight thousand kids gathered in Miami, Jazz. Eight *thousand*. There's gonna be a riot. We *have* to put these tickets on sale.'

I called Napier-Bell, George and Andrew, but none of them answered – they were all out, of course. It was Friday night and they hadn't given up booze. They were partying. Napier-Bell was probably down the Caprice, pissed and holding court, having a tea party with his boyfriends. I called the promoter in Miami. I could hear kids chanting in the background. He spoke like a man under siege.

'You're fucking crazy. You've gotta do these gigs. There's eight thousand kids and they're gonna tear my stand down, man. You're out of your fucking mind. You'll sell twenty-five thousand today alone!'

I put the phone down and went to have a cup of tea with Yazz. I didn't know what to do. As a general rule, OK, if you sell fifty per cent of the tickets in a day, you're gonna sell the whole place out before the show.

I phoned the promoter back. 'Listen, you can put the tickets on sale. But tomorrow, I want you to tell the whole planet that you've sold thirty-three thousand tickets in one day.'

BIG LIFE

'I said twenty-five thousand.'

'Sure. But tomorrow you're gonna say that you've sold thirty-three thousand, OK?'

I knew that in order to change everyone's mind about the stadium tour, we'd have to inflate the figures slightly, make them not just amazing, but mind-blowing. The next day, the promoter called me.

'We sold twenty-seven thousand, man. It's Wham mania in Miami!'

'No, we didn't,' I said. 'We sold thirty-three thousand, eight hundred and twenty.'

On Monday morning, I called George. I didn't bother calling anyone else. I told him the story about the messages from Rob Kahane, about the Miami radio stations, about the near riot at the box office, how I'd had to make a decision and how, in one day in Miami, we'd sold thirty-three thousand tickets. So yes, I lied to George. I lied to everyone. But it was a white lie.

By Wednesday, it was a phenomenon. We'd sold over thirty thousand tickets in one day, and so suddenly all the other promoters round America went into action. Not just that, we had calls from other promoters around America, wanting to put Wham! on in stadiums. People called from Phoenix, San Antonio, Detroit, Idaho, everywhere. And we said no to every single one of them because they went against my theory, which was all based around playing stadiums in places where homes had MTV.

[Pause]

Actually, that's not quite true…when all those other promoters were calling me up trying to get Wham! on in stadiums, after Miami had gone mad, I did agree to an extra gig in Detroit. The guy there offered us so much money. I couldn't say no. And, in the end, we didn't sell out that stadium in Detroit. We had to cloak off large areas of seating. I broke with my principle and that was a mistake. Because the principle worked. Skydel was wrong. It was a new era.

Hollywood Park went on sale and we sold forty thousand tickets in the first weekend. San Francisco sold out almost immediately – fifty thousand. We did Toronto the day after Springsteen. Fifty thousand. Sold out. The WHAMTRAK trains carried thousands of fans down to the Vets Stadium in Philadelphia. We didn't quite sell that one out, but it was extremely close. Close enough.

Years later, in Nantucket, an American guy with an eye-patch collared me in a record shop: 'I've always wanted to meet the man who fired Barbara Skydel,' he said. And he puffed on a cigarillo. 'They'd never lost an act, you know. And Barbara did *everything* she could do to destroy you. But the more they criticised you, the weaker they got. You destabilised a huge company, Mr Summers. You were the beginning of the end for Premier Talent.'

I went from being a wanker to being a genius, as you can in the music industry, though you're normally a wanker again by the following week, which is strangely reassuring. I remember George and Andrew shitting themselves backstage before the Hollywood Park gig. The lady who owned that racecourse knew who Wham! were now. She was trotting around on her pony backstage, predicting a third world war. Elton John showed up just before they went on. When sixty thousand people roar, it's a big sound. I mean festivals are great, but they're not as loud as sixty thousand teenage fanatics roaring at a racetrack at the height of a band's fame. It was a big, frightening sound.

We made that sound.

BIG LIFE

Macrobiotics

'The way you cook, Mr Summers, and the way you eat; it all needs to change.'

I was told this by a slender man in a mohair poncho. I'd gone for a consultation at a macrobiotic centre on Old Street, East London. I started eating at the restaurant there – a dingy place called East/ West. I was drawn to macrobiotics because I was looking for a cure for my face. I'm drawn to the idea of change, OK.

I was managing the biggest pop group on the planet. I was in a relationship with a woman I adored. But I had to change. Make-up wasn't a long-term solution. I wanted more. I wanted Yazz to love me forever. I had to change my face for me and for her.

Healing with food is all about Yin and Yang, OK. The importance of balance. The importance of sticking to grain, vegetables, fruits, salad, a little fish, rather than steak and booze, you know…rampant fornication fuelled by fifteen greasy spring rolls. The importance of seasonal, local food. Globalisation has really fucked our diets. It's fucked around with our health and our souls.

I bought every book on earth to do with macrobiotic eating. It was like reading Marx and Lenin in the seventies. My mind opened. I hired my own macrobiotic chef. She came and lived with me and Yazz. Yazz went macrobiotic to support me, I think.

[Pause]

She was beautiful and healthy. After becoming macrobiotic, my face remained red, OK, but I felt calmer. I wasn't so edgy. I felt stronger in my decision making and much fitter. I was still spotty, but they weren't such an angry shade of red.

Things were good with Yazz and me. We bought a flat in Belsize Park and we had a succession of macrobiotic cooks. We hosted macrobiotic dinner parties where we ate rice balls made of nori, salted plums and seaweed. I turned down the opportunity to be a Buddhist a lot during this period. I was obsessed with macrobiotics. I thought it was the answer to my face, to everything. I was looking into people's eyes and diagnosing them with allergies and life-threatening illnesses. I was trying to get everyone I met to change their ways. I was all about Yin and Yang. Even a quick lunch with me could turn into a nightmare – I'd accuse people of being too Yin or far too fucking Yang. I tried to make everyone balance what they ate. I was trying to single-handedly balance the Universe. But I wasn't balanced – I was completely macro-psychotic. And every night I washed the make-up from my face and looked. And there I was. Looking back. A bright red nose between my eyes.

TAPE #13
(13TH APRIL 2012)

China

I'm hungry. Are you?

[Exits room. Returns with a bowl of assorted seeds and nuts]

Going to China was a huge act.

[Eats handful of seeds and nuts]

Help yourself to these.

[Pause]

We were trying to prove how big we were, OK. Although it was unclear what Napier-Bell had organised. 'It's political, Jazzbo.' That was Napier-Bell's mantra – everything was political. 'We're on thin ice here, Jazzbo. Agree to everything!'

Lindsay Anderson insisted on eight camera crews. He wanted simultaneous coverage. Every morning I'd go into the office and find kilometres of telexes from China with endless stipulations. We took along a hefty security guard called Dave Moulder, too. And a gifted Portuguese trumpeter called Raoul. We had to take everything with us, from the PAs to the plectrums.

We flew first to Hong Kong and the world's press came with us. The tabloids, *Smash Hits*, the broadsheets, the TV news, everyone was involved; great photographers from all over the world came to document the first pop band in China.

Hong Kong had changed a lot since I'd been there in the sixties. There were many more people, huge skyscrapers and a subway. I visited the harbour, where I'd lived and worked as an army radiographer. I looked up my old hospital clerk, Harry Kwan. He was retired now, Harry, and surprised to see me again. I took him and his family out to dinner. I didn't look up my old Chinese girlfriend. It would have hurt too much, seeing her. And Yazz was with me. It would have been too sad… All the people you leave behind in life. My lovely Chinese girlfriend.

[Pause]

Where is she? She could sing, did I say? [Sings] *Yellow bird, high up in banana tree…*

[Pause]

It felt like we'd arrived in China uninvited. We had to give away tapes with the tickets so that people who came to the gigs knew the music. The audience in Beijing was a mixture of kids, soldiers and police. The atmosphere was stilted and Napier-Bell was constantly anxious. Even when we went to the British ambassador's residence, the ambassador seemed surprised to see us, as if he hadn't been expecting us. He organised an impromptu garden party.

Napier-Bell informed George and Andrew that, at all banquets (which, for some reason, we paid for), they should stand and thank the 'Travel Department of the All China Youth Federation'. Most nights, we'd find ourselves sitting at a tense table with dozens of Chinese dignitaries. Napier-Bell kept reminding George of the importance of his speech. George didn't really understand quite what was going on. I didn't either. Even Napier-Bell was lost in a labyrinth of his own bollocks and bluster. Words would ping between George and Andrew and the Chinese dignitaries, all curdled slightly in translation. At the first banquet, George got up and thanked the 'Travel Department of the All China Youth Federation'. Everyone applauded and it all seemed to make some strange, strange sense.

BIG LIFE

Mao had only been dead about nine years. They'd put on entertainment for us. There was a singer at one banquet with a great voice, and he was followed by a girl, a magician, a really unusual person – she got George up the front and tied his thumbs together. I looked around to check that the cameras were capturing the moment. What did I see? I see Lindsay Anderson, smiling to himself, watching the show. And I see fucking Martin Lewis, the producer, sitting there in his silly white three-piece suit. All the camera crew were sitting round on the floor doing nothing. This was fucking East meeting West. I was thinking, What are these guys thinking? I crept from my table and collared an American. 'Pick up your fucking camera and take some pictures of fucking East meeting West.' And of course he was like, 'Who the fuck are you?' And by the time I'd told him, it was all over, and George was sitting back down and politely thanking the 'Travel Department of the All China Youth Federation'. Later on that evening, Lindsay Anderson fell over. He had to go everywhere on crutches or in a fucking wheelchair.

Simon and myself and Yazz and George and Andrew, we were due to stay in Beijing to do a live TV interview with CBS America. Everyone else was moving on to Guangzhou. That had been a nightmare to organise, because it meant there would be empty seats on a Chinese Airways flight. That hadn't happened before. In the morning, when everyone else was supposed to be leaving, Dave Moulder, the security guard, came to me in the hotel lobby, looking a little fraught.

'Jazz, we've got a bit of a problem with the trumpeter, Raoul. He went to see the terracotta army yesterday. Now he's locked himself in his room.'

'Well,' I said. 'You'll have to fucking break the door down.'

TAPE #13

TAPE #13

'He thinks he's possessed by the devil.'

'Even so, Dave. Break his door down. He *has* to get on that plane. These people are inflexible. Put him in a straight-jacket if you have to.'

Me and Yazz spent a lovely morning walking round Beijing. Then, in the afternoon, George and Andrew did the CBS Breakfast News interview. Martin Lewis must have been there, too, because I remember he took a phonecall as we were sitting in the green room. All I could hear was him saying, 'Wow…amazing…wow… *amazing*.' Then when the call ended, Martin hung up and turned to me: 'Hey Jazz, someone's stabbed themselves on the plane.'

'What?'

'One of your guys has stabbed themselves on the plane!'

'Who?'

'Your trumpeter. They've flown back to Beijing. They put him in the ambulance and he was hanging out the back playing the Last Post!'

'Fuck,' I said. 'Fuck…*fuck*.'

I went back to the hotel and found Dave Moulder. He was meant to be ex-SAS, Dave. He'd done security for Led Zep, or said he had. He looked seriously unnerved for such a strong guy. He looked like he'd seen a fucking ghost.

'Raoul was sitting next to Shirlie and Pepsi,' Dave told me. 'Then half an hour into the flight, he pulls a knife from his bag, says the devil's inside him, and starts stabbing himself in the stomach. Shirlie started screaming and the plane went into a dive. The oxygen masks came down. They thought it was a hijacking!'

'Where's Raoul now?'

'Room seventeen.'

'How is he?'

BIG LIFE

'He's fucking possessed, Jazz. It reminds me of the Led Zeppelin stuff. I'm scared.'

'Don't be such a wimp.'

'I'm not going back in that room, Jazz. Not for anything.'

We had a gig in Guangzhou the following day. I needed to get things moving somehow. I got a guy from the British embassy over to the hotel, which didn't help much because Raoul was Portuguese. But they got a doctor involved, an Australian. He gave Raoul more sedative and suggested we get him into care.

'When's the next flight to England?' said Napier-Bell.

'In four days.'

'He's sick,' I said. 'We need a mental hospital.'

'That's going to be difficult,' said the doctor. 'The Chinese have mental hospitals. But they don't really ad*mit* to having them.'

'I'm calling the Portuguese embassy,' said Simon. 'He's *their* trumpeter, technically.'

'I've tried that,' I said. 'It's closed. And he's *our* trumpeter.'

It was midnight. George and Andrew were tucked up in bed. We had to leave in the morning. Nothing could alter that plan.

'Let's leave him here,' said Napier-Bell.

'How can we?'

'Let's get the Travel Department of the All China Youth Federation to help. Let's say Raoul's dangerous. When he wakes up he could start stabbing people. That'll panic 'em.'

Around one in the morning, Mr Chang from the Travel Department of the All China Youth Federation turned up at our hotel. He looked anxious and sleepy, dressed in a neat grey suit. He'd made a mint out of our trip, that was obvious. He was corrupt. Corrupt people act the same in every country. They smile a lot.

TAPE #13

'If Raoul wakes up,' I told him, via our interpreter Ling Ling, 'I'm afraid he might start stabbing people. You've got to put him somewhere safe, OK.'

Mr Chang summoned a Chinese doctor. He finally arrived about four in the morning, looking a bit like a baker, I thought, wearing a long white coat and a little baker's hat. By this time, no one dared go into room seventeen. Not Napier-Bell, not Yazz, who'd gone to bed, not Moulder or Mr Chang. Fuck it, I thought, I'll go in. I was scared. Of course I fucking was. But someone had to go in that room.

I pushed open the door and entered pretty gingerly. The curtains were drawn. A weak bulb flickered in a bedside lamp. On the wall there were red marks and smudges. A trumpet lay on the floor beneath the window, crossed with a strip of moonlight. The Chinese doctor and I crept slowly towards the bed. Raoul was sedated. He was breathing heavily. With great care, I rolled him over and gently pulled his pants down. With slow, quivering hands, the Chinese doctor prepared another sedative and injected it into Raoul's bare buttock.

'Right,' I said. 'Well done.'

I took Raoul in my arms. With difficulty, and with no help from the Chinese doctor, I carried the trumpeter towards the door. Halfway across the room, he groaned and I immediately dropped him on the floor. Dave Moulder, who'd regained his composure, came in and took Raoul in his arms and carried him down to the hotel lobby and out into a waiting cab. He was a strong guy, Dave. We sat either side of Raoul on the backseat. We followed a Chinese army jeep into the darkness outside Beijing.

The first psychiatric hospital turned us away. The doctor went in, talked to them, came out and shook his head. We drove on through the night to another institution. This time Raoul was accepted. Dave Moulder and me carried him into the foyer and sat him down in a pretty bleak waiting area. His bandages had loosened and I could see the damage he'd done to himself on the plane. I felt awful.

The institution was a sad place. It took me back to my Nettley days, my attempts to get out the army, my life as a radiographer. There were brown walls, stone floors, iron beds, thin mattresses. It was very basic, though the doctor on duty, a middle-aged Chinese guy, spoke good English.

I went outside and told the taxi driver to wait. When I returned to the hospital, Raoul lay on one of their iron beds. He was coming round. He was pretty groggy, but not as deranged as I'd feared. He seemed not too bad, but the doctor felt he should stay in the institution. In the interests of Raoul's safety, I agreed.

'And you must stay, too,' said the doctor.

'No, no. I must go to Guangzhou for the pop concert.'

'No, no, no. You *have* to stay here.'

'What, for an hour?'

'For the duration of his stay. And also, how will you pay?'

'Well, that's not a problem. You tell us what it is and we'll pay it, but I'm not staying…'

It was approaching six in the morning. I was somewhere near Beijing. Dave Moulder was panicking again and rabbiting on about how there was no way on earth he was fucking staying.

'Look.' I tried to charm the doctor. I held his arm and smiled. 'We've left a message with the Portuguese embassy. They will come and stay with Raoul, OK.'

'No. *You* stay.'

'I'll tell you what,' I said. 'Dave here will stay and I'll –'

TAPE #13

'I'm not fucking staying here, Jazz, you're not fucking leaving me –'

'Dave.' I ushered him towards the doorway. '*I* need to go. I need to find Napier-Bell and Ling Ling. I need to speak to the Portuguese embassy, wake George and Andrew up, sort the money out. I'm the manager, Dave, and I will come back for you.'

'Please, Jazz, don't leave me here, I'll –'

'I will come back for you.'

'You can't just leave me…'

I walked from the sad, grey building and out into an East China dawn. I climbed into the back of the taxi, light-headed, anguished, but also focused. I hadn't slept for a day. We drove on narrow dusty roads through what felt like rural China. Dense, verdant forests stood on either side and suddenly, through the trees, I saw a grand red and yellow pagoda. I recognised it from our journey to the hospital. It crossed my mind that I was viewing the pagoda from the same side of the road as I had earlier. In front of me, the driver looked nervous.

'Hey, where are we? Where are you going?'

The driver responded with a string of pained words I didn't understand.

'Please,' I said. 'You're lost. You're going the wrong way. We're lost.'

Without warning, the driver turned sharply in the road and I slid across the back seat. We were travelling at some speed down a tiny dirt track. The whole vehicle was shaking. 'Please. *Stop.*' My voice stuttered as the car moved through potholes and over large stones in the road. The driver braked hard and I slid down into the footwell. There was silence. Then, out of the silence, I heard voices.

I peered out the window. There were thin fucking chickens fighting in the dust. Two starving mules pulled a trap piled

161

high with turnips and parsnips. There were hundreds of thin, muddy-faced Chinese, all dressed in rags, really – chemises, battered sandals and coolie hats. Seriously gaunt fucking men and women in worn out cotton Mao suits. They approached the car. They looked stern, these people. They started beating the window with fingers and turnips and they're making strange sounds I hadn't heard at any Beijing banquet. I was like some rare beast in its cage. They were looking at me like I was from another planet. I was scared. They were pressing their noses against the windows – fifty of them surrounding the car, screaming at me in a complete fucking frenzy. The driver, meanwhile, starts punching his head very hard in frustration. I spoke some words of Cantonese I could remember from my days in Hong Kong, but none seemed to make any sense. My heart was beating like mad. At length, he composed himself and revved the engine. He turned the taxi round, sending dust pluming in the fragile light and scrawny chickens squawking and people scrambling to get out of our way.

I orientated us by the grand pagoda and we headed back towards Beijing. There were few tall buildings there in those days. I spotted the basketball stadium, where we'd done the gig, and was able to guide us there. I knew the Great Wall Hotel wasn't far from the stadium, maybe a mile away; if I could get there then we could find our hotel.

Yazz was sleeping. I kissed her forehead then went to wake Napier-Bell. I didn't kiss him. I dragged his duvet off his bed and told him to get his arse in gear, to get onto the Portuguese embassy. I showered and went for breakfast with Yazz. It was grupa, that's all I ate in China, with warm apricots. I could have done with some Dexys or some coffee, but I'd given all that up.

TAPE #13

After breakfast, our translator Ling Ling and I drove back to the hospital to wait for the Portuguese ambassador. Ling Ling was completely lovely by the way. And a complete oddity. She wasn't Chinese. She was American. Her parents had moved to China after the revolution because they wanted to live under Communism. The two of us arrived back at the hospital around nine. Three hours in an asylum had turned Dave Moulder into someone who resembled the inmates. I found him hunched in a rickety chair beside Raoul's bed. Raoul was sleeping.

'You came back!'

'Of course I fucking did.'

The Portuguese ambassador was pleased to hear Wham!'s trumpeter was a fellow countryman, but also disappointed, understandably, to hear about the events on the plane and that Raoul would miss the Guangzhou gig. He spoke to Raoul in Portuguese and there was something sad about that.

We agreed that the ambassador would stay and I'd pay the necessary money to his embassy once I was back in Hong Kong. Ling Ling, who had been clearing matters with the Chinese doctors, came into Raoul's ward and asked for a word.

'Jazz. They're saying you have to stay.'

'*Still?*'

'This is serious. They're saying you *have* to stay. Not Dave, not the ambassador. You're in charge, so *you* stay. That's how they see it.'

'Right,' I said. 'You and Dave go and get in the cab. Once you're there, wait for five minutes, OK.'

Dave and Ling Ling left and I sat down beside Raoul in the rickety seat. The doctor took Raoul's temperature. The Portuguese ambassador stood by the window whistling 'Careless Whisper'. I

163

covered my mouth and nose with my hands and concentrated on a patch of sunlight that was moving slowly across the floor. I counted to sixty in my head. Then I ran.

Down two flights of stairs. I jumped a flight in one go. I sprinted through the grim reception and burst through double doors and out into a lovely oriental garden. The morning sun was shining so fucking beautifully. I could see the taxi waiting on the road. I hurdled two miniature fences and ran as fast as I could. Doctors in the distance were shouting words I'll never know. Ling Ling opened the back door as she saw me racing towards the car. I dived in the style that Superman might have dived, if he'd been manager of Wham! For a moment, I was airborne, then I crumpled up, back in the footwell of a Chinese taxi, shouting, 'Drive! Drive! Drive!'

The car didn't move.

'Fucking *drive*!'

The car didn't move. Ahead of us, standing in the road with his arm outstretched, showing us his palm, was the Chinese doctor. He walked slowly to the window and insisted that the driver open it, which he did, and they spoke, and Ling Ling translated.

'These are gweilos,' the doctor said, pointing at us. 'You can't drive them back. I forbid you.'

The taxi driver looked really nervous. He didn't know what to do. He switched the engine off. The doctor retreated from the car and I thought, 'Fuck this.'

'Everyone out,' I said. 'Moulder, Ling Ling, get out, we're walking. I'll hold a bunch of money up and we'll get a lift.'

The doctor followed us for a while, shouting, but he got the message in the end: we had a plane to Guangzhou to catch, a pop concert to get to. There was no reason for us to stay now that the Portuguese embassy were involved. After a few hundred yards I turned and saw him walking back towards the hospital, his white coat billowing behind him.

It was huge, worldwide, the news that Wham! had experienced a crisis on a flight in China. It overshadowed Napier-Bell's attempt to start a Chinese record industry, which was a plan he'd concocted at some point along the way. I think that was the main reason for us going, to be honest. Napier-Bell organised a press conference in Guangzhou where he planned to announce a grand union between East and West and the emergence of a Chinese entertainment industry. But events had overtaken him. Wham! were global news. China made us bigger than ever.

That night, in my Guangzhou hotel room, I did interviews with the *New York Times*, the *Straits Times Singapore*, *Republicca*, the *Guardian*, *Le Monde*, *Bild Zeitung*, the *Sydney Morning Herald*, every newspaper you can think of. The Chinese hotel staff were inexperienced; any journalist that rang asking to speak to me or Napier-Bell would be put straight through. It happened all night. It had gone round on Reuters that Wham!'s plane had been hi-jacked in China. That was the headline: *Wham! Hi-jack in China!* I was on the front page of *The Times* in England.

The concert in Guangzhou was very different to Beijing. It was a smaller venue, full of kids. Hardly any army, police or party members. And these kids had scarves they'd made and banners saying 'Wham!' They were proper fans. Guangzhou was just over the border from Hong Kong, so they could pick up the radio stations. They knew the songs and, most of all, they knew how to act. They acted like Western pop fans. They danced and screamed and sang along. At the end of the set, they were all going absolutely crazy; they knew how it worked – they were screaming for an encore. The band were doing a costume change and the kids were chanting. It was amazing, the level of emotion, the hysteria. And standing there, doing nothing, wearing his beautiful three-piece white suit, was Martin Lewis, and, beside him, leant on his crutches, his eyelids drooping, was Lindsay Anderson. All eight cameras were pointing away from the audience and were filming the empty stage.

'What the fuck are you two doing? This is *history*. This is the first pop band in China! That's an empty fucking stage. It could be anywhere. Film the fucking kids!'

Lindsay was a legend. But he didn't give a shit.

It was also obvious what Napier-Bell had done in order to make the China trip happen. He'd done a deal with the Travel Department of the All China Youth Federation. Essentially, he'd booked us all on a package holiday. That was the reason we all had to stick together and stay in the same hotel, and why it was so tough for us stay in Beijing while the others boarded that doomed flight to Guangzhou. He'd not gone through the Cultural Ministry or anything so complex, he'd done it through the Travel Department. Far from being a piece of sublime international diplomacy, he'd taken Wham! on holiday. Napier-Bell acted like an international politician, but really he was much better than that. He had persuaded Mr Chang of the travel department to put on the gig in Beijing and, because we were there, things started to happen, like we went to see the British ambassador, who knew nothing about our trip. It was an amazing achievement. To book a holiday. To make history. And no one told the *New York Times* it was a package tour. Simon was a genius.

I called in at the Portuguese embassy in Hong Kong to pay Raoul's medical bills. I was so tired. Yazz and me flew to Hawaii for

TAPE #13

a week. We had a great time, staying at the Kawala Hilton, right on the beach. After a couple of days relaxing, I went into a newsagent's and asked for a copy of *Newsweek*.

'I've been in China,' I told the assistant. 'I need to catch up.'

'Oh,' she said. 'Did you happen to see Wham?'

TAPE #14
(14TH APRIL 2012)

Conversation #4

Nothing in life comes without thought. I'm more thankful for having a spotty face and red nose than I am for anything else, OK. Because having that face forced me to change the way I thought about life. I've changed the way I see the world. People can be so narrow-minded. Don't be. And if you are, recognise that fact and work to change your thoughts.

[Phone rings]

Hello Tim, can I call you back, I'm doing the book…La Roux? Yeah, I will. OK.

[Hangs up. Long pause]

You live, OK. You have a chance. Money complicates things for people really. The decisions I make have got fuck all to do with money. I don't want people to make albums out of fear, OK. If you get the music right, then the money comes…

Make sure you write that down.

No Mismanagement

Napier-Bell was so bored because his 'diplomatic missions' to China had ended. He'd spent too long out there getting fat. He decided we should be selling NOMIS Management. Every now and then he'd invite me to his flat and I'd shake the hands of glistening, slightly odious men with big suits, cuban cigars, cocaine eyes and flats in Monaco.

TAPE #14

Meanwhile, I had dinner with Harvey Goldsmith and Ed Simons, his business partner. Harvey told me about his experience with selling his company, which'd been bought by a big entertainment conglomerate called Kunic Leisure. Kunic Leisure owned stuff like the London Dungeon and some leisure centre in Scarborough.

'We could buy you,' Harvey said. 'Kunic are backing us. They'll give us the money. We're getting new offices in Oxford Street. We'll give you some cash. You could start your own label, or make films if you like.'

I went back to Napier-Bell and told him to forget those cowboys from the City and to let Harvey Goldsmith buy NOMIS Management. In November, we had a meeting very early in the morning with the chairman of Kunic Leisure. I can't remember his name. Something Hudd, I think. We had a nice meeting and, in the course of the conversation, he told us that Kunic Leisure was financed by a guy called Sol Kerzner, who owned Sun Hotels and was currently trying to get his money out of South Africa by buying up UK businesses. It's a bit like Zomba, the guy told us. Simon and I both new that Zomba were doing well and were backed by South African money.

[Pause]

Fucking *money*. Everywhere I looked, there was someone arguing about it, dreaming of it, or losing it, making it, or promising me lots and lots of it.

Pepsi Cola

'Mr Summers, don't hang up. I can make you a lotta money.' This was the first thing Jay Coleman ever said to me. It was March 1985. He called my hotel room in New York one morning. 'I

169

put the Pepsi advertising deals together,' he continued. 'I did the Michael Jackson deal. I did the Lionel Richie deal. I could make you a quarter of a million dollars.'

'You forgot a zero there, Jay.'

'I'm sorry?'

He was every bit the second-hand car salesman, Jay Coleman. A week later, he walked through the hotel lobby like he was striding across a Dagenham forecourt, surrounded by shiny new hatchbacks. He wore an ill-fitting suit, a yellow shirt and a completely atrocious tie. He reeked of aftershave. I think it was Brut. He repeated his offer of a quarter of a million dollars for Wham! to record a Pepsi advert for Europe only. The age of the brands had really fucking dawned. This was big business. This wasn't like dancing around selling blank tapes in Tokyo.

'If we do a deal, Jay, it'll be for the whole world,' I said. 'It'll be two and half million dollars and it'll be the ad that plays at half-time in the Super Bowl, OK?'

A couple of weeks later, Jay phoned me in London to arrange a meeting between me and Pepsi. A courtship began, but I agreed to nothing. In the meantime, we did China, we did the stadium tour. I took the idea of the Pepsi advert to George and Andrew. George, as ever, wasn't convinced, but I argued that if it was the Super Bowl advert, which is always pretty funky and runs for a year after its premiere, it would take us deep into the heart of the American market.

I met the Pepsi people somewhere in up-state New York. I was a bit blasé. 'We need to be very clever,' I said. 'I don't wanna do this unless the ad is thoughtful and cool. I don't want George and Andrew dancing round cans of Coke in the middle of Times Square. I'm more interested in the quality of the advert than I am the money.'

TAPE #14

'You mean cans of Pepsi?'

'The point is it has to be *good*.'

It was an interesting approach to take. But I meant it. I invited the Pepsi people to our show in Chicago and arranged a meeting with George and Andrew. In November 1985, the Pepsi lawyer came to London to hammer out the deal: Three million dollars. That's what we negotiated. It was an awful lot of cash.

George was in Los Angeles. He'd grown to like that part of the world. We were gonna shoot the advert just before Christmas in order to be ready in time for the Super Bowl in February. It was going to be a huge, high-profile, global campaign. We concluded the deal and then, one evening, George called me:

'Jazz, are you sitting down?'

'I'm actually sitting here reading a book on Taoism, George. It's –'

'I don't wanna do the Pepsi deal, Jazz. It's gonna run for a year all over the world. And it's gonna make Wham bigger than ever, right?'

'Exactly!'

'But Jazz...I want Wham to end.'

What Have You Done?

On the sale of NOMIS Management to Kunic Leisure, Napier-Bell and me would both receive six hundred thousand pounds. If we hit our targets over the subsequent three years, we'd get two and half million pounds each, which, considering my background, was pretty unbelievable.

In Simon Napier-Bollock's book, he claims that George had asked him, and not me, to manage his solo career. It's not true. I knew, having spoken to George, that I'd be involved. I was excited.

171

BIG LIFE

Me and Yazz got married at Lady Diane's, the macrobiotic hotel in Jamaica. We took her mum and dad over, Diane and Winston. Winston came from Jamaica originally. He hadn't been back to the island since he'd emigrated to England in the fifties. We stood at the altar together; I was dressed in black and Yazz was dressed in white. We were monochrome – it was pretty cool. Yazz looked liked some divine vision. And I stood beside her.

In January, I attended the American Music Awards. It was the perfect time to tell George about the Kunic Leisure Deal. Clive Davis of Arista was there with Whitney Houston on his arm. I introduced Clive to George and he tried to persuade him to record a duet with Whitney. I couldn't take my eyes off her that night. Whitney was so stunningly beautiful. She took my breath away.

Later, backstage, George was pissed off 'cause he hadn't won Best Single for 'Careless Whisper'. I'd been assured by the organisers that we would win. I guess they lied. They put me in the shit with George somewhat.

'Jazz, I don't wanna do a song with Whitney Houston.'

'I realise that. But what about Aretha Franklin? She's on Arista.'

'*Yes.*'

I found Clive and politely declined the duet with Whitney and asked about Aretha. His eyes lit up.

Regarding the Kunic Leisure deal, George was reassured by the involvement of Harvey Goldsmith and happy that Napier-Bell and me were making a bit of money. He was prepared for the inevitable headlines in the tabloids: *WHAM! SOLD FOR COOL £5m* etc.

George stayed in LA after the American Music Awards. He attended some parties and enjoyed himself while I returned to London. A few days later, I got a call from Rob Kahane at around midnight. A call at that time always meant one of two things: either something very good had happened, or something completely shitty had.

'What have you done, Jazz? What have you done?'

'Er...nothing?'

'Have you seen the headline on the front of the *Hollywood Reporter*?'

'Of course I fucking haven't.'

'*Wham sold to Sun City*, Jazz. *That's* what you've done. George knows about it. He's in a terrible state. He's beside himself.'

'What?'

'Jazz, after *all* your work. You've *blown* it.'

'No, I can't have.'

'You *have*. WHAM SOLD TO SUN CITY. You've blown everything.'

I'd always been against artists playing in South Africa. George and I had spoken about it. There was a song in the chart at the time, Little Steven's 'We Ain't Gonna Play Sun City Any more'. Rod Stewart and Elton John were both under the kosh for playing there. It was a red-hot political potato, I knew that. I fucking hated apartheid.

Napier-Bell, for some reason, was in China, still trying to get capitalism up and running. I couldn't get through to him. I called George in his LA hotel, but he wouldn't take my call. At about 3am, Napier-Bell called from Beijing.

'Jazzbo, what the *fuck's* going on?'

'Is Harvey owned by Sun City or not?'

'I don't know.'

'I've a horrible feeling we're fucked here, Simon. A horrible fucking feeling we're completely fucking fucked. Get back here. This is awful.'

BIG LIFE

I went to see Harvey Goldsmith in his new office on Oxford Street. He was with Ed Simons. I took a seat on a Chesterfield sofa and sighed. Then I swore a great deal and I was on the verge of tears, to be truthful. Harvey sat behind his desk, nervously sifting through some papers.

'Wham sold to Sun City? What is all this? Let's get this straight, guys. Who own Sun Hotels? Who owns Kunic Leisure? Does Sol Kerzner own Sun City?'

'Yes,' said Ed Simons.

'No,' said Harvey.

'Come on, boys. *Which*?'

'It's true,' said Ed Simons. 'Sol Kerzner owns Sun City.'

'Well,' said Harvey, folding his arms and raising his eyebrows. 'I didn't know that.'

I put my head in my hands and I could have cried and fucking cried. I tried to call George, but again he refused to take my call. Over and over, I called, but it was no good. I was banging my face against a brick wall.

The very next evening we were due to receive a BPI Award together for our China trip. Only three managers have ever won one. Me, Napier-Bell and John Reed, Elton John's manager. The award ceremony was held at the Grosvenor Hotel and they were just becoming televised.

George flew in from LA just in time for the ceremony. It was the first time I'd seen him. We took our seats at a circular table. George wore a cowboy hat and was bare-chested beneath his jacket. I stared at his hairy pectorals – I was so fucking crestfallen. Andrew wore a long leather trench coat. Me and Simon were in tuxedos, mine black, his white. Monochrome, but not particularly cool. As the award ceremony began, no one spoke. Then, during a pause

174

in proceedings, while all the other tables hit the booze and drugs hard, Simon broached the subject of the Kunic Leisure deal.

'I don't wanna talk about it, Simon.' George said. 'Let's just get this over and done with.'

'George,' I said. 'We *have* to talk about this.'

'Lunch then,' he said, not looking at me or Simon. 'The day after tomorrow.'

Norman Tebbit presented us with our award that night. I watched the presentation recently on YouTube. I watched myself walk across the stage towards his grubby smile. At the time, I was thinking about how I was about to shake the hand of one of Thatcher's most odious henchmen. I seriously thought about not doing it. But I did. I shook his sweaty hand. In that moment, my life couldn't get any worse. Although, on YouTube, I appear to be smiling a little, my hair swept back, my red face coated in make-up.

I discovered later that Tebbit's wife was in hospital at the time, having been injured in the Brighton bomb. Given that, it was the right thing to do, to shake his hand.

Two days later, we met George Michael and Andrew Ridgeley for lunch at San Lorenzo – a swanky Italian. Harvey Goldsmith made a long speech about how much he detested apartheid, about how he had no idea about the connection between Kunic Leisure and Sun City. 'It's all a very unfortunate misunderstanding,' he said. George listened carefully, looking down at his splayed fingers, not nodding – in fact not moving at all.

When Harvey finished, George looked at me.

'Why did you do this, Jazz? You know I'm gonna go solo.'

'We haven't done this deal, George. I want to walk away. I made a mistake.'

BIG LIFE

Harvey went to make a phonecall. Napier-Bell went outside to get air. Andrew was busy eating. He was pretty blasé about the whole situation. He'd grown used to being in the eye of George's storm. He was good at it.

'I'm gonna have a career for another twenty-five years, Jazz,' George said. 'Why did you do this?'

'We haven't signed, George. I don't support apartheid.'

'I'm really sorry, Jazz. Truly, I am.'

A day later, our secretary informed me that George had been in touch with her to book limos. He'd taken one trip to see Tony Russell, the lawyer, and one to see Dick Leahey, the publisher. I knew what that meant.

Simon and I concocted a press release: 'George Michael has parted company with NOMIS Management and intends to pursue a solo career in the music industry. At this stage, Andrew Ridgeley will continue with NOMIS Management.'

The next day, there was no mention in the press of all that dreadful Sun City business. Every headline read: *Wham! Split!* Even George acknowledged that it had been a cunning bit of management.

Sol Kerzner, years later, became friendly with Nelson Mandela. But it was how the whole thing looked and got reported that did for me and Napier-Bell. We'd gone from managing the biggest band on earth, to nothing – to worse than nothing, to people thinking we were racist. Simon Napier-Bell and I got a settlement from Wham! It was somewhere in the region of eight-hundred thousand pounds, out of which we had to pay the lawyers who'd worked on the now defunct Kunic Leisure deal, which cost us about a hundred and fifty grand. I think we came out with about three hundred and fifty thousand pounds each, which was the most money I'd ever

TAPE #14

had. But money didn't mean that much. It was the music I missed. We'd had a laugh and a lot of success, but Simon and I had little in common apart from Wham! He went his way; I went mine.

PART FOUR

TAPE #15
(29TH APRIL 2012)

Conversation #5

Oh, hello. I liked your band the other night…yeah, I did…there were three talented members. The guy on flute was good. The guitarist. And the singer. But the bassist was bad I'm afraid and the drummer needs to be knocked on the head. And really the singer's only half a frontman…he was *hiding* behind that keyboard, I think. Convince him to put the keyboard at the side of the stage, so when he goes and sits at it he's fucking Elton John, or fucking, Mr Wispy, you know, Coldplay's singer…I don't like the way he dances…yeah, Mr Wispy…I think the band needs to be electro-psychedelic, but they'll need a much more cosmic rhythm section…and some better songs…yeah…I've got Nobu booked for Saturday…I know…hey, by the way, if you're dealing with BMG, cc Hartwig on everything – they shit themselves. Who? No, no way, I don't trust him – never trust a hippie. At some stage we need to talk about La Roux. Could you get Tony Beard to give me a call when he gets in? All right, mate. See you.

Right. Here we are again…here we are. How are you feeling? Tell me this: why don't you eat more fruit?

The Birth of Big Life

If you're managing a massive band, everyone wants to fucking know you. When you aren't, it's like you've got the plague. I had a sick fucking feeling. Without Wham!, I had a sense of real loss. I missed George and Andrew. I was concerned my lifestyle might go down the pan. On top of that, everyone thought I was racist.

While I'd been away with Wham!, old Tim Parry had been busy becoming a producer and a manager himself. He'd managed a band called the March Violets, who were similar to Danse Society. He'd also been booking the Claridon for me, a real scrudgy bar beneath the hotel of the same name.

About a month after George Michael sacked me, Tim Parry walked into my office on Gosfield Street looking thin, slightly bedraggled, with his shoulders hunched and altogether unconfident and miserable.

'How are you, Tim?'

'Well…'

'What?'

'Well, I'm OK, Jazz…I'm producing the odd thing, managing the March Violets and…'

'And what?'

'The other night, at two in the morning, the March Violets' bassist phoned me up and called me a cunt.'

'Why?'

'Don't know.'

'What did you say to him?'

'I was sleepy, Jazz. I didn't say much.'

'He called you a cunt?'

Tim nodded.

'Number one, Tim. If he calls you at two in the morning to call you a cunt, he's the cunt, not you. Number two, phone them up right now, tell them to fuck off and let's go and find some great bands who won't call you up at two in the morning and call you a cunt. What do you think?'

182

'Yeah, I'd like that.'

'I haven't got a lot of money. I'll give you a hundred and fifty quid a week.'

Tim was perking up already. I was pleased because I was fond of him and he was such a clever young man. Within a week we flew up to Scotland to meet a band. I can't remember who they were. Tim'll remember – he's the anorak. We had a meeting with this cool three-piece Scottish band and I was full of bravado about how I'd managed Wham!, managed Danse Society and managed Tim in Blue Zoo. They went with someone else, that band, sadly, but a week or so later Tim found a band called the Soup Dragons. They weren't the biggest band on the planet, but they were fresh and had great songs. We were up and running, I thought.

East/West, the macrobiotic restaurant on Old Street I told you about, well, quite honestly, I found it a bit dingy. It was full of brown-rice-eating hippies and lost souls. I'd talked to a few people about starting a slightly more upmarket macrobiotic restaurant. In trying to think of a name, I'd come up with the name Big Life. After all, what did macrobiotic mean? I wasn't sure, but having looked it up, I discovered, essentially, it meant 'macro' – 'big', 'biotic' – 'life', and so I had this idea to open a cool café called The Big Life Café. The café didn't work out in the end, but I loved the name so much, it was so positive, we started Big Life Management and Big Life Music.

Although we'd started the company and started managing the Soup Dragons, we were, in managerial terms, back to being complete fucking wankers. I missed being a genius; I missed it very much. What we needed was a hit. We needed one little hit to bring us to life. But hits are strange and capricious wild beasts and they're more likely to bite your hand off than let you pet them. And hits breed hits, of course, and so your first hit is always the hardest.

By summer 1987, I was running low on cash. Yazz and me went to Provence with my daughter, Katie, and it was a time of reflection. I felt responsible for Tim Parry. He was such a great guy, knew so much about music – he'd be an asset to any record label in London. I phoned him from Provence and said I was concerned for him.

'Don't feel you have to stay with me, Tim, OK?'

'Jazz, are you firing me?'

'I'm saying, don't feel bound to my fate. You're really good, Tim. I've always known that.'

A couple of weeks later, we were at a Soup Dragons gig in Hammersmith. Tim told me about two guys called Coldcut. He was full of praise for them, saying how talented and cool these guys were. They were different, he said. They were fresh. It was a new era. These Coldcut boys weren't boys with guitars. They were producers, remixers, samplers. We got them a remix for Eric B and Rakim, a song called 'Paid in Full'. They sampled an Israeli singer called Ofra Haza, who died recently, but she was a sensational singer and this mix Coldcut did *made* Eric B and Rakim; they took off. We're talking about the birth of fucking sampling here. They had James Brown on there! 'Paid in Full' was an unbelievably good piece of hip-hop, OK.

Coldcut made their own song called 'Beats & Pieces'. We got it out in the clubs and went to press with it and, just before Christmas, we sold fifteen thousand copies. When that happens, without any major label co-ordination or much promo at all, you know you're on to something.

TAPE #15

'I'm telling you, Jazz. 1988…' Matt from Coldcut was lying on a desk in the Big Life office. '1988 is gonna be about house music.'

'Is it?'

'Yeah. And we've got an idea for a song. It's called *Doctorin' The House*. What we need is a singer.'

'I know a singer,' I said. 'Her name's Yazz.' I gave Tim the look, so he wouldn't reveal to Coldcut I was talking about my wife. 'Yes. You know, guys, I think this Yazz could be just the singer you need.'

Me and Yazz were skint. We stayed in London for Christmas 1987. 1988 began – the year of house music. We went to Utopia Studio in Primrose Hill to record 'Doctorin' The House'. Coldcut made these songs on little tape machines. They were so cool. They took one look at Yazz and rejoiced – she was so beautiful.

And the song was fantastic. Check it out on YouTube: 'Doctorin' The House'. Matt and John had a show on Kiss, which was a pirate station in those days. I contacted some guys called BigTV and asked them to make a video. They said they needed eight thousand quid. I didn't have that kind of money. Tim and me, Big Life Music, had four grand left in the world.

'We'll give them four grand now, OK,' I said to Tim. 'And four grand when the money comes in.'

'Jazz,' Tim said. 'What if the money forgets to come in?'

'It won't.'

'It might.'

'If that situation arises we'll fly to Madras and fake our own deaths. Agreed?'

'Jazz. I'm serious.'

'Fuck it!' I grabbed Tim by the shoulders, which I don't often do. 'We're gonna have a hit, Tim! Do you hear me? We're gonna have a hit!'

BIG LIFE

Radio 1 refused to play 'Doctorin' The House'. That's always a good sign. We did everything we could to promote it on pirate stations. The video was so great. MTV hammered it. We worked the clubs and the press like maniacs. 'Doctorin' The House' by Coldcut featuring Yazz entered the charts at number six.

Island Records offered us a deal on Coldcut and Yazz. They faxed it over. The fax had their little palm tree logo on it. It was such an awful deal. I wrote 'bollocks' on it and faxed it back. We had a hit. We were geniuses. We were in the game.

We made two appearances on *Top of the Pops*. Yazz doing this amazing dancing, owning the whole fucking show, blowing the minds of all the little *Top of the Pops* nerds and then Coldcut, Matt and Jonathan, at the back of the stage pretending to scratch records. It was different; it was fucking brilliant.

Within months, we were receiving advances from independent record companies all around the world who were releasing 'Doctorin' The House'. Independent labels were lively in the late eighties. We got to number eleven in Germany. The record went global. We got a deal with Columbia in America. It was such a fresh record. That's the secret to A&R. Being able to spot when something's fresh. That's what the world yearns for – *freshness*. Fresh food. Fresh music. Fresh thinking, OK.

We got a new office on Regent Street. One of the first people to visit us there was an interesting young man called Youth. Youth was the bassist from Killing Joke. He wore a suit that day, I remember, which I see now was slightly out of character. He wanted Yazz to join a band he'd formed with Jimmy Cauty from the KLF. The band was called…what the fuck were they called? Brilliant! The band were called Brilliant.

'Number one, Youth,' I said. 'Yazz ain't gonna join Brilliant. Number two, why do you want to form another band?'

186

TAPE #15

'To get an advance,' Youth said. 'To live for a bit. Maybe have a hit?'

'Youth, you know something, you can keep doing that, keep blowing advances and then starting again. But really you need to think bigger. We *all* do. We are our thoughts, Youth. You should be a producer.'

I Grab Tim Round the Collar Again

My wife wanted a record deal. Tim thought we should do it all on Big Life Records, our own label. I agreed, but I was married to Yazz, and living with her, so it was sort of a tricky situation.

I went round all the record labels to talk about doing a deal for Yazz. We're talking about an artist who's had a hit and been on *Top of the Pops* twice. But we still couldn't get a deal. London Records offered us something; Pete Tong liked Yazz and Coldcut and we had a meeting with Roger Ames. Roger Ames – I should say something about Roger.

[Pause]

Roger Ames has enjoyed a long ride on the magical merry-go-round of record labels, leaping from job to job on a pink plastic horse, making millions, doing deals and developing an ever-harder nose. He's a hussler. A money-maker. A businessman. I really like Roger, but me and Tim Parry are a different species. We just rent little offices in London and look for artists we believe in. We've no corporate masterplan.

'The important thing for me, Roger,' I said, 'is money to make Yazz videos.'

'Why?'

It was 1988 and the head of London Records was querying my desire to make videos for an artist as beautiful as my wife Yazz.

BIG LIFE

Roger offered us such a shitty deal. I walked out of the meeting feeling completely dejected. Yazz's lawyer, Alexis Grower, thought it was pretty shitty, too.

Do you know something? Years earlier, it was Alexis Grower who encouraged the Late Show to sack me, after they heard I worked at North Middlesex Hospital as a radiographer. I daresay Alexis was trying to sue my mother for letting me float around in her womb. He dreams about suing me while cleaning his teeth. When Yazz sang on 'Doctorin' The House', I phoned Alexis and asked him to be her lawyer. I admitted I wasn't only Yazz's manager, her A&R man and her label boss, I was also her husband. I wanted Alexis to represent Yazz because I knew he wouldn't bend to my will.

'Why would we give Yazz away?' Tim kept saying. 'We've had a hit.'

Coldcut came to see me about a song called 'The Only Way Is Up'. It was a mid-tempo, soul-type song. We could all hear how good it would sound as an acid house record. I played it to Yazz that evening. She walked round our Belsize Park flat singing it all night.

We put Coldcut and Yazz in Livingston Studios in North London. A couple of days later they played the song to us. We couldn't believe it, Tim and me – it was so *awful*. Coldcut had made Yazz and 'The Only Way Is Up' sound like one of Pete Waterman's wet train-set dreams.

'No,' I said. 'This isn't right. What have you done?'

'We thought you wanted a pop record.'

'That's not how this works, boys. Do it your way, not Pete Waterman's, for Christ sake.'

I sent Youth into the studio to play bass on the track and, in fairness, once the lads realised that it was what *they* did that was cool, not what Stock Aitken Waterman did, the music became fresh; they nailed it.

Pete Tong phoned Tim and told him he still wanted to sign Yazz. Tim explained that we were doing it ourselves on Big Life Records. Capital Radio were playing 'The Only Way Is Up' six weeks ahead of the release. They loved it. It was buzzin up in the clubs and we were making the video.

Roger Ames called, of course.

'Summers,' he said, in his deep Trinadadian accent. 'It's a fuckin smash and I wannit.'

'But you offered me a shitty deal, Roger.'

'You didn't have this smash, Summers. I'll give you seventy thousand pounds and seventeen points retail. For one song, Summers.'

That was a superstar royalty and a lot of money. Tim was sitting opposite me as I spoke on the phone. As I repeated the terms of the deal to Roger, Tim turned pale. 'You know what, Roger,' I said. 'We're gonna have a hit with this ourselves. It's a thanks but no thanks, I'm afraid.'

Tim and me were silent for a while once I'd hung up.

'That's a lot of money to turn down, Jazz.'

'Fuck it.' I grabbed Tim round the collar again. 'It's a hit, Tim! I can *feel* it!'

My beautiful wife Yazz was number one for six weeks. Not on London Records or on Island Records, but on Big Life Records, our own little label. She and I celebrated on Sunday evening at our flat. We drank champagne. It was my first drink in five years.

'The Only Way Is Up' was a massive record. You've heard it, right? [Sings] *The only way is up!* It was big worldwide. We had a huge single, but no album. We didn't even have a follow up single!

BIG LIFE

Tim Parry brought his guitar round to our flat in Belsize Park and he wrote 'Stand Up For Your Love Rights' in the living room with Yazz, while I listened to Chet Baker quietly in the kitchen, eating salted plums and pumpkin seeds. It went to number two. We booked out Livingston studio and in three and half weeks we wrote and recorded the first Yazz album.

It was around this time when I started managing a band called Blue Zone, OK. Now, I didn't think they were the greatest act I'd ever managed, frankly. But they had something. They were from Rochdale near Manchester and had this singer, Lisa, whose voice was…well…totally beautiful.

TAPE #16
(30TH APRIL 2012)

The Pace of Popular Culture

Did I tell you I nearly managed P Diddy? We had a meeting by a swimming pool one afternoon in LA. He was quite a cool guy, really, P Diddy. He had an English butler who kept topping up my sparkling water. It was a stinking hot day and he's a taciturn bloke. I told him he was talented and needed to get in the studio and make some music. He looked at me for a bloody long time and I looked at him. He was wearing a pretty impressive tracksuit. 'Maybe you're right,' he said. I never heard from him again.

[Pause]

We had three acts in our first year at Big Life: Yazz, Coldcut and De La Soul. We sold well over a million albums and, as a result, the major labels came sniffing around, including old Maurice Oberstein – he of the high voice, remember. Maurice was a good guy. He'd let Wham! do the Maxell tapes ad in Japan, all those years ago.

It's a funny industry, music. All these people circling round, switching companies, signing acts, dropping acts, chasing new things. Roger Ames, who I told to stuff it with Yazz, went from London Records to run Polygram in the UK, then he went to Warner Brothers, then EMI, and now he's working at LiveNation. These guys are chameleons; I don't envy them.

William Goldman said, 'Film executives know nothing.' It's true of record executives, too; they know nothing! They're spirited into companies by fluke, nepotism, circumstance, sycophancy, foul play or, often, by tripping over a great artist on their way to sign an absolute stinker. All you people who love music out there, be empowered by this fact: the people in charge know nothing. *You* can be in charge. Especially today. An American with a big bouffant told me 'Careless Whisper' wasn't right for radio. A guy once told me 'Bittersweet Symphony' didn't have a chorus so couldn't be a single.

How are we doing for mint tea, because I didn't finish telling you about Wham!'s China film, did I?

[Long pause]

When we returned from China, Lindsay Anderson began his editing process. It was all very hush-hush, Lindsay this, Lindsay that, Lindsay's editing process is sacred and secret. This went on for ages. It was July before I was invited to an edit suite in Soho and all they gave me was endless cups of tea, not mint, just normal. It was nearly August when they agreed to show me the first cut. I sat there watching *Wham! in China*, sipping tea, thinking, 'Fucking hell, this is the slowest film I've ever seen in my life.' It was glacial. It was slug-in-slowmotion slow.

My hero, Lindsay Anderson, who I was falling out of love with as it was, didn't seem to get it. I put his cantankerous nature down to artistic temperament and the fact he'd fallen over in Beijing. 'Lindsay,' I said. 'This is great. There's just a couple of things. The music isn't quite right. The timing of it. Do we need a music video editor?'

'No.' Lindsay's voice really was exquisitely posh. 'To do so would spoil the pace of the movie.'

'Sure,' I said. 'But at the same time, this is the biggest pop band in the world. There needs to be a certain vivacity to the film, don't you reckon?'

TAPE #16

'We'll think about it,' he said.

How many more fucking cups of tea till it's finished? I didn't ask, but I wanted to. He promised me that in three weeks we could do a first showing. I walked round Soho, highly stressed, trying to figure out a way to improve it. It was *so slow*. There was one bit when Andrew Ridgeley was taken to the English Corner in the middle of Beijing, where a bunch of people got together to speak English. It was lovely, but it went on for ten minutes, and before we even got there we were treated to five minutes of a Chinese guy playing trumpet. It was tedious. A couple of weeks later I went down to the suite and Lindsay wasn't there.

'It's not very fast, is it?' I told one of his assistants.

'It's the way Lindsay wants it.'

'Sure,' I said. 'But it's quite slow, right?'

'Well, Lindsay's worried it's a little swift.'

'Is he?'

'Yes, he is.'

There was nothing I could do but arrange a screening. George and Andrew came down, Napier-Bell, Lindsay, I think Harvey Goldsmith was there. It was a summer's day in Soho and we all gathered round a screen in the dark. It was purgatory. It was snail's pace. George left the moment it ended. I could tell he was agitated throughout. But he was always lovely and polite, so he shook Lindsay's hand, thanked him and fled.

George called the following day. 'Jazz, it's George, that movie… that movie! It's *so slow*.'

'It's very slow, isn't it?'

'We can't let it out like that!'

I went to see Lindsay and told him again that it was a bit leisurely. 'I respect you, of course,' I said. 'But the boys don't think it suits

193

their audience. I think we need to get a new editor on board. The budget's going up and up, Lindsay.'

I'd pissed him off; that was clear. 'Quite honestly, Mr Summers, quite honestly, you don't understand cinema. I have, after all, made a great many films. Really, this is *my* movie.'

'But please, you have to respect what George is saying. He's paying for it.'

That was another mistake. Lindsay looked down his nose at me. Talking about money with a radical filmmaker is an error. '*Maybe.*' He was seething. '*Maybe* I can cut a little from the English Corner sequence. Give me another few weeks.'

I did. I gave him a few weeks and then we had another screening. Again, George left the moment it finished. Even Harvey Goldsmith, a real optimist, fell fast asleep. Napier-Bell and I took Lindsay Anderson to a Chinese restaurant in Soho. We sat upstairs and told him just how desperate the situation was.

'We need to speed this movie up, Lindsay. We're not joking around.'

'You're a typical producer, Summers. You'll just fuck it up. If I let you touch this film, you'll just fuck it up.'

'I take it,' I said, 'that you're not prepared to re-edit the film.'

'That is correct. Quite honestly, I'm *tired* of you.'

'I'm *tired* of you. I'm *tired* after watching your fucking film, sir.'

'You'll fuck it up, Summers. I know producers like you –'

'Lindsay Anderson! You're one of my heroes and I'm sorry to say this: you're fired.'

Napier-Bell's mouth fell open. He looked at me like I'd groped the Queen. He began to frantically apologise to Lindsay.

'No, Simon,' I interrupted. 'I've had enough. Who the fuck does this bloke think he is? He's wrong. It's slow. It's too slow. Too much fucking trumpet!'

TAPE #16

I stormed out of the restaurant and left Napier-Bell with the bill. I'd fired Lindsay Anderson because he was a cantankerous old git and I couldn't listen to him plodding on in his plummy voice about how shit I was and how his film's too fucking swift when it's the slowest fucking film I've ever seen in my life. I mean, I wanted a proper film – nothing too poptastic – but he'd delivered something that would've lulled an art-house audience to sleep. And he really did treat me like a red-faced retard. And I wasn't that. I was passionate about the film idea.

'I resign,' said Martin Lewis.

'Fine,' I said. 'Fuck you.'

I phoned my friend Strath Hamilton, who signed the Late Show to Decca in the seventies, but lately was in LA, working in Hollywood. He actually went on to be heavily involved in the *Mighty Morphin Power Rangers*. Strath and I had tried to get a film of The Long March off the ground once, an epic tale of the Red Army's retreat. He was impressed I'd sacked Lindsay, so I revealed I didn't really know what I was doing.

The Wham! movie, *Foreign Skies*, got finished fairly quickly with Strath's help, and also a good guy called Andy Morahan. I went to see it at the Gate in Notting Hill and, I have to say, I felt proud of what we'd done. We edited it pretty well in the end. It was funny and profound and George was quite amazed with how we'd turned things round. And it wasn't too poptastic, but nor was it slow. You should check it out.

People Hold On

Lisa Stansfield has an amazing voice, OK. She was in Blue Zone with Ian Devaney and Andy Morris. They'd made an album which, frankly, I

195

didn't believe in. Tim and Yazz convinced me to work on it. 'You can't let them down,' Yazz said. So, for the only time in my life, I went through the motions with an album. I worked without passion. I hated it.

I remember Jonathan from Coldcut telling me he loved the b-side to the new Blue Zone song and planned to play it on Kiss, the pirate station. I was surprised by that. I didn't think they were fresh enough for him. And then one day I went home and found Yazz dancing round our living room to Blue Zone. Again, I was kind of surprised. She said she couldn't stop playing it.

'Which song?'

'This one! The b-side.'

She played me a song called 'Love is a Big Thing'. It was Lisa Stansfield singing soul, but the beats were funky and current. Tony Blackburn made the song his Record of the Week on Radio London. He also said, 'Any record company that makes this a b-side needs their head examining.' I invited Lisa, Ian and Andy to the flat. At last, I could be honest with them.

'Lisa Stansfield, the soul singer, with beats!' I said. 'That's your future! What do you think?'

Ian Devaney pulled a scruffy looking cassette from his bag. He tossed it across the table and said, in his thick, Rochdale accent, 'There's plenty more where that came from.'

The song on the cassette was called 'All Around The World'. I played it three times and, finally, I understood the power and potential these musicians had.

'You've written a global number one,' I said.

'Right,' said Ian Devaney. 'Well that's good, isn't it?'

Christmas 1988, Yazz and me were in Paris. She invited her limo driver to dinner at the Bandouche. Yazz was on Mercury in France and they joined us, too, her plugger, markerting guy and a few others. Jack Nicholson, the actor, he was at the Bandouche that night. In true Hollywood style, he told Yazz, 'It's great to meet you, I *love* your record!' Nicholson really swooned over her that night.

Yazz was more interested in talking to her limo driver, this French guy. They'd lit a candle, Yazz and him, at the Sacré-Coeur the previous day, and they were reflecting on the spiritual atmosphere there. I felt distant. She'd been doing promotion in Paris for three days without me.

Two days later, on a plane to Tokyo, she insisted on sitting next to her PA, instead of me. I could hear them giggling to each other from where I was sitting. She booked herself a separate room in Japan. She said she couldn't stand the fact that I was always talking business in the bedroom.

Shortly after we checked in, I saw a bunch of red roses being delivered to her room. I bribed a Japanese bellboy and he told me the flowers were from Paris. When I confronted Yazz, she told me they were from her French promoter. I knew how unlikely that was. She'd never even played in Paris. I knew that wasn't true.

I left her in Tokyo and flew to New York to see my friend Sabato.

I knew the feeling; I'd felt the same when she left me for the German model. I phoned her once I'd landed in America. She told me she'd been in an earthquake. She was fine, but I was beside myself. That night, I showed Sabato the video for Yazz's single, 'Stand Up For Your Love Rights'.

'She looks *sensational*,' he said.

When it was finished, he turned to me.

'Jazz, are you crying?'

'I love her so much.'

'And she loves you, Jazz. You *know* she does.'

BIG LIFE

Sabato recommended a book called *Living in the Light* by a woman called Shakti Gawain.

'Read it,' he said. 'Promise me you will, Jazz.'

A fire ripped through Sabato's apartment block that night. We were evacuated onto Varrick Street and I remember I bumped into Mica Paris among the evacuees. I called Yazz in the morning to tell her. I told her I'd see her in London on Friday.

'No, Jazz,' she said. 'I'm going to Paris with the girls. I need to get away from all the earthquakes and fires.'

I couldn't face the flat in Belsize Park, knowing that Yazz was in Paris. I flew to Jamaica and booked into the macrobiotic hotel, Lady Diane's. In some ways, it was the worst thing I could do. Everyone there was asking about Yazz and asking why I was alone. I sat and stared at the porch where Yazz and I had delivered our vows. It wasn't too busy in March, the hotel, but there was a couple of women having lunch at an adjacent table. They must have seen how fucking blue I looked because they invited me to join them. They were Jamaicans.

'Is there a spiritual bookshop on the island?' I asked.

'In Jamaica? You must be joking! What book do you want?'

'It's called *Living in the Light*.'

'OK, there isn't one bookshop in Jamaica that'll sell you that book, but I tell you what, what are you doing today?'

'Nothing.'

'I think I know where I can find you a copy.'

The woman smiled and placed her hand on mine. I don't remember her name. But there's a proverb, isn't there, it's something like: *When the student is ready, the teacher appears.* After lunch, the woman went home and returned with *Living in the Light* and also another book.

198

TAPE #16

'I think this one might help you, too.'

She gave me a book called *You Can Heal Your Life* by Louise Hay. I didn't read it straight away. I read *Living in the Light*. I stayed up all night reading it and it took my mind away from Yazz and the visions of her in Paris. It helped me to re-frame my view of the Universe. The following day, I read the beginning of *You Can Heal Your Life*. It seemed a bit Californian kooky to me. It was full of affirmations and ideas about self-love and I wasn't so sure. I read a bit, but lost faith.

I stayed at Lady Diane's for five days. I got up. I applied my make-up. I read. I moped around. I exercised on the beach at dawn each day. I performed an exercise to try and rid myself of all my rage. I stood on the shore and waved my arms quite frantically for an hour and then, to finish, I screamed at the top of my voice at the Caribbean horizon. Jamaican fishermen watched from their little boats. It took away my anger a little, but nothing could get rid of the fear and the hurt.

I phoned Yazz in London when I knew she'd be back. I dialled our private number, the one that the record companies and paparazzi didn't have. She'd recorded a new message on the machine: *Oh, Boo… Oh, Boo, I'm just popping out. I'll call you later.*

I redialled and listened to that message three times. Then I walked to the sea shore in tears.

On the plane back to England I bumped into Chris Blackwell. Chris was the founder of Island Records and a real legend in our business. We had a nice chat about Big Life's great success and how I'd written 'bollocks' when Island faxed me a record contract for Yazz. But, the truth is, flying above the earth that day was the lowest moment of my life. I opened up the Louise Hay book again.

199

BIG LIFE

It's hard to explain, but I read it in a different way. I was desperate. One of the first affirmations she suggests in the book is simply to tell yourself that you like yourself. I repeated that affirmation – 'I like myself' – for the entire flight, sitting there, looking at the seat in front of me, saying it over and over again in my head. After two hours, I fell asleep and woke up in London.

Yazz's brother, Pete, drove me home from Heathrow. I found Yazz in the living room. She was having extensions put in her hair. My macrobiotic cook, Vivien Lee, was preparing seaweed and nori balls. In spite of everything, I was happy to see Yazz. She stood and hugged me very loosely. I must have looked terrible because Vivien took me into the sitting room and spoke to me.

'Everything that you see, Jazz, is sometimes not real.'

I didn't know what Vivien meant. Maybe she meant that what's going through your mind can radically affect reality. I didn't confront Yazz about the phone message I'd heard. I tried to be positive and loving. When the hairdresser left, I sat down with her.

'What's going on?'

'I want to get my own flat, Jazz.'

Big Life had just paid her a royalty cheque for well over a million quid. I knew she could afford to buy a flat. She'd had the second biggest-selling single of 1988. Cliff Richard beat us and that's not the end of the world.

'Are you in love with someone else, Yazz?'

She said nothing.

'Who's Boo? Is he the limo driver?'

She looked away.

It was my birthday. We ate at the Caprice and afterwards we went to Café des Artistes to dance. I danced with her. I ran my fingers through her long blonde extensions. I held on to them. We danced to 'Eternal Flame'.

It must have been tough and quite suffocating for Yazz, being married to her manager. We'd go to bed talking about a remix and wake up and discuss video ideas. She found a flat around the corner in England's Lane. She took me to see it and I warned her about buying a place above a Chinese restaurant. The smell seeps in, see. But she bought it.

Within the week a paparazzi was camped outside my house with a lens on his camera as big as a howitzer. Every morning I drew the curtains and saw him there, watching me, smoking a cigarette, talking on a massive grey mobile phone.

Yazz was the biggest popstar of 1988. The fact her husband was called Jazz, well, the tabloids loved that and found it funny, and I suppose it is, in a way – Jazz and Yazz.

She was half living with me and half living in England's Lane. We were preparing for her first ever tour. She was on the phone to Boo morning, noon and night. The phone would ring and I would answer it and hear him breathing. It hurt. I felt like exploding, but I was in love. The tour had sold out and 'Fine Time', her new single, was in the top ten. In the video, she tossed a house key into the air. In real life, she bought an extension for the phone in our flat, so it went into the bedroom she occasionally slept in.

'You need to be careful, Yazz,' I told her. 'We're about to go on tour. On tour, you're vulnerable. We're married. You're going on children's television. I need to manage this situation, as your manager, not your husband. Be discreet. For your career and our business.'

I held it together for three reasons. One, I loved her. Two, I didn't want to fuck her career up. And three, I didn't want mine and Tim's work to all be for nothing. I told Yazz's press officer about the affair. She'd known Yazz and me for years and she had to be ready in case the story blew up in the tabloids.

They did extensive dance rehearsals for the tour up in North London. Yazz was such an amazing dancer. I drove up to the rehearsal studio on the eve of the tour and, while I was there, I got a call from the press officer.

'Jazz, there's a reporter on the prowl. He knows everything. Someone's sold the story. I'm sorry.'

'Fuck...*fuck*. Tell him to call me, OK. Give him this number.'

I didn't go back into the rehearsal studio. I waited by the phone for the journalist's call. He was from the *Sunday People*. The phone started ringing and I took a deep breath.

'Hello, Jazz, how are you feeling today, eh?'

'Absolutely great, thanks.'

'Well, well.' He had this artificial, sneery voice. 'That's not what I hear, Jazz. I hear you blew up today. I hear you're splitting up with Yazz.'

'Really?'

'I hear she's shagging a Frenchman and she's moved out.'

'That isn't true, I'm afraid. We *have* bought a flat round the corner from ours. She needs space to write and escape. That's all. She hasn't moved out.'

'Well, what about this affair?'

'Nonsense,' I said. 'I'm with her now. We're rehearsing. Five minutes ago she was sitting on my knee, very happy.'

'You're lying to me, Jazzy. Come on. Open up. She's shagging some frog. She doesn't deserve loyalty.'

'I tell you what, mate. There's a lot of shit flying around about everyone. But you should be careful what you believe. You wanna check your source. Because you are so *far* from the truth, OK. Yazz was sitting on my lap five minutes ago. We're planning a family. Everything you've just said is the biggest bunch of bullshit, so if you wanna print it, fine, print it. I'll sue your paper and earn a fucking fortune. I love clothes and so does Yazz. We'll buy a whole new wardrobe with your money.'

I put down the phone. I closed my eyes and rested my forehead against the wall, taking some deep breaths, trying to slow my heart – it was thrashing round like a caught fish.

[Long pause]

I knew who had leaked the rumour. It was a girl who was working on the tour. I pulled Yazz out of rehearsal and told her what had happened. 'Number one,' I said. 'Number one…we can't have that girl on the tour. Number two, I'm going to come on the tour with you, OK. We need to protect your image.'

'You're not staying in my room.'

'I understand that. We're going to have adjoining rooms.'

'I don't want that.'

'Because you want Boo with you. I realise that. I am jealous and I am hurt. But I'm trying to protect you. If he comes on tour with you, it will *kill* your career. The papers will bribe the chambermaids, Yazz. That's what they do. He can't come anywhere near you. If you have to, get him a hotel room in London and visit him there. But that's a risk. We're doing a press call in Sheffield next week and you're going to sit beside me and we're going to be planning our future together.'

Day after day, while we were on tour, I sat in my adjoining room, listening to Yazz speaking on the telephone next door. Really, it turned me inside out, that experience. We went to Dublin, I remember, and my heart was breaking. The Edge from U2 sent her flowers. I sat on my bed and listened as she spoke to Boo on the phone. There were rumours around the band that Yazz was having an affair. That was inevitable. When I got on the tour bus to travel to Belfast I could hardly breathe because of the shame. I was twisted inside. I sat on the tour bus, just behind Yazz. I returned to my affirmations, as I had on the plane flying home from Jamaica. When you're in love with someone as deeply as I was, and when you know they're in love with someone else, and when you're having to sit on a tour bus with that person, and your face is so red…

[Pause]

It was hard.

The stress and the emotions I was dealing with had harmed my face. My nose was terribly red and I hadn't applied any make-up. I sat still on the bus and repeated the affirmations from the Louise Hay book. I told myself that I loved myself. I did that non-stop from Dublin to Belfast. I looked out of the window at the passing towns and fields, or at the back of Yazz's head, because she was in front of me, and I said to myself, 'I love myself, I love myself, I love myself.'

This will sound strange, I think, but it's true: I bounced off that bus in Belfast feeling energetic and happy. I was like a different person. I was lively. I bantered with our staff and even enjoyed the gig. I was full of energy and a desire to work. Those simple affirmations have such a profound impact.

In the days that followed, I sat down in front of hotel mirrors, as Yazz spoke on the phone in the next room, and I would say, 'I love myself, I love myself, I love myself.' I would say, 'Jazz Summers, you are a divine expression of life and I love and accept you as you are right now.' I said that over and over again.

I bought an old Art Deco mirror for the flat in Belsize Park. For weeks, months, I sat in front of it and repeated those affirmations.

TAPE #16

I used to sit there for hours. If I hated my face, the Universe made my face worse, so I taught myself to love my face in that lovely old mirror.

'I am willing to release the pattern within me,' I repeated, 'that is creating the need for Anger.'

'I am willing to release the pattern within me,' I repeated, 'that is creating the need for alcohol.'

For so long I'd had this grotesque face. I wanted to drag the skin from my skull in rage. But that day, as I bounced off the bus in Belfast and started telling jokes, I was changing my mind. ('I love the skin on my nose and face, I love the skin on my nose and face, I love the skin on my nose and face.') We did the press call in Sheffield and Yazz hinted that we were planning a family. After that, the tour continued and I returned to London. I knelt down in front of the mirror in my bedroom and said, aloud, 'I love and accept you as you are right now.' I said, over and over again, 'I love the skin on my nose and face. I love the skin on my nose and face. I love the skin on my nose and face. I love the skin on my nose and face.'

Me and Yazz separated that April. I lived alone in Belsize Park, working hard on my affirmations – 'I forgive you, Yazz, for hurting me (twice). I forgive you. I set you free.' In May, old Maurice Oberstein at Polygram bought fifty per cent of Big Life. Tim and I got a big cheque. We felt invincible. We felt anything we put out would be a hit. As part of the deal, Yazz got half a million pounds and a great new record deal. I had more money than I'd ever had; I bought a Saab convertible.

I was extremely lonely. I think I thought Yazz's relationship with Boo was an infatuation and that she'd come back to me. But that wasn't going to happen. I'd attended her birthday party in Soho.

BIG LIFE

That was depressing. Although she'd ended things with Boo, she told me, she was with someone else. I ended up just wandering the streets that night.

I was a sponge for new ideas. Anything I thought might help me with the pain. I turned to another Shakti Gawain book. This one was called *Creative Visualisation*. In it, there was a technique called the Pink Bubble Technique. It sounds pretty wacko maybe, but what you do is you visualise the object of your desire in a pink bubble. Then you let it go. You let it float away. The book was so convincing that I tried the technique. In May 1989, I visualised Yazz pregnant with my child. I let that image of her float away in a pink bubble. It sounds peculiar. So why did I do it? Well, I loved her. That's it. I *adored* her...

Stop recording.

TAPE #17
(1ST MAY 2012)

Rio

Sabato visited London. Last time I'd seen old Sabato I'd been really cut up over Yazz. He asked me how I felt about her. 'You know what, Sabato.' We were walking on Primrose Hill on a beautiful summer morning, beneath a wide blue sky. 'I've let go of Yazz today,' I said. And it was true. The affirmations allowed me to set her free. And that's what you're supposed to do to people you love, if you can, you set them free. It's what I want to do with the music I love, OK – set it free.

That evening I got a phonecall.

'Jazz?'

'Yazz?'

She was in Portugal, staying with friends and family in a rented villa. I didn't feel a twist of pain when I heard her voice. I felt OK.

'How are you?'

'I'm not too bad, Yazz. How are you?'

'I want to get married, Jazz.'

This was inevitable. I knew one day we'd have to get a divorce and so even this news felt bearable.

'Who are you marrying?'

I half expected her to say the gardener at the villa she was staying at.

'*You*, Jazz. I want to marry *you*.'

'You already did me, Yazz.'

BIG LIFE

'I want to marry you again. Because I love you. And I want to have your baby.'

'You're not serious -'

'I'm coming to London. I've got to see you.'

The first thing that rushed into my head was the pink bubble. I'd put her in a pink bubble. Had it actually *worked*?

I took the day off and waited for her in the flat. I was so nervous. I didn't want to sink down into that pit of fucking despair again. I took extreme care over my make-up. I remember walking down the hall to answer the front door. How apprehensive I felt, and how hard my heart beat. And there she was, standing on the doorstep in the bright sunlight. She looked amazing. Her hair was short again and bleached blonde. She wore a black cowboy hat, a short floral dress and a denim jacket draped over her shoulders.

She was only in London for one day for a dentist appointment. The following day, I went to France with Tim Parry and my friends and, while I was there, I phoned Yazz and told her I was still in love with her. She repeated that she loved me. I arranged to go and join her in Portugal.

Me and my daughter Katie, who was five, flew out to Lisbon the following week. The change in Yazz was strange. It was miraculous. We kissed by the pool and it was everything I could have hoped for. We made love that night, and although it wasn't perfect, we spoke about how it would take time. A day later, we made love on the beach. Each day, Yazz's macrobiotic cook dangled a pendulum above Yazz's pubis. It was an old wife's tale: which way the pendulum turned determined whether you were pregnant or not. They were doing that every other day. After Portugal, we went to Ireland for the weekend. We made love and, on our return to London, she went to the doctor. And yes, she was pregnant.

TAPE #17

Yazz and I had made a film in Portugal, a documentary about her that included some concert footage. We were busy releasing that and I was working hard at the label on De La Soul and Coldcut. One of the main conditions of us getting back together was the separation of business and pleasure. I shouldn't accompany her on her promotional trips. That was the right way to do it. I wished we'd thought of that sooner. We didn't make love again after we found out she was pregnant. In actual fact, we stopped a lot of our intimacy. One morning, I went to kiss her and she turned her face away.

'What is it?'

'Nothing.'

'Yazz, what *is* it?'

She wouldn't say. She left the room. The next four months were the strangest of my life. On one hand, I was ecstatic to see my second child grow in the body of the woman I adored. On the other hand, Yazz was pulling away from me yet again. Though we lived together, the distance between us was unimaginable. To live with someone under those conditions was the hardest thing. There was no friendship. We'd created a human being, but there was a desert between us.

I wondered whether I'd performed the pink bubble technique wrong. I'd imagined Yazz pregnant, sure, but I hadn't imagined myself with her in the bubble. Maybe that was a mistake on my part. My head was all over the place. I agonised over these thoughts.

When Lisa Stansfield released 'All Around The World', we didn't have a clue about its chart position during the week. You had to listen to Radio One on Sunday evening with everyone else. The previous year, when Yazz was number one with 'The Only Way Is Up', Lisa Stansfield used to phone Yazz and me every Sunday,

209

just after seven, to say well done. The weekend after 'All Around The World' was released, Yazz went away with friends to stay in a country house. I sat by myself and listened to the charts. 'All Around The World' entered at number one. I turned the radio off and stared into space. A minute later, Lisa called and she was jubilant. Tim Parry called, jubilant also, but Yazz didn't call. It was a moment of success, I suppose – 'All Around The World' was on its way to becoming a global sensation. But I was upset. When Yazz returned the following day, she didn't greet me. I went to hug her and she turned away. She went up into the spare room. She was four months pregnant.

[Pause]

I could have punched my way through stone walls. The following evening, we attended the premiere of the film we'd made. It was embarrassing for Tim Parry, I think, the way Yazz ignored me, didn't want to be anywhere near me. You know how socially awkward that is, right, when a couple is publicly so fractured. Yazz was tactile with the film's director, I remember, and I suppose there's nothing wrong with that. At midnight, she wrapped herself in the duvet and didn't speak to me. I lay down beside her, but barely slept.

In the morning, I followed her into our downstairs bathroom. She stooped to wash her face and I saw my reflection in the mirror. I hadn't put my make-up on yet. My eyes stared out from a jail of damaged skin.

'I'm *angry*, Yazz. I'm so angry I could punch you...I don't want to do that. You want to go, Yazz. Go!'

It was November 1989. And that was the end. I was in love with her and already in love with the child she was carrying. But I couldn't take any more pain. I was back behind the starving line.

TAPE #17

To alter the pain inside me, I sat in front of my bedroom mirror and spoke.

'I'm living in a beautiful and well-balanced flat,' I repeated. 'Everything is bright and perfect in my life.'

'I love myself,' I repeated. 'I am lovable and everyone loves me. I bring joy back to the centre of my heart. I give love to all.'

'I am willing to forgive Yazz for hurting me (three times). I forgive you darling. I set you free.'

'The skin on my nose and face is now completely clear of all red marks, spots and blemishes. The skin on my nose and face is now completely clear of all red marks, spots and blemishes.'

My relationship with Yazz had driven me to despair. I wouldn't have made it back without the help of Louise Hay's book.

Yazz, these days, lives in Spain. We keep in touch because we both love our daughter, Rio. On reflection, I know a woman can change dramatically when she's carrying a baby. Maybe Yazz couldn't help the way she was. Maybe I wasn't strong enough. Whatever it was, it's over now. And because of the love and because of the pain, Yasmin Evans was my greatest teacher.

It was difficult visiting my daughter Rio, being in Yazz's house with her new lover. I'd sit beside Rio, who was one or two years old, and I could see she was thinking, who's this? I used to walk around the park with her, telling her about life and music. But those visits were worth it, because these days we see each other all the time, Rio and me.

Dream

I went to Boozios in Brazil for Christmas. I went with Sabato and Mark Dean – Deano, who I hadn't seen since the Wham! days,

211

since CBS shat on him from the top of Soho Square. Deano didn't know whether he was coming or going, I don't think. He'd got into rebirthing and macrobiotics. We were all in a bit of a state. Hence Boozios. It's the St Tropez of South America. I took my macrobiotic cook, Vivien Lee, and Sabato got two girls to come along, Isabella and Marine.

After Yazz, the last thing I wanted was a relationship. A couple of loving bunk-ups in Boozios would have been nice, but I didn't want anything serious. I wanted to be single. But Marine was very attractive. Although she had alopecia at the time, I remember. She was about to get married and she and her fiancé were doing a lot of coke. That's why her hair was falling out. I advised her to alter her diet, knock the marching powder on the head and we ended up in bed together.

Marine and me were together four years. Those years, my late forties, were wired and fucking all over the place. I started to drink wine again. Looking back, although we managed Soul II Soul and Lisa Stansfield, we really concentrated on getting Big Life songs in the chart. We lurched from hit to hit, from debt to debt, from studio to studio, from bailout to bailout. It seemed like every month I'd be asking Polygram for more money. The pressure was enormous, but we had hits. We always had hits.

I started drinking wine each night with my dinner. The pressure was getting to me. Me and Marine drove round France together and I thought I could control it. Only drink with dinner, I thought. Only drink fine wine. Only drink at weekends. Soon, I was drinking four bottles of wine a night, every single night. That put paid to my French girlfriend, really, the drinking, plus all our affairs.

On my fiftieth birthday, in 1994, I was so drunk. I was with a lady called Ineka by then, who I'd just moved in with. She had to carry me up the stairs and put me into bed. I'd thrown a massive party at the Groucho Club in Soho. I looked at the pictures the following week and, despite the make-up, my nose looked awful, my face was horrendous.

In 1997, after ten years of hits, Big Life Records went bust. I remember I got a phonecall from the editor of *Music Week*.

'Fucking great,' I said. 'You wanna write about us now we're fucking bust!'

'Jazz, do you know how many hits you've had?'

'*No I do not.*'

'Fifty Top 40 songs in ten years!'

I was surprised to hear that. But it was true. We'd run one hell of a little record label. We had 'The Only Way Is Up', of course, but there were others. We did 'Naked In The Rain' by Blue Pearl, 'I'm Free' by the Soup Dragons, we signed the Orb. We had a number one album with *UFOrb*. Naughty By Nature, Damage, De La Soul. In 1993, we released 'Iron Sky' by Mega City Four – that's the first fucking Britpop single. Listen to it! In 1994, we released 'Come Baby Come' by K7. Remember that? [Sings] *Come, baby, come, baby baby come…* But I wasn't tired. I'm still not tired. I was in my mid fifties in the late nineties. But take away the nine army years and I was still in my prime.

[Pause]

I'm still in my prime.

[Pause]

Let's go out for a meal this evening. Let's eat some beautiful food.

Towards the end of 1996, we got a call from Peter Kooner. He was reviving D:Ream and needed a manager. I'd known Peter since way before he started D:Ream. He was a great songwriter and he really stuck at it.

The Labour Party approached us to ask if they could use 'Things Can Only Get Better' for their 1997 election campaign. I spoke to Peter and he liked Labour, so we went for it. We agreed to go along and play the song at the party conference in 1996, where Tony Blair made his famous 'Education, Education, Education' speech, remember? We went along and met Blair and the Labour Party started using the song. We were very co-operative. Peter would regularly perform at Labour Party meetings.

As 1997 began, New Labour's campaign really gathered momentum. The Sunday before the election, Peter was asked to go and sing 'Things Can Only Get Better' in St Albans. Blair and Blunkett were speaking and Peter was performing at the end of the night. I accompanied him as his manager and afterwards I met Blair backstage with Blunkett and Michael Levy (who'd signed Blue Zoo). I looked at Blair and said, 'You're gonna be prime minister on Friday morning.'

'Really,' Blair said. 'How d'you know that?'

'It's in the air, Tony. Michael knows. It's in the air. You're gonna walk it.'

Blair looked at me. It was like he was thinking, who's this pundit?

'Tell him, Michael,' I said. 'You *know* when you release a record whether it'll be a hit or not. It's in the air. You just *know*. I'm working on a song called *Bittersweet Symphony* at the moment. We're having some real fucking problems, but it's gonna be a hit. I can *feel* it. And you're gonna be prime minister.'

The following Friday, I attended the party at the Royal Festival Hall. Peter performed 'Things Can Only Get Better' in the foyer and it was an amazing night. Alan McGee was there. Tony Russell

TAPE #17

was there, the ball-breaker lawyer, because he likes Labour. And then, funnily enough, Richard Branson shows up.

'Hey Richard.' I shouted at him from across the room. 'What the fuck are you doing here? I thought you were Thatcher's blue-eyed boy!'

He completely ignored me.

PART FIVE

TAPE #18
(16TH JULY 2012)

Conversation #6

Last week was strange at Big Life. Tony Beard, one of our senior managers, walked out. He took La Roux and Klaxons with him. Elly from La Roux called to thank me for all the hard work I put in, breaking her in America. That was nice of her. She told me Tony understands her music more than I do.

[Pause]

I suppose I have to accept that. It isn't true. But I have to accept it's how she feels. Klaxons didn't phone me or email. That's not especially graceful, is it? Even so, I'll miss managing those acts.

[Stands. Goes to window]

I stood by the swimming pool late last night, listening to the insects go quiet… Have you had breakfast? You should. It's a good meal. I eat a bowl of fresh fruit every day. Have you noticed?

[Pause]

Tony Beard told me he was worried about the future. He's worried about the music industry and about his acts not making it. 'These are hard and brutal times, Jazz,' he said. 'Fifteen years ago, you could pick up a couple of average bands a year and earn fifty grand. You can't do that any more.'

Average bands? I've never once tried to find an 'average' band. Neither has Tim Parry. The old ways are dying. That's clear. Let them, I say. I saw a band called Savages the other night. Four fearsome, utterly formidable young women. Brilliant songs and

219

attitude – intense and joyous. I wish I was managing them. When they played, it was fantastic. And you know what, passion is the future.

[Pause]

You recording?

[Long pause]

If my artists don't support me then I can't do my job. I need their backing, OK, or how can we work? Lisa Stansfield was being ripped off in Italy I remember. She was performing in a tent in Rome. The gig had sold out, but other ones had been poorly promoted and she hadn't been paid. She needed me.

'Eh, Jazz, ciao!' I flew to Italy. I was greeted by a guy called Francesco. He approached me, arms spread wide, all set for a huge embrace. 'Benvenuto!' He'd done a good job publishing Lisa in Italy, but he was screwing up the promotion and it was slippery, not to pay her. 'Jazz, benvenuto!'

'No benvenuto, Francesco,' I said. 'No hug for a promoter who's screwing up.'

I told Lisa to stay in her hotel room and not come out.

'Lisa ain't playing,' I told Francesco. 'You owe us for three gigs, plus tonight, that's a hundred grand. And I want it today, in cash, before she goes on stage.'

'Impossible.' He shook his head and his lower lip bloomed. 'It's Saturday, Jazz. How can I get so much cash on a Saturday? You'll get it on Monday when the banks open. So go get Lisa, yes?'

'If you'd have paid us for each gig, you'd only owe us forty grand. It's your problem, Francesco, not mine. No money, no gig.'

At moments like that what matters is faith. I'm not gonna change my mind. I'm not gonna back down. I'm not gonna listen to the excuses of an unscrupulous man. Lisa Stansfield had faith.

TAPE #18

She backed me. She stayed in her room until Francesco sulked into the lobby carrying two big brown paper bags.

A manager needs an artist's support. I don't always get it. Sometimes Fat Deiter wins, you know. Sometimes…sometimes you end up standing beside a drum kit on a street in Frankfurt in the snow.

[Pause]

That's a flashback. A metaphor.

I need to think.

TAPE #19
(16TH JULY 2012)

The Verve

'History has a place for us,' said Richard Ashcroft, OK, in an interview in something like 1993. 'It may take us three albums,' he said. 'But we will be there.' He was talking about the Verve. What a thing to say, eh. What a brilliant fucking truth to speak.

People say rock bands are like families, but they're worse, I think. Being in a band ain't easy. The Beatles couldn't stay together, could they? Or Oasis, or the Jam, or...I don't know...the Eagles.

Put a family in a Transit van and send them round the world with free booze, fornication, drugs, adulation, ridicule, ask them the same twenty questions fifteen times a day, make them go on stage every night, sleep in strange beds, film and photograph them all day long, get them in millions of pounds of debt, then ask the family to go into a studio twenty hours a day and make a second album. Do you see? These are intense situations, bands.

The 1990s was a different era. Lots of excess, like the eighties, but less about glitz. It was rock's return, Britpop, I suppose, and I was interested in that. I'm always interested in things changing. I loved the Verve. They were a heavyweight band, full of gloom and love and totally profound. They spoke to me. Four beautiful, miserable northern lads who brought the world to its knees.

Tim Parry first met Richard Ashcroft because Youth was producing them. This was 1996. The Verve had released two albums and were about as big as a cult band could get. Tim kept telling me about these

222

amazing demos he'd heard – songs like 'Sonnet', 'The Drugs Don't Work', 'Lucky Man'. The members of the Verve were on the dole at the time. They were £1.2 million in debt to their label, Virgin. I was clean and eating big amounts of broccoli. I ate it raw and sometimes I dipped it in hummus. I ate a lot of carrot, too. Nice fresh chopped carrot and a dollop of hummus, OK. It was funny, meeting a group of lads like the Verve. They were all childhood friends from Wigan and they probably thought, who's this strange southerner who doesn't drink or do drugs and eats raw broccoli?

[Pause]

Do you know how volatile the Verve are? Do you, though? They were really fucking volcano volatile. They were famous for it. Most people, like I did, think the turbulence came from the relationship between Richard Ashcroft and the guitarist, Nick McCabe. But the more I learnt about it…

[A phone rings]

Alexis Grower, what does he want?

[Answers phone]

Alexis, how are you? I'm right in the middle of my book so you can fuck off.

Mick and Keith

Youth was in the studio putting the finishing touches to *Urban Hymns*. Tim and me were down, listening to the songs, thinking, these are fucking amazing! The album's a masterpiece.

'You haven't used any samples on the album, Youth, have you?' Tim asked.

'Yeah, we did actually,' Youth said. 'There's one on *Bittersweet*. We sampled Andrew Loog Oldham…'

BIG LIFE

'You did what?'

'Yeah,' Youth said. 'The loop, it's from *The Rolling Stones Songbook*.'

Tim assures me I turned pale. A shadow crept across my soul.

'Which Stones track?'

'*The Last Time*.'

It felt like winning the lottery but losing the ticket. I knew who owned the copyright for that era of the Rolling Stones. It was a man called Allen Klein. Allen Klein, former manager of the Rolling Stones, former manager of the Beatles. Klein was notorious. A breaker of deals, balls – all that kind of thing. He ran a company called ABKCO. For 'Bittersweet Symphony' to exist, we'd have to come to an agreement with Allen Klein regarding how we share the publishing royalties.

'There's no way we can emulate those sounds, is there, Youth?'

'I'm afraid not.'

'Fuck.' This was me. I had my eyes closed. 'Fuck, fuck, fuck... *fuck*!'

The Verve hadn't sampled an original Stones track. They'd sampled Andrew Loog Oldham's reworking of the original. But it came down to two things: Mick and Keith. They were registered as the writers of the original song *and* the Loog Oldham version.

I didn't know Allen Klein. I knew his assistant, Iris Keitel. We'd had a lot of success with 'I'm Free' with the Soup Dragons. We turned a Rolling Stones b-side into a big hit and ABKCO had agreed synchs and ads for that song. Maybe they'd feel the same about 'Bittersweet Symphony'.

I called Iris Keitel in America and attempted to charm her. It all seemed to be going rather well until I told her, tentatively, about the sample on 'Bittersweet'. Here, the tone changed. 'Oh,' she said.

TAPE #19

'Yes, I know about this. This is that Verve band, isn't it? Some *idiot* from EMI phoned me about this yesterday, offering us fifteen per cent. I told him to fuck off, Jazz. Fifteen per cent! I already told them to fuck off. You needn't have called.'

'Iris,' I said. 'It could be huge, this song.'

'Listen, Jazz. Fifteen per cent is a fucking disgusting royalty. They've stolen our music! I told EMI's idiot yesterday. We don't like people stealing our music. We don't like it. I've spoken to Allen. We're not going to agree to this.'

I summoned every ounce of charm I had. I tried to transmit goodwill down the phone: 'Iris, this is a great song. Please. Let's talk about a really good split. Good money for Mick and Keith. Good money for the Verve. Fair's fair. They've sampled the Stones, but they've created a beautiful song.'

'No.' Iris really snapped at me. 'We're not going to do it, Jazz. Listen to me. *We're not going to let you use it!*'

'Right,' I thought. 'That went well.'

I was able to find an address for Andrew Loog Oldham in Bogotá. I needed allies – people that might believe in the music more than the business. Andrew was a good guy. He'd managed the Stones in the sixties and of course he'd actually made the music that had been sampled. I wrote to him in Colombia.

I phoned Nancy Berry, who ran Virgin Records in America. She liked the Verve and was friendly with Mick Jagger and Keith Richards. She loved 'Bittersweet Symphony', too. I told her about the response from ABKCO and asked if there was any chance she could play 'Bittersweet' to Mick and Keith. Those two were bound to put music before business.

'Sure,' Nancy said. 'I'm seeing them at a video shoot tomorrow. I'll take it down.'

225

BIG LIFE

Next, I went to speak to the Verve. It might be, I told them, that Iris' approach is simply how ABKCO open negotiations. Or, I said, it might be that they simply won't let us use the song. I warned them that they might lose *all* of their publishing royalties on the song. We agreed that 'Bittersweet Symphony' was such an important piece of music, we had to keep fighting for it.

Andrew Loog Oldham, meanwhile, faxed me a letter from Bogotá. 'Alas,' he said. 'I like it!' He wasn't hopeful about our chances with ABKCO, though; he thought Mick and Keith were probably our best bet. 'But remember,' he said, 'they love their money too, and are hardly likely to remember where they knocked the song off in the first place.' I got the feeling Mick and Keith might not be overly eager to put music before money. Andrew was a good guy, but he knew which side his bread was buttered. 'I like to help adventures,' he concluded, 'but not at the cost of my "gold watch"…'

I called Iris at ABKCO and she said I was wasting my breath. She was still refusing to let me talk to her boss, Allen Klein.

The only person I knew who would be able to get to Allen Klein was Nancy's husband, Ken Berry. Ken was the head of EMI worldwide, and owned the copyright on the more recent Rolling Stones material, via Virgin. I felt sure there was a deal to be done between him and Allen Klein. Nancy hassled Ken and a meeting was put in place. Even so, I met with the Verve and prepared them, once again, for the eventuality that they'd lose all of the publishing royalties on 'Bittersweet Symphony'.

Then something very unexpected happened.

'I've got some great news!' This was Nancy, the following week. 'Ken's spoken to Allen and Allen's agreed to let the song be released. He's agreed a fifty-fifty split on the publishing!'

TAPE #19

'Fucking hell,' I said. '*Really?*'

'They're gonna send you the paperwork straight away. Pretty cool, huh?'

'Nancy, I love you. And I love your husband! I don't know what he's got on Allen Klein, but I'd love to see the photographs!'

I was delighted. I called up the band and they were ecstatic, too. It was what they deserved, at the very least, a fifty per cent royalty on the song they'd written.

The following week, the contracts arrived at Big Life. Everything was in order. The agreement to use the sample was all correct. But then, when I checked the publishing contract, it didn't quite make sense. ABKCO had sent Richard Ashcroft a cheque for a thousand dollars, which they said was payment for writing the lyrics of 'Bittersweet Symphony'. The publishing contract wasn't fifty-fifty, as I'd expected. It wasn't fifty per cent the Verve, fifty per cent Jagger/Richards. It was one hundred per cent Jagger/Richards. I looked it over half a dozen times, looking for a side note or an amendment or something. But there was nothing. It was wrong.

I phoned America, feeling pretty perplexed. 'Nancy, this is really embarrassing. All the paperwork's come through fine, but it's *not* fifty-fifty. It's one hundred per cent Jagger/Richards. This doesn't make sense. Can you check with Ken?'

She called me back the following day.

'Hi, Jazz. I spoke to Ken. He's spoken to Allen. And the contract *is* right. And it is fifty-fifty.'

'It ain't right, Nancy. And it ain't fucking fifty-fifty. I've got it in front of me. It's one hundred fucking–'

'No,' she said. 'The contract is right. And it is fifty-fifty, Jazz... it's fifty per cent Mick, fifty per cent Keith.'

227

BIG LIFE

When 'Bittersweet' was nominated for a Grammy, the song was attributed to Mick Jagger and Keith Richards. It baffles me, really, how they could bare that, Mick and Keith. Maybe they're so used to having money and greatness bestowed on them, they just nodded, banked the cash and went with it.

We were asked to put the song on a Vauxhall advert. We declined because the Verve aren't into that, so ABKCO re-made the song without the vocal and gave Vauxhall permission. Everyone thought it was the Verve, but it wasn't. It's the same when the football comes on TV in England. Richard's sons tell him his music's on, but it isn't, not really, and that hurts him. And me.

[Pause]

Iris Keitel said she didn't like people stealing her music, but ABKCO took so much from Richard Ashcroft. They stole the soul of that wonderful piece of music he'd created, and that's very different than sampling. It's perfectly legal, but it's legal robbery. The split should have acknowledged the contribution of both parties. But business is business and music is music; I guess that's how ABKCO saw it. ABKCO has sold that music around the world, undervaluing what the Verve created. They're toe-rags. I never cashed that cheque they sent Richard as payment for the lyrics. It was offensive. I don't think Richard even knows they sent it.

I met Jackson Browne (he wrote that wonderful Nico song, 'These Days', as well as loads of others) in Hawaii, Christmas 1998. It was Jackson who told me where the Rolling Stones got 'The Last Time' from. It's a traditional song, performed by a group called the Staple Singers. Look it up on YouTube. That's corporate rock 'n' roll, I suppose.

TAPE #19

Do You Hunt?

It reminds me of this time when I was managing Soul II Soul. You're too young to know how fucking amazing they were, maybe. Do you know Jazzie B? You should. He's a legend. He calls me *Uncle*. I don't know why. But he does. I've known Jazzie since he was on the street with his soundsystem, way before Soul II Soul broke through. I had dinner with him at Chen Du in Camden once and he asked me to manage him. And I did. I managed him for three years. We did a *Best of Soul II Soul* album and all sorts. I'm always bugging him to form Soul II Soul II, a group of young musicians who could be a Soul II Soul for now.

While I managed him, me and him had to go out to America for a court case. A couple of strange Floridians, siblings, a brother and a sister, were suing him. They claimed they'd written the song 'Keep On Moving' and that Jazzie B had stolen it. They believed they'd sent the song to Atlantic Records and somehow it had been passed on to Jazzie, and he'd passed it off as his own. It was totally and utterly ridiculous, but Jazzie and I had to go over to fight the case.

Virgin Records hired this tanned and unbelievably macho lawyer to defend Jazzie. He was a nutter. He objected practically every five seconds by bursting out of his seat like someone had held a lit match to his arsehole. The court adjourned for the weekend and this Mr Macho guy invited Jazzie and me up to a mansion overlooking Malibu Beach for Sunday lunch and a tactical discussion. The lunch he offered was meat, meat and more meat. I couldn't eat any of it. Mr Macho was marching round in white Speedos, eating ribs and chicken wings and telling me and Jazzie about all the people he'd destroyed in courtrooms across California.

'Do you hunt?' he said.

BIG LIFE

'No,' I said.

'Jazzie,' said Mr Macho. 'Don't tell me you don't hunt either.'

'I'm sorry,' Jazzie said. 'I can't say I do.'

'Do *you* hunt?' I asked.

'Oh, yeah, *I* hunt, sure I do. I hunt deer with a bow and arrow.'

The next day, in court, Mr Macho objected to something. He leapt from his seat and charged across the courtroom into an area where lawyers were forbidden. All of a sudden, sirens sounded and metal bars came from nowhere and Mr Macho was trapped in a cage before the judge, shouting his head off and trying to break free. The jury filed out and Mr Macho was banned from the court.

The brother and sister were making all sorts of accusations of Jazzie B. Chief among them was the fact that he wasn't what they called 'a musician'. How could he have written 'Keep On Moving' when he wasn't a musician? Their lawyer was really sneery and confrontational.

'Admit it, Jazzie B, you're not a musician!'

'I do admit it,' Jazzie said. I really felt for him, having to stand in the witness box. 'I'm a DJ.'

'A DJ?' This lawyer was bland and tanned and had an unbroken breadstick up his arse. 'How can a *DJ* possibly write a song?'

'Well,' Jazzie said. 'I put beats together, get people in to play, people who follow my vision…'

'What? So how do you know what you're doing? How do you make decisions?'

I think, in that moment, the situation finally got to Jazzie. He was being accused of fraud; his entire authenticity was being questioned. He was being defended by a hyperactive huntsman and now he was being accused of not being able to write songs. But, rather than lose his temper, he stood calmly in the witness box. He looked at the members of the jury. He looked at the judge, at the brother and sister who were accusing him, at the aggressive, sneery lawyer, and he said, 'I do it from here.' He tapped his heart. 'I make music from here.'

And it was clear to everyone in that courtroom that they were in the presence of an artist. Jazzie was so honest, dignified and magnetic. He's a big, cuddly guy and he was so real in that moment. The case was thrown out not long after. I love Jazzie B. He really ought to get Soul II Soul II going, don't you think – I think that's a great idea. I'd rather have Soul II Soul II than boring old JLS. We're a good team – Jazz and Jazzie! But he calls me Uncle.

Don't Bore Us, Get to the Chorus

Don't become one of those music biz nerds who listen to pop songs like they're listening to the weather forecast. Sometimes songs don't conform to conventional structures. You have to trust how a piece of music makes you *feel*, OK.

The Verve's A&R man was a guy called Dave Boyd. I remember meeting old Dave to discuss which song should be the lead single from *Urban Hymns*. We ate in a lovely Indian on Mortimer Street called Gaylord. He's tucking into his potato pakora, Dave Boyd, and he's glancing up at me saying, '*Space and Time*, Jazz. It's gotta be *Space and Time*, right?'

'No, Dave,' I said. 'It's gotta be *Bittersweet Symphony*.'

I saw a great big fucking red question mark appear above his head.

'Really? *Bittersweet Symphony*? I really think it should be *Space and Time*.'

A week later, in a boardroom at Virgin Records, Tim and me are telling a bunch of pretty cool music guys that the lead single from *Urban Hymns* has *got* to be 'Bittersweet Symphony'. And they're looking at us, saying, 'Ooh, I'm not sure about that, fellas. It takes a bit of a listen.' Takes a bit of a listen? It's an anthem. 'It's not got a chorus,' someone piped up. And suddenly I can't take it any longer. I start banging on the table, rattling all the teacups. 'It's one long fucking chorus!' I completely lost it. 'It's an anthem! Listen to it! It's one long fucking chorus!'

Trust your gut. If it feels right, it's right.

[Long pause]

If you don't know when it feels right then you're in the wrong industry.

Georgia

Marine, my French girlfriend, in true French fashion, had an affair. That was OK. I'm friends with the guy now. He's a lovely man. There was a lot of love between Marine and me, but not enough lust, I suppose, so we both had affairs.

Mine began in 1992. It was with a woman called Ineka. I'd first met her in 1989, when she came to pick up some tickets for a Yazz concert. She was Yazz's best friend from school, you see. She was so lovely. I'd feared she'd be a bit off with me, because off all the grief between me and Yazz. But she was sweet.

After that, we'd run into each other every once in a while and I always thought she was very wonderful. It was a passionate affair. Me and the beautiful Ineka. I loved her. And one day she came to me and told me she was pregnant. The moment she said that, I felt this presence, this child, I suppose, trying to get through into the world. I was so excited – I wanted this baby, but I couldn't put pressure on Ineka. After all, we were having an affair. I was living with another woman.

TAPE #19

I told Ineka I'd support her, whatever she decided. The following day, when she told me she intended to keep the child, I wept with joy. Georgia was a mistake. I can't deny it. But what a glorious one. The most beautiful mistake I ever made.

[Pause]

I needed to say that. Have you met Georgia? You should. She's an amazing person.

Circus Animals

Urban Hymns sold eight million copies in eight months in 1998. These days, maybe Gaga sells like that. Adele does, I suppose. *Urban Hymns* made the Verve one of the biggest bands on earth. It's still about the fifteenth best-selling album in UK history. You can check that, can't you? I think it's about fifteenth. Think about that. *Fifteenth*!

In late 1998, I flew to Munich at short notice. I took a fresh pair of underpants, a Comme des Garçons shirt and a piece of paper – a fax. When an album does as well as *Urban Hymns*, you're entitled to renegotiate the band's record deal. Virgin Records had faxed me the terms of the new deal and I headed straight for Heathrow.

Going to see the Verve was often nerve-wracking. They were playing at a venue in Munich called the Circus. The smell of exotic excrement hung in the air. Elephant and horse and lion. Animal excrement and sawdust, that's what I remember. I held the fax in my hand.

Richard Ashcroft was the first to emerge from the backstage area. He was with Kate, his wife. He looked tired and thin. He brushed his long brown hair away from his eyes and nodded at the piece of paper.

233

BIG LIFE

'Come on,' he said. 'What's the deal?'

'We should wait for the others.'

'No,' he said. 'Come on. Tell me.'

'Well,' I said. 'Whether or not you ever sell another album ever again, I've negotiated you a guaranteed twenty-three million pounds.'

'Jesus.'

'Twenty-three million,' I said. 'Ten million on signature, five million for the next two albums, guaranteed, not options, and three million pounds immediately towards back royalties. I've got you a twenty-two per cent royalty on *Urban Hymns*, twenty per cent on your back catalogue, twenty-four per cent on future albums. If you wanna make a solo album, there's a three million pound advance. If Nick wants to make an instrumental album, he'll get a million quid up front. The bottom line is,' I said, 'it's a guaranteed twenty-three million quid.'

Richard looked over my shoulder. I followed his gaze. He was looking at the stage. A bunch of roadies were busy setting up the lighting rig, positioning Richard's monitors and lifting enormous great speakers into place. I turned to face him and smiled.

'Amazing,' he said. 'That's amazing, Jazz. Thank you.'

Nick, Pete and Simon filtered through from the backstage area. When they heard the news they were ecstatic. Once they'd signed the contract, they'd each be millionaires. That night, I stood by the sound desk and the Circus went wild. They played with such conviction and fury, and yet there was so much fucking *freedom* and sadness and vulnerability in those songs. They were at the height of their powers.

Did I ever tell you I managed Embrace?

[Pause]

TAPE #19

Me and Tim managed Embrace with a guy called Tony Perrin. In fact, Tim found them on a cassette they sent to the Big Life office.

The evening after Munich, back in London, I got a call from the Verve's Tour Manager – Pete Gunn. The band had celebrated on the tour bus after the Circus gig, he said. Nick McCabe had partied all night and, as a result, Pete Gunn, who sounded really fucking stressed, had had to break into Nick's hotel room to get him to the next gig on time.

Embrace were doing a midnight show at HMV, Oxford Street. Their debut album was due out on the Monday. As I walked there, at around eleven at night, my phone rang – Pete Gunn again. I stopped outside a closed Topshop and plugged my ear with my fingertip, so I could hear what he was shouting.

'It's all gone off here, Jazz! Seriously. It's all fucking gone off!'

'What's happened?'

'Something happened on stage. Then in the dressing room, Nick starts saying how much he enjoyed the gig. Richard threw a bottle. Nick threw a hat-stand and the whole thing went off. I've got Simon and Richard on tranquillisers. I don't know where Nick is. I'm worried, Jazz. I'm worried they're breaking up. They wanna cancel the tour!'

The Verve splitting up was the only thing that could prevent the new deal going through. I was on twenty per cent of those advances. If they spilt, I'd lose four million pounds. I told myself not to think about the money. All I should think about is: how the fuck do I keep these boys together? Another album like *Urban Hymns* would take them into U2 territory. I knew that. They were headlining V and Slane Castle that summer. We had an American tour booked.

BIG LIFE

The Good Will Out, Embrace's debut album, was set to go in at number one. And it did. But my head was full of the Verve as I watched Embrace at HMV. I took Tim to one side and told him it was possible the Verve were splitting.

Richard Ashcroft rented a flat in Barnes, not far from Hammersmith Bridge. He wasn't in a good state when I went to see him. The tour was cancelled by then. We'd blamed that on ill-health. Richard was sitting on his sofa, all pale and troubled. I took him a book called *The Power of Now* that had just been published. He was all strung out between the past and the future.

'I don't know, Jazz,' he said, locking his thin hands together and closing his eyes. 'I honestly don't know what to do.'

The next time I saw Richard I was with Tim Parry. We ate salad sandwiches at a little restaurant just off Cavendish Square. He sat in front of us, looking into space.

'The last thing I wanna do is split this band up again. It's an amazing band. This is really difficult…but if I go solo,' he said, turning to me, 'I've only got my own problems to carry.'

And so the biggest record contract I ever negotiated never got signed. Radio 1 listeners voted 'Bittersweet Symphony' the Best Song Ever. At the 1998 Brit Awards, the Verve won the awards for Best British Group and Best British Album. Youth won Best Producer. We were well on our way to being the biggest rock band in the world.

And it was over.

The chemistry that made the magic, destroyed the fucking magic, too. Nick McCabe couldn't carry on. The band toured America, played the V Festivals and Slane Castle without him. They were never as good without Nick.

TAPE #19

Robbie Williams was third on the bill that day at Slane. I remember him buzzing off the fact he was standing on the spot that Richard Ashcroft would later stand on. I watched from the wings and thought Robbie was a great entertainer – amiable and charming, but also that he was right to be humble in the shadow of Ashcroft.

I was so desperate for answers I consulted a numerologist about Nick McCabe and Richard Ashcroft. I sent their dates of birth to a woman in America who I really trusted. I thought she could give me some perspective on their relationship – how I might be able to help them. But she came back and said, 'Jazz, these two people *need* each other. There's no problems between them at all. In fact, their numbers combine magically.'

I visited Richard shortly after he signed his solo deal with Virgin. We sat together in his living room, drinking tea.

'How's Nick?' he asked. 'Have you seen him?'

'We had lunch last week,' I said. 'He'll do something, I think, but he said the only place he'd like to gig was in his back garden.'

'If you see him again, please give him my best. I really love that guy.'

Richard gave me an inquisitive look. He must have read my thoughts, because he put down his mug, brushed his hair from his eyes and smiled.

'Jazz,' he said. 'The Verve splitting ain't about Nick McCabe.'

'So who is it about?'

He didn't say.

He never has.

The thing is, right…I'd only managed the band through *Urban Hymns*. A lot of stuff had happened before. There were deep rifts – horrible tensions.

237

BIG LIFE

Simon Jones, the bassist, had married. Simon's one of the nicest blokes you'll ever meet, OK, and he was totally besotted with his wife, an American girl called Myra. And she's lovely, too – really funny and gutsy. But she was a real rock 'n' roll girl, Myra. She had a lot of love for the lifestyle and her partying could sometimes get out of hand.

People think managing a band is just about managing the different members. It ain't. Bands come with all sorts of other people you have to manage. And they're usually the hardest people to keep a lid on. On tour, everyone's jumbling around in the same stinky bag: musicians, roadies, wives, caterers, drivers. Things get messy.

It was nearly ten years since they'd been boys in Wigan, innocently starting a band. They'd grown up. They'd changed as people. All the tensions were pushed into the silence, and that affects the music eventually. Guys like U2 and Coldplay'll go on forever probably, like the Stones. They've figured out how to stay together. The Verve couldn't do that.

A year later, in 1999, I was managing Richard Ashcroft as he attempted the transition from front man in a band to solo star. I was managing another northern lad, too, called Damon Gough – Badly Drawn Boy. Every manager in the industry wanted to manage Damon, you know, but he chose me and Tim. I think it was because we were the only managers who talked about music at the interview. That's our trick! Everyone else was promising him multi-million pound deals and all that stuff. Damon's debut album, *The Hour of Bewilderbeast*, won the Mercury Prize. It's one of my favourite ever albums. Damon turned up and played when I won the Peter Grant Award. He stood on stage and said he loved Tim and me. He said he'd be with us until he died. He's a lot younger than me, so I'll die first. But he'll be with me till I die.

Back in 1999, Big Life were moving into a new property, on Chalton Street, King's Cross, where we're still based today. We decided we'd celebrate the move with a sushi party. I was supervising the buffet when Richard Ashcroft phoned.

'Jazz. How are you?'

'I'm surrounded by raw fish, Richard. How are you?'

'I've got bad news, Jazz.'

'Are you coming to our party?'

'I don't want you to manage me any more.'

I was holding a chopstick and a bowl of wasabi. 'Why's that?' My heart was thumping. 'It's not working, Jazz.' I went outside into the street. 'Richard, let's go for a cup of tea.'

But his mind was made up. He was sorry. He was gone. It hurt like a lover leaving, OK. I looked at the sky. He meant the world to me.

Dave Boyd came to our sushi party. It was a very raw event all round. I suppose I looked a little white around the gills. I don't remember much. All I could think about was losing Richard. Dave Boyd greeted the news of my sacking with such surprise. 'Oh my god!' he said. 'Jazz, that's terrible!'

Years later, I learned that it was Dave Boyd himself who convinced Richard to sack me. He'd gone round to Richard's house three nights in a row and done everything he could to persuade him. I've no idea why he wanted me out. I think it might have been something to do with his Christmas bonus.

Sooner or later, as a manager, there's a chance you could get fired. You can't walk out of a record deal, not really, not easily, but no court in the land can make you work with someone day in day out that you don't want to work with. I've been fired in all sorts of ways. It was brave of Richard to call me directly – I always like that way, though it hurts and it's sad.

My favourite sacking was Lisa Stansfield. We'd sold ten million records and she'd written some sensational songs, and then, ten years on, she invited me for tea at the Mayfair Hotel, her and Ian Devaney, her band-mate and husband. 'Jazz,' she said. 'When we started working with you, we were kids…it's time to grow up now. It's time to leave home.' It was sad, but it was lovely and I stood and hugged her and Ian. And she stays in touch, Lisa. At big moments, she supports me.

A manager lives and works between a rock and a hard place – between an artist and a record label, between 'them' and 'us'. The other day an A&R man contacted one of my artists and told them I was slow and old and out of touch. He persuaded her to fire me by email. But when we spoke, she changed her mind – she saw I was passionate, that I believed in her. She's a fucking great rapper, this girl. Some time passed and the A&R man called me up, making a load of weak excuses, saying he'd been misunderstood. 'I hope this doesn't sound sanctimonious,' I told him. 'But I forgive you completely for what you did. Let's move on.' I wouldn't have done that twenty years ago. But it felt great, forgiving him for trying to fuck me. I felt fresh.

TAPE #20
(8TH JULY 2012)

God

Why I ever agreed to manage Eternal I'll never know. The experience fucking haunts me. I met them at Chen Du. I went in and there were these two sisters: Esther and Vernie Bennett. I knew about them because, you know, they were big time. I'd seen them on TV, videos, billboards. I took a seat and they were all very kind and well-behaved. It was explained to me that Eternal had recently gone from being a foursome to a duo of sisters.

The following day, over breakfast, I informed Tim we were now the managers of Eternal. I can't say he was pleased. He looked, I recall, as though the milk in his tea had soured slightly. Tim being Tim, he was aware of their past success, their hits. He knew they were signed to EMI. We rolled up our sleeves and set about A&Ring the new Eternal album. And you know what, it was a great record. Fuck knows what it was called, but it was good, I remember. I think it was just called *Eternal*.

Esther and Vernie cost EMI an absolute fortune. Everything they did cost big money: their hair, their clothes, their nails, their shoes, their styling, their travel. They used to live within a half mile of each other in Purley in Surrey, but every time they came to a meeting in town they demanded a car, often a Rolls Royce, and they refused to travel together, so EMI would have to send two separate limos for them. It was outrageous. If they had their hair extensions done, special hair was flown in from America. Getting them on television cost a fortune. They did Party in the Park in 1997 – four songs. It cost EMI £30,000 for that show. All on limos, stylings, hot chocolate and hair and nails.

Big Life had a girl called Sarah Bowden, who I assigned to Eternal's day-to-day business. She'd only been working with us for three or four weeks and so, I suppose, wasn't completely sure how we operated.

Esther and Vernie went to LA for a photoshoot. They were staying in the Peninsula Hotel. Vernie Bennett called up Sarah Bowden back in London, where Sarah lived in a bed-sit in Bethnal Green.

'Sarah?'

'Hello?'

'Sarah, this is Vernie.'

'Oh, hi Vernie.'

'Sarah, could you call room service and find out where my hot chocolate is?'

'Sorry?'

'Twenty minutes ago, I ordered a hot chocolate. I'm a little worried, Sarah, because it hasn't arrived yet. Could you find out where it is?'

'Sorry, Vernie, where what is?'

'My hot chocolate.'

'Oh. It's one in the morning here, Vernie...'

'Can you just call them up, Sarah?'

She should have politely told Vernie to do it herself, which is the Big Life way – no nonsense big time behaviour, if we can help it.

'Vernie, I can't call from here because my phone doesn't dial internationally. The best I can do is go round to my sister's. I'd have to call from there.'

242

TAPE #20

'OK.'

'It's a half an hour walk.'

'OK.'

'Right.'

Sarah got up, got dressed and walked across East London in the middle of the night to her sister's house, where her sister was also sleeping. Having woken her and explained the situation about the hot chocolate, Sarah decided to give Vernie a quick call. After all, it had been nearly forty minutes since the initial conversation.

'Hi Vernie, it's Sarah –'

'Oh, Sarah, it's arrived! I'm drinking it! No need to call.'

'Oh…'

It became obvious that some of the media had turned their back on Eternal. I spoke to Doctor Fox about getting them on the Capital Radio Breakfast Show, but he said absolutely no way.

In my opinion, the Universe was turning its back on Esther and Vernie Bennett on account of their ludicrous behaviour and their ridiculous demands for hot chocolate.

I had lunch with them before the album came out, to discuss their publishing situation. After all the work, I felt I deserved some money.

'You know something, Jazz,' Vernie said. 'I think God is watching down on us. Because the songs on this album were written *after* our previous manager and *before* you started managing us. So we won't be paying any management commission on these songs under any circumstances.'

'Vernie,' I said. 'God might be looking down on you. But he sure as hell ain't looking down on me. I've worked so *hard* on this record. You should really consider what you're doing here.'

BIG LIFE

The people at Big Life called them Fester and Ernie. The public had decided they didn't like them. It was simple. What's her name had left the band. What is her name? She married a footballer. *Louise.* They'd been tyrants on TV and bitchy in the press. Sammy, my lovely step-daughter, saw a poster of Eternal on Kilburn High Road. Someone had sprayed the word 'Evil' across it.

We always keep champagne in the office to celebrate a hit. The head of EMI called me and told me the band had called a meeting and stipulated that I be excluded from it. That was the last straw. I had to resign.

I heard the cork pop from a bottle. My staff were celebrating the end of Eternal, drinking champagne at ten in the morning.

I sent a fax.

To: Esther and Vernie Bennett
Re: Eternal
Dear Esther and Vernie,
It is with great pleasure today that I resign as manager of Eternal. Esther, you have a wonderful talent, please look after it. Vernie, I shall pray for you.
Sincerely,
Jazz Summers

TAPE #21
(8TH JULY 2012)

Mannequins in a Skip

I can close my eyes and be back there, sitting on a drum-stool in Malacca, playing with the Shades of Blue.

We played Singapore. We had Singaporean groupies who weren't girls but trannies. We'd pile off to Boogie Street after the gig to parade around and shout and dance and drink. A trannie called Marilyn loved the way I drummed. She used to beg to sit on my knee and I let her once or twice. Boogie Street was a long cacophony of transvestite brothels, bazaars, shouting hawkers and noodle bars. Gambling dens, dancing soldiers, sailors, swarms of running rats and gangsters. I'd stumble the back streets of Singapore, falling in and out of monsoon drains, searching for Boogie Street. I had a knife pulled on me once. Marilyn sprang from the darkness, from nowhere. She knocked my assailant clean out with her floral handbag – it was full of rocks.

[Pause]

I always blew her a kiss if I saw her on Boogie Street.

[Long pause]

Towards the end of 2001, Keren McKean, Big Life's Scottish scout, introduced me and Tim to a band called Snow Patrol. They'd had two albums out on an independent label and now they were dropped. They had a publishing deal with Sony, too. I'd seen their name about, you know, but just the odd glance in the back of *NME*. I took their demo tape home.

BIG LIFE

Sony Music had to pay £40,000 to continue with Snow Patrol's publishing deal. We phoned them up and asked for the money because the band were completely skint. Sony asked for an extension on their option until the band got a record deal. They didn't believe. We needed money to make some new demos, keep them alive, do some gigs. After some consideration, Sony dropped the band.

They didn't have a record deal or a publishing deal, but they had a song called 'Run' and a song called 'How To Be Dead'. Me and Tim made the decision to sign their publishing to Big Life Music. We gave them £50,000, which was a lot of money for us to lay down. But we believed. This song 'Run' was fantastic. Do you know it? [Sings] *Light up! Light up!*

Armed with the demos, me and Tim went round every single record company. Pretty much every single record company on earth. We went to EMI, Island, Sony, Epic. We sent the songs everywhere. I remember we were at EMI one day, talking to some guy who knew much more about Snow Patrol than Tim and me did. He was telling us about their early singles, songs from their second album, all sorts. We played him 'Run' and he seemed to like it. But would he sign a band in that situation? No way. No one wanted to sign a band they believed had already failed.

We played the tracks to this bloke at Mercury. He was Northern Irish, like the band. I sat him down in our office and played him 'Run'. I said, 'This is an anthem! Listen! *Light up! Light up!* It's an anthem!'

He said he'd be in touch. He wasn't. And this fucking festival of indifference went on for many months. In the middle of the summer, I phoned Korda Marshall at Mushroom Records. I knew Korda pretty well. We went over to see him and he introduced us to his new head of A&R, Max Lousada. They had this big oak table in their meeting room. I could feel I had a chance. I felt good. I handed Korda the CD and instructed him to put on a song called 'Chocolate'.

'Yeh,' Korda said. 'That's a great song.'

'Now play this, OK. *How To Be Dead.*'

Gary Lightbody's voice filled the room. It sounded great. That's not always the case when you're pitching a band to a record label. Sometimes you realise it's not gonna happen. You can taste defeat in the air. Korda and Max sat side by side with their arms folded, faces blank, not giving much away.

'Right,' I said. 'Korda, listen to this one. This one's called *Run.*'

All through 'Run' they kept their arms folded. Occasionally, Korda looked out of the window, watched cars drive by or clouds cross the sky. When the song finished, he and Max gave Tim and I flat smiles. It was as if we were somehow embarrassing ourselves.

'Right,' I said, when 'Run' finished. 'Play that song again. Play it again, Korda. Play that fucking song again.'

'Really?'

'Turn it up,' I said. And when the chorus came on I stood up in front of them and said, '*Listen*, it's an anthem! *Light up! Light up!* It's an amazing song!' Korda and Max sat there looking about as interested as a pair of old mannequins in a skip. 'You know what,' I said. 'I've always wanted to say this to someone and I never have, but I'm gonna say it today…if you two don't get that, you're fucking deaf. I'm out of here.'

That was the tip of the iceberg. Seriously. The *tip.* The tip of a huge iceberg of rejection. Tim and me stood in boardroom after boardroom, listening to 'Run', watching A&R men sip cups of tea, massaging stress balls, looking out the window, falling asleep. And

BIG LIFE

I banged on so many fancy tables and sang, so many times. [Sings] *Light up! Light up!* Sometimes we got close. Often, we got nowhere. Until, finally, a man called Jim Chancellor, a new arrival at Fiction Records, drove up to Glasgow and, having met the boys and heard them play, agreed to sign Snow Patrol. Jim was a godsend.

How did I keep going through all the failure? How did I take all that snooty rejection? I believed. I believed. A lot of people thought Snow Patrol were boring, but I believed their hearts were pure and that their songs, songs like 'Run', that made up their third album, *Final Straw*, were honest and true and they moved me. I'm not afraid to admit that. Snow Patrol moved me.

The problem was they were extremely uncool. And that can be a very tedious problem in the music industry. It can be a very tedious problem in your personal life, too. People love cool things. People love new things, hot things and buzzing-up things and hyped things and trendy things and Snow Patrol weren't any of these things. They were about as hip as mannequins in a skip.

The band went out on a little tour. They played a strip club in High Wycombe. They were really having to work the toilet tour. Although Zane Lowe played 'Spitting Games', their first single, Radio 1 were more likely to playlist a *Mein Kampf* audiobook than a Snow Patrol single. I'm serious.

I wanted Snow Patrol to play at the Universal Sales Conference. I wanted to get Lucien Grainge involved. Lucien was the head of Universal and an all round huge cheese; I elbowed him in his ribcage during their performance.

'You're right, Jazz,' he said. 'This *Run* song. It's a hit!'

'I know! It's a fucking anthem. *Light up! Light up!*'

Lucien became someone I could bug. I started bugging him about getting Snow Patrol on the radio. I called him up and bugged

248

him about Snow Patrol on a daily basis. Do people know Lucien Grainge? No? Lucien Grainge is a kind-eyed, jovial, diabolically powerful guy. But basically he's good. He's done ABBA, Amy Winehouse, Eurythmics, U2. Everyone's got a Lucien Grainge song on their iPod. I kept bugging him about 'Run'. Eventually, he put the big pressure on Polydor to prioritise the band.

I took the head of Radio 1 to watch Snow Patrol support Grandaddy at Brixton Academy. When Snow Patrol played, there was probably only about ten lines of people standing at the front watching. But when the band played 'Run', these people all sang along at the top of their voices. They threw their hands in the air. I looked at the head of Radio 1 and smiled. 'See?' I said. 'It's an anthem. *Light up! Light up!*

Sometimes, you know, I make an explosion to grab people's attention. I once walked into a meeting about Snow Patrol at Fiction Records in Chiswick. The Head of Radio Promotion was there. I took a risk. But life's a risk! 'I'm really not happy.' I pointed at the guy. 'In fact, I think you're fucking Snow Patrol up!' The whole room lit up like a sparkler. 'But do you care? Do you really want *Run* on the radio?' People were demanding I apologise. 'Does it really *matter* to you? Because it *matters* to me. It *matters* to the band. But does it *matter* to you? I be*lieve*. Do *you*? You've got a nice job here. You'll get another song next week, right? No, I'm not gonna apologise. I think he's fucking it up.'

I spent Christmas 2003 in Bali. While I was there I received a text. It said 'Run' had been added to the first Radio 1 playlist of the new year. We were on our way. That's all you need sometimes in life, momentum. How do you get momentum? Belief and perseverance! 'Run' went to number four in the UK and, on the back of that, we re-released the album, *Final Straw*. We sold one and half million copies. A lot of credit goes to the producer, Jacknife Lee. I'd picked him because he was different. He wasn't rock or indie. When you're picking a producer, don't always go with the obvious choice, OK. Often, as with Snow Patrol and Jacknife Lee, it's about putting different specialities and interests together. Also, Jacknife was relatively untested at the time, so he was cheap.

In February 2003, I said to Steve Strange, the band's agent, 'I don't want to be on the second stage at V. I want to be on the main stage. I don't care if it's two o'clock in the afternoon, get them on the main stage.'

'Why?' he said, thinking it might be better to be high up the bill on a second stage.

'Because by the summer, *Run* will be a huge song. It will be the anthem of the summer. I can see it,' I said. 'I can just picture it. We'll have the biggest crowd of the day, singing: *Light up! Light up!*'

At V, I bumped into Korda Marshall. He came running over, shouting my name. 'Jazz, Jazz, why didn't you bully me into signing Snow Patrol?'

Snow Patrol played the main stage at two in the afternoon. There were fifty-five thousand people there, all singing 'Run'. That was a special moment. I'd sang 'Run' to suited goons in endless boardrooms the previous year. I'd sung 'Run' to people who were checking their phones. And I'd been ignored. But now, on a sunny day in England, I listened as fifty-five thousand people sang that song. [Sings] *Light up! Light up!* And I saw how happy they were.

BMG were looking for songs for Natalie Imbruglia. Jacknife Lee and Gary Lightbody had a go at writing for her and, after a couple of days in the studio, they came into Big Life to play us the results. They played a song called 'Chasing Cars'.

TAPE #21

'Gary,' I said. 'You're not giving this to Natalie Imbruglia.'

'No?'

'That's the biggest song on your next album.'

'I was thinking that,' said Jacknife.

They had another song called 'You're All That I Have'. It was another cracker. A perfect lead single. In later weeks, whenever I visited the band in the studio, it was so obvious they were writing a big record. They'd cracked it! Gary was writing wonderful songs and Jacknife Lee had found their sound. In April 2006, we released *Eyes Open*. The first part of the year was all about set-up.

I travelled to America and met with Interscope to discuss 'Chasing Cars'. 'You can go to every radio format with this,' I said. 'This song knows no fucking genre. Go to pop. Go to rock. Go everywhere. This song will connect with people all over America!'

And I knew, sitting there in that office, that not one of these Americans believed me, or believed in the song. It's so frustrating. Brenda Romano, head of radio at Interscope, waved me away like I was insane. And if Brenda Romano doesn't want to take a record to radio, it doesn't go. Full stop. 'Brenda,' I said. '*You're* insane. You've got to take this record to Pop Radio and also to Hot AC [Adult Contemporary].'

Bugger Brenda. This was a new era. It wasn't just radio that could break a song. Certain TV programmes had started really pushing contemporary music. And the Internet had changed the way people listened. If you heard a song you liked on TV, you wouldn't just tap your foot and smile. You'd unfold your laptop and type fragments of the lyrics into Google.

Alex Pastavas got Snow Patrol on *The OC* when we were promoting *Final Straw*. She was at ABC by the time we came with 'Chasing Cars'. We invited her down to our show in LA. Building

251

relationships is crucial, OK. Treat people well. Don't be a dick. I firmly believe that our long-term relationship with Alex was what made her pick 'Chasing Cars' for the finale of a show called *Grey's Anatomy*.

Did you see it?

[Pause]

It brought a lump to your throat, the end of that series. And it was because of 'Chasing Cars'. The song whipped up such a storm on *Grey's Anatomy*. And like I say, this was a new era: all over America people reached for computers and typed lyrics or guessed at the song's title. This was May 2006. YouTube had arrived the previous year. The day after *Grey's Anatomy* aired, 'Chasing Cars' appeared in the iTunes Top 10. I phoned up Brenda Romano.

'Brenda,' I said. 'We gotta go to Hot AC.'

'Yeah, fine!'

'When are you going to Pop Radio?'

'Going?' she said. 'We've gone!'

They only believe when they see it in front of them. You've got to believe *before* you see it. That's the trick.

'Chasing Cars' got into the top five of the American chart. It was the first time a British band had done that in fifteen years. It was the last ever song to be played on *Top of the Pops* in the UK. Channel 4 viewers voted it the number one song of the noughties. They were given a Q Award recently and Gary mentioned me personally in his speech. Snow Patrol sold out an arena tour. It was amazing. They were huge. We sold over two million downloads on 'Chasing Cars'. We sold out an Australian tour. We sold a million albums in America. We outsold Take That and the Arctic Monkeys in the UK. We were riding so high. Towards the end of January 2007, I went to New Zealand with the band. From there, we were going to go and do some sold out shows in America. I got a text from Tim: *Call me urgently*.

Back in London, Tim had intercepted an email. The email was addressed to one of our employees who looked after Snow Patrol's day-to-day affairs. I won't say her name. She was on maternity leave and so Tim was following her emails, checking we didn't miss anything. The email was from the PA of a guy called Peter Mensch. It mentioned a meeting between Peter and the band that was due to take place in America.

Peter Mensch is head of a management company called Q Prime. One of our own employees was arranging for Peter Mensch to meet with Snow Patrol behind mine and Tim's back. People might know Q Prime because they manage Metallica, Muse and Red Hot Chilli Peppers. I knew that there was only one reason why Peter Mensch would be meeting with Snow Patrol.

I didn't know what to do. I was with the band, working, but I knew they were in the process of abandoning me. These days, when sorrows come, I don't drown them. I meditate. I looked at myself in my hotel mirror. I couldn't make sense of it. There are no accidents in life. If George Michael hadn't sacked me (and he did so with good reason) I would never have done all the things I've done.

I flew to San Francisco with Snow Patrol. Calm. I was calm, but I was so upset. I felt ill. Couldn't eat or sleep. I thought it was flu, but it was grief.

'Gary,' I said. 'I've heard something and I'm upset. An email that talks about a meeting with Peter Mensch. Have you not got the basic decency to talk to me about this first?'

There was a horrible meeting in San Francisco. Me and the band. They weren't happy with things, things to do with a song they'd written for the *Spider-Man* film, a Disney deal they wanted out of. I felt vulnerable. But we know what we do in life, don't we? We know what we give, how hard we try.

Me and Tim had taken Snow Patrol from nowhere. We'd taken them from the basement bowels of nowhere. We'd spent eighteen months getting them a record deal – it had been an almost impossible task. And an exhausting one. In the subsequent years, we worked night and day to break them all over the world. And yet we were going to get fired. For what? For doing an amazing job?

When I manage someone, I give them life and soul. Blood, sweat and tears come out of me. If we'd fucked up, that's different – but this? We were sitting on top of the world.

I remember Tony Wadsworth, who's head of the BPI now, he called me after Snow Patrol sacked us. He couldn't believe it. No one in the industry could. Everyone knew what we'd done for them, mainly because they'd rejected us when we were trying to get the band signed! When I walked into Interscope in LA in 2009 to play Jimmy Iovine La Roux's debut album, he said, to a room full of people, 'We all miss you on Snow Patrol, Jazz.'

I was in Istanbul in 2008. I had a Turkish girlfriend. This was a few months after they'd sacked us. Gary Lightbody called.

'Jazz,' he said. 'I know what you did for us. I really, really know and I wanted to phone you and say thank you.'

He's a lovely guy, Gary. He's quite nervous in conversation. It took a lot of strength for him to call me that day. And I really appreciated it. Every time I see them, it's all right. Gary always gives me a hug. There's something in their music. I felt it. Something true. It was just another chapter, I suppose…of love and music…time…

Let's leave it there.

TAPE #22
(10TH JULY 2012)

Conversation #7

I'm gonna play you a Scissor Sisters song later called 'Let's Have A Kiki'. It's buzzing up online as we speak, OK, on YouTube. Radio 1 won't play it in a million fucking years. They'd tell you Scissor Sisters are too old. What are they gonna do, read out the band's birth certificates? 'Let's Have A Kiki' – Radio 1 listeners would love it. Although I think it's got the word 'motherfucker' in the chorus. Still, I'm gonna play it to you later. I'm so happy I manage Scissor Sisters. They're *such* a great band. Such a great bunch of people, too. And they did it. They've channelled the Universe. They remembered how to write songs, how to love music, how to love each other. They've made music without fear.

Did I tell you I'm managing Boy George? He called me up, out of the blue. I've been trying to get Culture Club back together. It's not easy, getting four guys with a lot of history to reunite. But George *wants* it. He doesn't *need* it. The others need to *want* it, too, not just *need* it.

[Long pause]

You watch…sometimes I need to feel fire in me. Boy George is healthy and balanced and he knows what he wants. He wants to make a great Culture Club record – not just throw the band back together and tour the world for a bit of cash. If the rest of them start dithering, then fine – we'll make a Boy George album. He's a cultural icon. His voice is more beautiful than ever. You watch…

next week. I'm gonna give everything. You watch...Monday morning...where were we? Switch that fucking thing on.

Bittersweet

In September 2006, I met Richard Ashcroft in a restaurant near Harrods. A few months before, I'd watched him sing 'Bittersweet Symphony' with Coldplay at Live 8. I missed him. And maybe he missed me a little. We hugged the moment we saw each other.

I started to manage him again. He was about to embark on his own arena tour and commence work on his third solo album. But then, a few months later, he called me up and said, 'Jazz, it's a beautiful day...I've been thinking about what a great band the Verve were.'

Richard once likened putting the Verve back together to me moving into a small house with my three ex-wives. As hard as that sounds, I think putting the Verve back together is probably a little more challenging. Even so, it lit my heart up, the idea of them reuniting. Tim Parry suspected things wouldn't be quite so turbulent this time, that people would have changed. They were a bit older, they'd had kids, but the band were still young enough to be relevant. The world always cries out for soul. And the Verve still had that.

We booked a comeback tour: two gigs each in Glasgow, Blackpool and London. It was the music story of the year. We released their first studio jam on NME.com and the Internet lit up like a skyscraper at night. People loved it: the groove, the soul, the complete fucking authentic beauty and majesty of the Verve.

[Pause]

Listen. I'm addicted to music and I'm addicted to life. I've been addicted to sex and drugs and booze. Some people can balance

TAPE #22

Sobriety and Intoxication, but I can't. And neither could Nick McCabe.

The tensions began to surface at the very first gig at Glasgow Barrowlands. Nick wanted it to be like it had been in the band's early days. He wanted the band to group-hug after they played. Whereas Richard, by 2007, had developed a ritual of leaving the venue a matter of seconds after a gig ended. Nick couldn't understand that. But, of course, Richard wanted to go to the hotel and hug his wife and children.

From Glasgow, the tour went to the Empress Ballroom in Blackpool. On the second night there, Myra showed. This was the real test. It was the first time all the characters had been together in the same room for nine years. I was nervous as hell. I was watching everything carefully. I noticed how friendly Myra was being – she was being lovely to everyone except Richard's wife. That worried me. With the Verve, multi-million pound deals were always tightly entwined and jeopardised by the smallest social acts.

The truth is, I could taste bitterness in the air like fag smoke. They were back together, sure, but there was no forgiveness, no dealing with the past, with the demons. What was it? What was the problem? I used to rack my brain. I used to meditate to try and find answers.

[Pause]

There was huge unprocessed anger towards Richard. After all, when the Verve split in 1998, the other band members and their families were denied the lifestyle that comes with being in a huge rock band – the wealth, the status, the travel and adulation. And you know what, if you can't forgive – I should know – you become angry.

BIG LIFE

Backstage in Blackpool, I walked into a dressing room and found Simon Jones sitting alone with his bass guitar, drinking a pint of Guinness. He looked nervous and pretty forlorn.

'You all right, Simon?' I said.

'Sure.'

Suddenly, Myra burst into the room.

'Who the fuck does he think he is? *Richard Ashcroft*. He thinks he's some kind of fucking superstar. Who the fuck fucks off straight after a gig?'

'Myra,' I said. 'Calm down. You need to let go of this anger. It'll hurt you.'

She was venomous – so *angry* with Richard and his wife. This was about more than someone leaving a gig early. This type of anger was years in the making. It ran so deep. It was spectacular. The only person I'd known be that angry before was me.

After Blackpool came two shows at the Roundhouse in Camden. During soundcheck on the first night, Richard tried to speak to Simon, but Simon Jones struggles with confrontation. It didn't go well. After that, Richard didn't really talk to anyone. He turned his guitar up extremely loud. I stood at the sound desk as this deafening fucking noise came out of Richard's amp.

They played an amazing gig that first night in Camden. It was a press frenzy. Jimmy Page sat beside me and spent a lot of the gig saying how great Nick McCabe was. Despite the obvious tensions, the gig was a triumph. I went backstage afterwards, excited. Richard had already left, of course, but I wanted to congratulate the rest of the band on such a fantastic show.

'Jazz, wait.' The tour manager grabbed me in the corridor. 'Don't go in the dressing room,' he said. 'It isn't safe.'

'I have to. I'm the manager.'

258

TAPE #22

Pete Salisbury, the band's drummer, came out and warned me not to go in.

'I have to,' I repeated. 'That was a fucking amazing gig. I'm the manager.'

I opened the dressing room door and Nick McCabe descended on me, shouting and swearing, blaming me for everything. What had I done? I had no idea. But I suppose the anger they felt towards Richard had to be directed somewhere. And I'm the manager – managers take the blame. Simon Jones was slumped in his seat, looking at the wall. Pete Salisbury tried to pacify Nick, but it couldn't be done. It was terrible. It was like stumbling into one of hell's inner circles. It was the booze, of course – too much booze, too much unsaid, too much fucking time, too much potential genius, too much at stake.

Later that night, Myra left an angry rant on Richard Ashcroft's answering machine. His children heard it. That was it as far as he was concerned, and I could understand. She sent me a bunch of texts, too…I've got copies of them somewhere.

I travelled home from the Roundhouse in complete shock, totally exhausted, and I went to bed and stared at the ceiling.

After hearing the answering machine message from Myra, Richard wanted to stop the band there and then. But there were Verve fans flying into London from all over the world for the second Roundhouse gig. He had a duty to play. They all did. And despite a really poisonous soundcheck that I could barely watch, the Verve played. And it was one of the best gigs I ever saw. Chris Martin was there. We'd had news that the arena tour had sold out. We were getting rave reviews in the press and online. Nick had swung from Intoxication back towards Sobriety. I'd done that myself, many times. He apologised for attacking me the previous night. 'If the

259

BIG LIFE

Verve don't work out, Jazz,' he said, 'I could be a guitar tech!' But it was only a reprieve. The problems remained.

We had millions of pounds of festivals booked. We also had a new album to release and millions of fans around the world excited and facing disappointment. We had American tours and Japanese gigs booked. As in 1998, we had to soldier on.

It was horrible. Everywhere we went, I had to arrange huge numbers of dressing rooms, book separate hotels, separate catering arrangements. I had to make complex plans to ensure that certain people arrived at the venues at different times and did not meet. Shortly before the arena tour, Richard cut his hair short and he dyed it blond. He did that in protest, I think. He was really suffering.

On tour in Germany, I received a voicemail from Nick McCabe. He was ranting and I hardly understood a word. He was screaming at me, making demands. Richard told me that while on stage that night, Nick looked like he despised the world. He had an alcohol problem. I know about that problem because I'm an alcoholic. I wrecked the CBS Record Conference in 1984. I probably looked like I despised the world that night in Torquay.

Japan was tough. Richard had warned me that playing there would be difficult for Nick; I should have listened. They played at sunset at Summer Sonic in Osaka. I'd travelled there with Richard and, as usual, we arrived about fifteen minutes before we were due to play. The backstage area was full of caravans and outside one sat Pete Salisbury.

'All right, Pete?' I said.

'Let's just get this over and done with,' he said.

During the gig, I found I was watching everything Nick McCabe did. There was something strange about him. Something loose about that hunched figure. He used a thing called a bottleneck a lot; you put it over your finger so you can play slide guitar. Normally, he handed it to his guitar tech, but during this gig he was throwing it wildly. At the end of 'Lucky Man', he smashed his guitar against his amps. Richard took this for an old-fashioned rock 'n' roll gesture, so he started smashing his acoustic guitar to bits. The back of the guitar came off and Richard fanned himself with it. The strings of 'Bittersweet Symphony' began. It looked to me as though Nick was dancing with his guitar tech, but I think maybe they were wrestling.

I anticipated the fact that Richard wasn't going to come on for the encore. I ran like hell to the backstage area to join him in the people carrier at the bottom of the ramp. I got there too late; Richard had already left. Nick McCabe came storming down the ramp and I knew immediately he meant to attack me. He looked like Quasimodo on acid. I recalled the time, years ago, when I'd thrown that bloke down the stairs at my folk night – the night Tracey the Go-Go Dancer warned me I might murder a person one day.

Being sober, I was much more nimble than Nick. I dodged as he went for me. He took a towel from round his neck and spun it above his head like a lasso. He whipped me once and grazed the side of my eye. His security man bear-hugged him and dragged him away kicking and screaming. In the dressing room, he threw a chair and broke a mirror.

Back in Osaka at the hotel bar, all the horror was so horrible it began to seem quite funny – me nursing my eye with a napkin. Ashcroft looked at me and said, 'Jazz, I want you to buy a gun. And I want you to buy a silver bullet. And if ever, *if ever* I suggest putting the Verve back together again, don't even think about it – shoot me in the head!'

BIG LIFE

It wasn't all bad. There were days when we found balance and those days were great. We got to Glastonbury on a Sunday afternoon. I could hear Neil Diamond in the distance, singing 'Sweet Caroline'. Leonard Cohen was running late, which meant our set might have to be shortened. Richard arrived at the very last minute and collapsed on a sofa in his dressing room.

'I feel like shit,' he said, squirming on the couch. 'I feel like absolute shit.'

I didn't see how he was going to get through the gig. I went out and stood by the sound desk, the place I always watch my acts from. Melvin Benn, who runs Glastonbury, came over all excited; he said it was the biggest crowd he'd ever seen on a Sunday night. They were packed up to the fence and waiting for the Verve.

I've seen a lot of gigs in my life. I've seen the Stones, Zeppelin, the Yard Birds, Springsteen, the Who, Blood Sweat and Tears. But that night, their playing, his voice, those songs; it was breathtaking. The Verve at Glastonbury was my ultimate experience of being in the music industry. After sunset, under the stars, it was heaven.

Mark Cooper, who runs *Later with Jools Holland*, texted me as the gig was ending: *Where are you? This is amazing!*

Zane Lowe texted: *This is the best gig ever.*

My phone went crazy. The crowd were as good as the band. It's on YouTube. Everyone should watch it. Richard came offstage and left Glastonbury immediately. He called me from his car and he was buzzing, joyous. It was a momentous gig. And that night, the band didn't give a fuck that Richard had left straight away. They understood that deeper forces were dictating their emotions and this moment in their lives. They embraced each other. They were ecstatic.

I drove back from Glastonbury, after the most amazing gig. There was no anger on that night. All I felt was sadness. Here was an amazing band. And I knew we only had four or five more gigs to play.

The following month, the new Verve album, *Forth*, went to number one.

I think Richard Ashcroft's one of the greatest songwriters Britain has ever produced. Nick McCabe's one of our truly great guitarists. But they're vulnerable guys, OK. Ashcroft seems strong and brash, but he's a sensitive, gentle soul. They both are. Richard takes on all the problems of the Verve; he can't just ignore things. He tries to lead and to shoulder it all, but he's not strong enough; no one is.

Nick apologised for what happened in Osaka. I cared for him a lot; I think he knew that.

'You need help,' I said. 'I'll help you. I've been where you are.'

He came to Big Life for a meeting the following month. He had a rucksack on. In the middle of the meeting, he pulled out a can of Guinness and drank it.

I forgave Myra for her texts and suggested she and Simon talk to a counsellor, a wonderful woman called Indi who'd helped me a lot over the years. I think it worked out pretty well. They sent me a box of candles and soaps to say thanks. They're good people, Simon and Myra. It was hard for them. It was hard for everyone, having to be in such a turbulent situation.

We all need help. I've had a lot of help in my life and I've tried to help others, too, as best I can.

The Verve need to forgive each other. I sometimes think forgiveness is more powerful than love. But practicing forgiveness ain't easy. It took me years and years of hurt to learn. I forgave Nick instantly for whipping me with a towel.

BIG LIFE

When the Verve were on it, Ashcroft on song, the rhythm section, Simon and Pete, laying down enchanting, soulful grooves, they were spellbinding. And on top of that you had Nick McCabe. He never played the same thing from one night to the next. You'd need three guitarists to replace him. Ask Chris Martin how good the Verve are. He'll tell you. At Live 8, he introduced 'Bittersweet Symphony' as 'the best song ever written, sung by the best singer in the world'.

The last Verve gig was V Festival in Chelmsford. Before they went on, Richard got the whole band together and he embraced each of them. On stage, he said, 'Thank you Pete Salisbury, thank you Simon Jones and thank you Nick McCabe. This is the Verve.'

A few weeks later, Nick phoned me. He'd found a place where he could go. It was ten grand for ten days. I paid half and, to my knowledge, he hasn't drunk since.

TAPE #23
(29TH JULY 2012)

Handcross

I was down the hospital in Woolwich when I was nineteen. This guy comes in carrying a cardboard box.

'Hey, Jazz,' he said. 'I need you to X-ray this.'

He handed me the box and seemed relieved to be parted from it. I asked what it was, but he only repeated that the contents needed X-raying.

'I'll leave you to it,' he said. 'X-ray its teeth.'

I set the box down and lifted the lid. Looking up at me from inside was a severed head. It was jet-black, but speckled all over with gold flakes. Eyelids, lips, cheeks and nose – all of them black and gold. I learned later that the head belonged to an Egyptian princess, but it felt more like a child's head. I lifted it. This head, I thought, is thousands and thousands of years old. I lay it on its side and supported it with foam. I X-rayed her.

There's so much I haven't told you.

I'm intuitive. I always have been. I once wired myself up with a spy device before a meeting with a record executive. Intuition told me the guy was going to be slippery. And he was. He phoned my artist afterwards and said that I'd blown up during the meeting, that I'd lost my temper. But I hadn't. I had a recording to prove I'd stayed calm.

[Pause]

I managed Devo for nine months. They were complete characters - very serious. They were spiralling down at the time and when I'd

BIG LIFE

finished managing them they were completely obscure. They took *everything* seriously. Each night they went on stage with flowerpots on their heads.

Listen to the bassline on Devo's song 'Whip It'. It's nearly the same as the 'Pretty Woman' bassline, isn't it? Roy Orbison – he's one of my heroes. Me and Napier-Bell were asked to manage him in the eighties. We met him in LA.

'It's an honour to meet you, Roy,' I said.

That was all I could manage. I just sat there, thinking, this guy sang 'Running Scared', 'Pretty Woman', 'Crying'. This guy changed my life.

We didn't manage him in the end. You win some, and other times all you get is a weird lunch. Me and Tim had a weird lunch with Sigur Ros. We were in the running to manage them and we loved the music, but as soon as we sat down in the restaurant, something felt wrong. Steely-eyed Icelandic musicians surrounded me. One of them asked me my exact age.

'Oh my god,' he said. 'You're even older than my dad!'

[Very long pause]

Rock 'n' roll's dead. The business model is. The *spirit* of rock 'n' roll lives on. The other night I had dinner with a guy called Skrillex. He's fucking twenty-four. He doesn't care about signing record deals or getting in the charts. He cares about making records, sticking them on YouTube and taking things from there. Skrillex reminded me of me and Richard Digance in the seventies. We didn't care about the charts. We wanted to get out there.

We're managing this great band at Big Life called London Grammar. The singer, Hannah, she's got an amazing voice. They've got this song called 'Strong'. It's a hit! Tim and me had a disagreement about the beat last week. I still shout loud from time

266

to time. I shout loud when I'm passionate. People were saying the song needs a hip-hop beat so it sounds up-to-date. But I don't care whether it's up-to-date or not because emotion is timeless. It is, isn't it?

Hip-hop was born out of a New York power cut – people looted instruments and turntables and made music with them. People seized the equipment. These days, the equipment is the laptop. It has changed music forever. The laptop is as significant to musical history as the electric guitar.

When the electric guitar came along I was a kid. And suddenly we had 2-track recorders and people could make fucking great records in any old room, like Joe Meek did, who recorded 'Telstar' on Holloway Road, above an umbrella shop. He hanged himself, sadly, Joe Meek – killed his landlady and hanged himself. But what wonderful music he made…

[Pause]

When I was a kid it took me years to save for a drum kit. A kid now can jump on his mum's computer and make a beat in seconds. If I was in my teens today I'd be sneaking out of X-ray departments, making music on laptops, taking my laptop into clubs. I'd be more interested in getting played on Annie Mac in the night time than on the breakfast show – that comes later. I'd have forty thousand followers on twitter. My mates'd be making videos for YouTube that we weren't even in. We'd have a shit load of likes on Facebook. We'd be going round, stirring it up, plundering the whole of rock 'n' roll for inspiration, pinching Elvis basslines and building songs. And when Artificial Intelligence comes in, I'll be plundering the sounds of the future. I'll be touring the world holographically. I could make a hologram of me and pack him off to play drums in Hamburg. Give it a year or so and the Beatles'll be heading back there, too. Four, fresh-faced hologram Beatles, playing the Reeperbahn every night of the year.

The future needs music companies. Music companies that will embrace the new rock 'n' roll. The new rock 'n' roll is piratical. It's not corporate. You can be a pirate. Go and be one. You don't even need to collect egg boxes to soundproof your bedroom any more. Just put your headphones on and get cracking. Life is...life is turning disasters into opportunities. Turn impossibilities into dreams.

We can't cure the industry by tinkering. Forget 'them and us', think 'us'. There's still a lot of music lovers working at record companies. Some great people who want to make things work and embrace new technology. More so now than ten years ago in fact. But the old ways are dying.

A Head of Promotion recently told me he'd got one of my acts on two big television shows in the UK. We're not talking E4. We're talking *Strictly Come Dancing* and the Royal Variety Show.

'The problem is, Jazz,' he said, 'who's gonna pay the costs?'

'You are, aren't you,' I said. 'You're the record company.'

'We can't, Jazz. There's no guarantee it'll lead to sales.'

Two marketing guys, who I respect enormously, sat me down and said, 'Jazz, we know your act have sold millions of records, but we're not gonna put out a Greatest Hits. They just don't work any more.'

Blimey, I thought. The death of Greatest Hits. They were the life-blood of the music industry. Greatest Hits used to pay the Christmas bonuses, pay the rent, raise cash to launch a couple of new acts. 'A few years ago,' one of them said, 'we'd spend money on marketing and we'd know, almost exactly, where the album would chart the following week. You paid the money and the record sold. But, Jazz, the thing is...we don't know any more.'

TAPE #23

Currently, record companies pay a lot of money for whatever's hot on YouTube, OK. Second albums become tricky because there's no aura of discovery. The public move on quickly. The economy fetishises the emergence and not the development of an artist. But take a band like the Black Keys – they stuck at it, made several albums, and they're massive. The music companies of the future need the resources and the aptitude to develop artists capable of having long, beautiful, fascinating careers.

The Digital Age enables an artist to make a song in their bedroom, acquire a digital fingerprint for it, and start collecting money. It's possible. Every time the song gets a view on YouTube or a play on the radio or on Spotify, a micro-payment could trigger, paying a sum of money directly into the artist's bank account. It's possible. David Bowie says it: music's gonna be like water. In the future, you'll pay for entertainment – for books, television, films, music, like you pay for water.

Because music flows in the Digital Age. It's a universal energy. We shouldn't try and trap it. Let it flow. Let it flow and the good music will touch people and become valuable. The money will come if we let the music flow. I had a guy in last week, twenty years old, who didn't *want* to sign a record deal. He wants to post his songs on SoundCloud and take it from there. In the past, everyone wanted to sign to EMI like the Beatles. That's changing. It's changing as we speak.

[Pause]

I haven't always succeeded. But when I lay my head on the pillow at night, I believe in what I'm doing. What other people say about me is none of my business.

[Pause]

I once managed a global star – an immoral brat. He was rude to the staff at Big Life. He held impromptu orgies. He trashed hotel rooms in the nineties – threw scrambled egg across a carpet. What kind of man trashes a hotel room post-1975? That went out the window with fucking Keith Moon's television. I'd cautiously pick my way across the debris of his orgies in the morning. He always demanded the presidential suite wherever he went. I remember once, in Cleveland, we could only get him the *vice* presidential suite.

'Who the fuck's in it, Jazz? Kick 'em out. I'm not playing unless I get it. Who the fuck's got it?'

'Bill Clinton,' I said.

[Pause]

Bill Clinton…

There's so much I haven't said.

[Very long pause]

I was lurching round Covent Garden pissed in 1977. They wouldn't let me in the Zanzibar. I'd been thrown out the week before for getting drunk with one of the Zombies. The next place to go in Covent Garden in those days was the Rock Garden. I knew the doorman there. I floated down to get more pissed and Talking Heads were playing. My vision was blurred and my head was spinning, but even so, the music moved me. It kept me going.

[Phone rings]

Hello? Yeah, we need to sort out the kick-drum on *Wasting My Young Years*. It needs to be four to the floor…hello? *Hello?* This new phone I've got is absolutely *hopeless*. It cuts out every time I –

[Phone rings]

Hello, yeah, we need to change the kick-drum on *Wasting My Young Years*. Where's he mixing on Sunday? I wanna go down… hello? *Hello?* This phone is completely fucking –

[Phone rings]

TAPE #23

Hello…yeah, so, could you email me what studio he's in 'cause I might just pop down. I'll be in London. We need to get the beat right on *Wasting My Young Years*. Have you seen the logo? It's fucking great. London Grammar – it looks so strong…right…all right.

I went on a wonderful journey with my face. I saw kinesiologists, numerologists, acupuncturists. I saw the osteopath, Michael Skipworth. He held me in his arms. He said there was an awful lot of energy trapped inside me.

To change my skin, I had to change my whole self. That's what the record industry needs to do – think holistically, change fundamentally. The Indian sages said it: as in the macrocosm, so in the microcosm. Even Klaxons said it: 'As above, so below.' Sometimes you've got to ask yourself, am I in the Universe, or is the Universe in me?

I meditate every morning, to see things clearly. It was during meditation in 1994, when my daughter Georgia was one, that I realised I had to stop drinking. I take great care in what I eat. You've seen. I do. I'm inspired by an elderly man I met on a Miami beach at dawn. He wore light denim jeans and a white linen shirt. The sun was coming up. He'd slept on the beach, this man.

'Hey, your name's Jazz.' I had a name-tag on. I was attending a macrobiotics conference. 'What a great name,' the man said. 'What do you do, Jazz?'

'I manage Lisa Stansfield.'

'That's great!'

His name was William Dufty. His books showed me how my diet could connect me to nature. They showed me how food could bring me in line with the Universe. He was married to the silent music star, Gloria Swanson.

BIG LIFE

A guy called Tienko Ting activated my natural chi. I felt this huge bright light behind my eyes. All my old hockey and drinking injuries came back to life. Tienko taught me to throw my body round all chaotically – to keep the energy moving. I did this for six years, in the basement of my house. Georgia used to watch me through the keyhole. 'Dad's doing his jumping around again,' she'd say. Although I kept wearing make-up, I could see that the redness was moving round my face.

I was cleaning my teeth, getting ready to go out for dinner one Saturday. I wiped my mouth and was about to apply my make-up when I looked at myself. The skin on my cheeks and my chin were clear. My nose didn't look too red at all. But I couldn't really believe it, so I put on make-up and went out to dinner. The following Monday, I got up and I looked in the mirror again.

[Long pause]

I went to work without make-up.

Dad taught me drums when I was four. He taught me to box when I was three. I never liked punching. My dad was a fantastic boxer. We had his belts and trophies on display.

In the military school, you had to box, whether or not you were in the team. I wasn't in the team, so I'd just climb into the ring and go through the motions, throw a few punches, block a bit. I might win one fight every now and then, but often people knocked the shit out of me. When Dad asked how I was doing in the boxing, I lied.

'Great,' I said. 'I'm on the team. I've won six, drawn one.'

Dad once told me a story about his childhood. He told me that when he was young he'd had eczema on his scalp. It got so bad he went to hospital to have it looked at. In the adjacent bed was an old guy who'd been injured in the trenches during World War One. This old guy gave my dad some cream to rub into his scalp. Dad said his whole face broke out in terrible red spots. The following day, he got in the ring with this kid who was a notoriously strong boxer. Dad said the kid was terrified by his red face. Dad knocked him out with two punches.

When I was fifteen, I used to tell that story as if it was me and not Dad who it had happened to.

[Stands. Goes to the window. Long pause]

I went to primary school in Handcross in Sussex. It was a little country village. I was an outsider because I came from Portsmouth. You tended to play with the other outsiders. I played with a kid who came from Durham. This kid was pretty tough. He always had boots on. We were playing on the rec after school one day. He was on the swing and I picked up a piece of wood and threw it at him for a joke. The wood scratched his finger and he leapt off the swing and attacked me. He picked up a big piece of wood and threw it at me. It hit me in the head and blood burst from my eye. I couldn't see. He kept punching me. I went down on the ground and curled up in a little ball.

Dad used to cycle past the rec on his way home from work. He cycled past that day and he heard me screaming. He stopped his bike and came over. He pulled the kid off me and lifted me up by the collar of my shirt.

'Hit him, Jazz. Hit him back. I've taught you. *Hit him.*'

I was in tears. Blood streamed from my eye and dripped onto my shirt and trousers. Dad told the kid to piss off. He put me on the back of his bike and cycled the two of us home. He didn't show me any love. He was very cold to me. He washed at the sink as Mum made tea.

'Jazz is yellow,' he said to her. 'He's got no guts.'

BIG LIFE

I sat in the living room, dabbing my eye with a wet cloth. In the years that followed, I must have blocked that day from my memory. It returned to me when I performed the affirmations of forgiveness for Dad.

Louise Hay teaches you to go back and change these events. I went back in my mind to the rec near the primary school in Handcross. But this time, when Dad came over and pulled the kid off me, he didn't instruct me to hit him. This time, Dad told the boy that fighting is not right. And he told me I was brave for not fighting back.

I created my red nose and spotty face to scare people off, so I wouldn't have to fight with them. I created my red face with thoughts and with rage, because I wanted to be tough, a big boy. These days my face is completely clear. I have repeated affirmations of forgiveness for Dad. It doesn't matter what you're going through, never stop learning and trying to improve. You have to find strength. You have to forgive others and love yourself. That's life. You have to live.

OK, we're done. Go and put the kettle on. I need to call Tim.

THANKS (JAZZ SUMMERS)

Thank you to my beautiful wife and best friend Dianna, who pushed me into writing this in the first place, collared Joe Stretch and supported both of us wholeheartedly throughout our adventure together. To Joe Stretch, who didn't feel he was collared at all. Joe, it has been an amazing experience working with you. To Tim Parry, for putting up with me for thirty years, without whom a lot of this book wouldn't have been possible. To Kat Kennedy, for her total dedication, objectivity and friendship, and to all the staff at Big Life. To our spiritual partners Naim, Gavin and everyone at Quartet Books. To Jany Temime, for her Provençal hospitality. And last but not least, to Peter Saville, for the privilege of working with you again.

P.S. Tim Parry has rewritten his song, it's now called 'Working With You Is Like Banging My Head, Banging My Head, Banging My Head, Banging My Head Against A Brick Wall'!

THANKS (JOE STRETCH)

Thank you, Jazz, for picking up the phone. Thank you for your belief and generosity, for the conversations we recorded, and the ones we didn't. Huge love to Dianna for being cool and wise. Thanks to Gavin, Kat, Jocelyn and, finally, to Rolf, for those elegant luncheons and rickety rides through Provence.